lake county

public library

The Family Book of Verse

Books by Lewis Gannett

CREAM HILL
SWEET LAND

Books Edited by Lewis Gannett

THE FAMILY BOOK OF VERSE
MAINSTREAM OF AMERICA SERIES

The Family Book of Verse

SELECTED AND EDITED BY

Lewis Gannett

HARPER & ROW, PUBLISHERS

NEW YORK and EVANSTON

Grateful acknowledgment is made to the following for permission to reprint selections included in this book:

"America the Beautiful" by Katharine Lee Bates, from *Poems*; by permission of E. P. Dutton & Co., Inc.

"The Yak" and "The Frog" by Hilaire Belloc, from *Cautionary Verses*, published 1941 by Alfred A. Knopf, Inc.; by permission of Alfred A. Knopf, Inc., and Gerald Duckworth & Co. Ltd.

"Nancy Hanks" by Rosemary Benét, from *A Book of Americans*, published by Holt, Rinehart & Winston, Inc., copyright 1933 by Rosemary and Stephen Vincent Benét, copyright renewed 1961 by Rosemary Carr Benét; by permission of Brandt & Brandt.

"Mud" by Polly Chase Boyden, from *Child Life Magazine*, copyright 1930 by Rand McNally & Company.

"So Sweet Love Seemed" and "I Never Shall Love the Snow Again" from *The Shorter Poems of Robert Bridges*; by permission of the Clarendon Press, Oxford.

"The Soldier" and "The Old Vicarage, Grantchester" from *The Collected Poems of Rupert Brooke*, copyright 1915 by Dodd, Mead & Company, copyright 1943 by Edward Marsh; by permission of Dodd, Mead & Company, Sidgwick & Jackson Ltd., and McClelland & Stewart Ltd.

"The Donkey" by G. K. Chesterton, from *The Wild Knight and Other Poems*; by permission of E. P. Dutton & Co., Inc., J. M. Dent & Sons Ltd., and Miss D. E. Collins.

"Lepanto" by G. K. Chesterton, from *The Collected Poems of G. K. Chesterton*, copyright 1932 by Dodd, Mead & Co.; by permission of Dodd, Mead & Co. and Miss D. E. Collins.

iv

The Family Book of Verse

BOOK ONE

Notes of Ecstasy

The great poets knew that life was worth living. They experienced rapture; they communicated ecstasy. Shelley soared with the west wind and the skylark; Keats traveled in realms of gold where a thing of beauty was a joy forever; Coleridge woke from a drugged dream to drink the milk of Paradise; Wordsworth's heart leaped up at sight of a rainbow; even Browning sang of the wild joys of living; and Tennyson heard soft music. Our own Emily Dickinson tasted a liquor never brewed, and Edna St. Vincent Millay could not hold her world close enough. Next to the many things called love, sheer joy has moved the poets most.

The poems in this section have little in common except the note of ecstasy. That is enough. Chronology here, in general, is reversed.

┼ God's World

O world, I cannot hold thee close enough!
   Thy winds, thy wide gray skies!
   Thy mists that roll and rise!
Thy woods, this autumn day, that ache and sag
And all but cry with color! The gaunt crag
To crush! To lift the lean of that black bluff!
World, world, I cannot get thee close enough!

Long have I known a glory in it all,
   But never knew I this:
   Here such a passion is
As stretcheth me apart. Lord, I do fear
Thou'st made the world too beautiful this year;
My soul is all but out of me,—let fall
No burning leaf; prithee, let no bird call.

EDNA ST. VINCENT MILLAY

⟋ Figs from Thistles

FIRST FIG

My candle burns at both ends;
   It will not last the night;
But ah, my foes, and oh, my friends—
   It gives a lovely light!

SECOND FIG

Safe upon the solid rock the ugly houses stand:
Come and see my shining palace built upon the sand!

EDNA ST. VINCENT MILLAY

Euclid Alone

Euclid alone has looked on Beauty bare.
Let all who prate of Beauty hold their peace,
And lay them prone upon the earth and cease
To ponder on themselves, the while they stare

At nothing, intricately drawn nowhere
In shapes of shifting lineage; let geese
Gabble and hiss, but heroes seek release
From dusty bondage into luminous air.
O blinding hour, O holy, terrible day,
When first the shaft into his vision shone
Of light anatomized! Euclid alone
Has looked on Beauty bare. Fortunate they
Who, though once only and then but far away,
Have heard her massive sandal set on stone.

EDNA ST. VINCENT MILLAY

You, Andrew Marvell

And here face down beneath the sun
And here upon earth's noonward height
To feel the always coming on
The always rising of the night:

To feel creep up the curving east
The earthly chill of dusk and slow
Upon those under lands the vast
And ever-climbing shadow grow

And strange at Ecbatan the trees
Take leaf by leaf the evening strange
The flooding dark about their knees
The mountains over Persia change

And now at Kermanshah the gate
Dark empty and the withered grass
And through the twilight now the late
Few travelers in the westward pass

And Baghdad darken and the bridge
Across the silent river gone
And through Arabia the edge
Of evening widen and steal on

And deepen on Palmyra's street
The wheel rut in the ruined stone
And Lebanon fade out and Crete
High through the clouds and overblown

And over Sicily the air
Still flashing with the landward gulls
And loom and slowly disappear
The sails above the shadowy hulls

And Spain go under and the shore
Of Africa the gilded sand
And evening vanish and no more
The low pale light across that land

Nor now the long light on the sea:

And here face downward in the sun
To feel how swift how secretly
The shadow of the night comes on . . .

ARCHIBALD MACLEISH

Barter

Life has loveliness to sell,
   All beautiful and splendid things,
Blue waves whitened on a cliff,
   Soaring fire that sways and sings,
And children's faces looking up
Holding wonder like a cup.

Life has loveliness to sell,
   Music like a curve of gold,
Scent of pine trees in the rain,
   Eyes that love you, arms that hold,
And for your spirit's still delight,
Holy thoughts that star the night.

Spend all you have for loveliness,
  Buy it and never count the cost;
For one white singing hour of peace
  Count many a year of strife well lost,
And for a breath of ecstasy
Give all you have been, or could be.

SARA TEASDALE

There's Nothing Like the Sun

There's nothing like the sun as the year dies;
Kind as it can be, this world being made so,
To stones and men and beasts and birds and flies—
To all things that it touches except snow,
Whether on mountain side or street or town.
The south wall warms me: November has begun,
Yet never shone the sun as fair as now
While the sweet last-left damsons from the bough
With spangles of the morning sun drop down
Because the starling shakes it, whistling what
Once swallows sang. But I have not forgot
That there is nothing, too, like March's sun,
Like April's, or July's, or June's or May's,
Or January's or February's—great days;
And August, September, October, and December
Have equal days, all different from November.
No day of any month but I have said—
Or, if I could live long enough, should say—
"There's nothing like the sun that shines today."
There's nothing like the sun till we are dead.

EDWARD THOMAS

The Donkey

When fishes flew and forests walked
　　And figs grew upon thorn,
Some moment when the moon was blood,
　　Then surely I was born.

With monstrous head and sickening cry
　　And ears like errant wings,
The devil's walking parody
　　Of all four-footed things.

The tattered outlaw of the earth,
　　Of ancient crooked will;
Starve, scourge, deride me: I am dumb,
　　I keep my secret still.

Fools! For I also had my hour;
　　One far fierce hour and sweet:
There was a shout about my ears,
　　And palms before my feet.

G. K. CHESTERTON

We Poets Speak

(FROM *Sister Songs*)

We [poets] speak a lesson taught we know not how,
　　　　And what it is that from us flows
The hearer better than the utterer knows. . . .
　　　　　　The poet is not lord
　　　　　　Of the next syllable may come
　　　　　　With the returning pendulum;
　　　　　And what he plans to-day in song,
To-morrow sings it in another tongue.
　　　　　　Where the last leaf fell from his bough,
　　　　　　He knows not if a leaf shall grow;
　　　　　　Where he sows he doth not reap,
　　　　　　He reapeth where he did not sow;

He sleeps, and dreams forsake his sleep
    To meet him on his waking way.
Vision will mate him not by law and vow:
    Disguised in life's most hodden-grey,
By the most beaten road of everyday
She waits him, unsuspected and unknown.
    The hardest pang whereon
He lays his mutinous head may be a Jacob's stone.
In the most iron crag his foot can tread
    A Dream may strew her bed,
    And suddenly his limbs entwine,
And draw him down through rock as sea-nymphs might
    through brine.
But, unlike those feigned temptress-ladies who
In guerdon of a night the lover slew,
When the embrace has failed, the rapture fled,
Not he, not he, the wild sweet witch is dead!
    And though he cherisheth
The babe most strangely born from out her death,
Some tender trick of her it hath, maybe,—
    It is not she!

FRANCIS THOMPSON

Spring

Nothing is so beautiful as spring—
    When weeds, in wheels, shoot long and lovely and lush;
    Thrush's eggs look little low heavens, and thrush
Through the echoing timber does so rinse and wring
The ear, it strikes like lightning to hear him sing;
    The glassy peartree leaves and blooms, they brush
    The descending blue; that blue is all in a rush
With richness; the racing lambs too have fair their fling.

What is all this juice and all this joy?
    A strain of the earth's sweet being in the beginning

In Eden garden.—Have, get, before it cloy,
Before it cloud, Christ, lord, and sour with winning,
Innocent mind and Mayday in girl and boy,
Most, O maid's child, thy choice and worthy the winning.

GERARD MANLEY HOPKINS

I Taste a Liquor

I taste a liquor never brewed,
From tankards scooped in pearl;
Not all the vats upon the Rhine
Yield such an alcohol!

Inebriate of air am I,
And debauchee of dew,
Reeling, through endless summer days,
From inns of molten blue.

When landlords turn the drunken bee
Out of the foxglove's door,
When butterflies renounce their drams,
I shall but drink the more!

Till seraphs swing their snowy hats,
And saints to windows run,
To see the little tippler
Leaning against the sun!

EMILY DICKINSON

Fall, Leaves, Fall

Fall, leaves, fall; die, flowers, away;
Lengthen night and shorten day;
Every leaf speaks bliss to me
Fluttering from the autumn tree.
I shall smile when wreaths of snow

Blossom where the rose should grow;
I shall sing when night's decay
Ushers in a drearier day.

EMILY BRONTË

Let Me Enjoy (*Minor Key*)

Let me enjoy the earth no less
Because the all-enacting Might
That fashioned forth its loveliness
Had other aims than my delight.

About my path there flits a Fair,
Who throws me not a word or sign;
I'll charm me with her ignoring air,
And laud the lips not meant for mine.

From manuscripts of moving song
Inspired by scenes and dreams unknown,
I'll pour out raptures that belong
To others, as they were my own.

THOMAS HARDY

The Year's at the Spring
(FROM *Pippa Passes*)

The year's at the spring,
And day's at the morn;
Morning's at seven;
The hill-side's dew-pearled;
The lark's on the wing;
The snail's on the thorn:
God's in His heaven—
All's right with the world.

ROBERT BROWNING

David's Song

(FROM *Saul*)

Oh, the wild joys of living! the leaping from rock up to rock,
The strong rending of boughs from the fir-tree, the cool silver
    shock
Of the plunge in a pool's living water, the hunt of the bear,
And the sultriness showing the lion is couched in his lair.
And the meal, the rich dates yellowed over with gold dust
    divine,
And the locust-flesh steeped in the pitcher, the full draught of
    wine,
And the sleep in the dried river-channel where bulrushes tell
That the water was wont to go warbling so softly and well.
How good is man's life, the mere living! how fit to employ
All the heart and the soul and the senses for ever in joy!
Hast thou loved the white locks of thy father, whose sword
    thou didst guard
When he trusted thee forth with the armies, for glorious
    reward?
Didst thou see the thin hands of thy mother held up as men
    sung
The low song of the nearly-departed, and hear her faint tongue
Joining in while it could to the witness, "Let one more attest,
I have lived, seen God's hand through a lifetime, and all was
    for best"?

ROBERT BROWNING

The Splendor Falls

(FROM *The Princess*)

The splendor falls on castle walls
    And snowy summits old in story:
The long light shakes across the lakes,
    And the wild cataract leaps in glory.
Blow, bugle, blow, set the wild echoes flying,
Blow, bugle; answer, echoes, dying, dying, dying.

O hark, O hear! how thin and clear,
  And thinner, clearer, farther going!
O sweet and far from cliff and scar
  The horns of Elfland faintly blowing!
Blow, let us hear the purple glens replying:
Blow, bugle; answer, echoes, dying, dying, dying.

O love, they lie in yon rich sky,
  They faint on hill or field or river:
Our echoes roll from soul to soul,
  And grow for ever and for ever.
Blow, bugle, blow, set the wild echoes flying,
And answer, echoes, answer, dying, dying, dying.

ALFRED TENNYSON

There Is Sweet Music Here

(FROM *The Lotos-Eaters*)

There is sweet music here that softer falls
Than petals from blown roses on the grass,
Or night-dews on still waters between walls
Of shadowy granite, in a gleaming pass;
Music that gentlier on the spirit lies,
Than tired eyelids upon tired eyes:
Music that brings sweet sleep down from the blissful skies.
Here are cool mosses deep,
And through the moss the ivies creep,
And in the stream the long-leaved flowers weep,
And from the craggy ledge the poppy hangs in sleep.

ALFRED TENNYSON

Music

Let me go where'er I will,
I hear a sky-born music still:
It sounds from all things old,
It sounds from all things young,
From all that's fair, from all that's foul,
Peals out a cheerful song.

It is not only in the rose,
It is not only in the bird,
Not only where the rainbow glows,
Nor in the song of woman heard,
But in the darkest, meanest things
There alway, alway something sings.

'T is not in the high stars alone,
Nor in the cup of budding flowers,
Nor in the redbreast's mellow tone,
Nor in the bow that shines in showers,
But in the mud and scum of things
There alway, alway something sings.

RALPH WALDO EMERSON

Magic Casements
(FROM *Ode to a Nightingale*)

Thou wast not born for death, immortal Bird!
No hungry generations tread thee down;
The voice I hear this passing night was heard
In ancient days by emperor and clown:
Perhaps the self-same song that found a path
Through the sad heart of Ruth, when, sick for home,
She stood in tears amid the alien corn;
The same that oft-times hath
Charmed magic casements, opening on the foam
Of perilous seas, in faery lands forlorn.

JOHN KEATS

13

A Thing of Beauty
(FROM *Endymion*)

A thing of beauty is a joy forever:
Its loveliness increases; it will never
Pass into nothingness; but still will keep
A bower quiet for us, and a sleep
Full of sweet dreams, and health, and quiet breathing.
Therefore, on every morrow, are we wreathing
A flowery band to bind us to the earth,
Spite of despondence, of the inhuman dearth
Of noble natures, of the gloomy days,
Of all the unhealthy and o'er-darken'd ways
Made for our searching: yes, in spite of all,
Some shape of beauty moves away the pall
From our dark spirits. Such the sun, the moon,
Trees old and young, sprouting a shady boon
For simple sheep; and such are daffodils
With the green world they live in; and clear rills
That for themselves a cooling covert make
'Gainst the hot season; the mid-forest brake,
Rich with a sprinkling of fair musk-rose blooms:
And such too is the grandeur of the dooms
We have imagined for the mighty dead;
All lovely tales that we have heard or read:
And endless fountain of immortal drink,
Pouring unto us from the heaven's brink.

JOHN KEATS

On First Looking into Chapman's Homer

Much have I travell'd in the realms of gold
And many goodly states and kingdoms seen;
Round many western islands have I been
Which bards in fealty to Apollo hold.
Oft of one wide expanse had I been told
That deep-brow'd Homer ruled as his demesne:

Yet did I never breathe its pure serene
Till I heard Chapman speak out loud and bold:
—Then felt I like some watcher of the skies
When a new planet swims into his ken;
Or like stout Cortez, when with eagle eyes
He stared at the Pacific—and all his men
Look'd at each other with a wild surmise—
Silent, upon a peak in Darien.

JOHN KEATS

Ode to the West Wind

I

O wild west wind, thou breath of Autumn's being
Thou, from whose unseen presence the leaves dead
Are driven, like ghosts from an enchanter fleeing,

Yellow, and black, and pale, and hectic red,
Pestilence-stricken multitudes! O thou
Who chariotest to their dark wintry bed

The wingèd seeds, where they lie cold and low,
Each like a corpse within its grave, until
Thine azure sister of the Spring shall blow

Her clarion o'er the dreaming earth, and fill
(Driving sweet buds like flocks to feed in air)
With living hues and odors plain and hill:

Wild spirit, which art moving everywhere;
Destroyer and preserver; hear, O hear!

II

Thou on whose stream, 'mid the steep sky's commotion,
Loose clouds like earth's decaying leaves are shed,
Shook from the tangled boughs of heaven and ocean,

Angels of rain and lightning! there are spread
On the blue surface of thine airy surge,
Like the bright hair uplifted from the head

Of some fierce Maenad, even from the dim verge
Of the horizon to the zenith's height,
The locks of the approaching storm. Thou dirge

Of the dying year, to which this closing night
Will be the dome of a vast sepulchre,
Vaulted with all thy congregated might

Of vapors, from whose solid atmosphere
Black rain, and fire, and hail will burst: O hear!

III

Thou who didst waken from his summer dreams
The blue Mediterranean, where he lay,
Lulled by the coil of his crystalline streams,

Beside a pumice isle in Baiae's bay,
And saw in sleep old palaces and towers
Quivering within the wave's intenser day,

All overgrown with azure moss and flowers
So sweet, the sense faints picturing them! Thou
For whose path the Atlantic's level powers

Cleave themselves into chasms, while far below
The sea-blooms and the oozy woods which wear
The sapless foliage of the ocean, know

Thy voice, and suddenly grow gray with fear,
And tremble and despoil themselves: O hear!

IV

If I were a dead leaf thou mightest bear;
If I were a swift cloud to fly with thee;
A wave to pant beneath thy power, and share

The impulse of thy strength, only less free
Than thou, O uncontrollable! If even
I were as in my boyhood, and could be

The comrade of thy wanderings over heaven,
As then, when to outstrip thy skiey speed
Scarce seemed a vision—I would ne'er have striven

As thus with thee in prayer in my sore need.
O! lift me as a wave, a leaf, a cloud!
I fall upon the thorns of life! I bleed!

A heavy weight of hours has chained and bowed
One too like thee—tameless, and swift, and proud.

V

Make me thy lyre, even as the forest is:
What if my leaves are falling like its own!
The tumult of thy mighty harmonies

Will take from both a deep, autumnal tone,
Sweet though in sadness. Be thou, Spirit fierce,
My spirit! Be thou me, impetuous one!

Drive my dead thoughts over the universe,
Like withered leaves, to quicken a new birth;
And, by the incantation of this verse,

Scatter, as from an unextinguished hearth
Ashes and sparks, my words among mankind!
Be through my lips to unawakened earth

The trumpet of a prophecy! O Wind,
If Winter comes, can Spring be far behind?

PERCY BYSSHE SHELLEY

To a Skylark

Hail to thee, blithe spirit!
   Bird thou never wert,
That from heaven, or near it,
   Pourest thy full heart
In profuse strains of unpremeditated art.

Higher still and higher,
   From the earth thou springest
Like a cloud of fire;
   The blue deep thou wingest,
And singing still dost soar, and soaring ever singest.

In the golden lightning
   Of the sunken sun,
O'er which clouds are bright'ning,
   Thou dost float and run,
Like an unbodied joy whose race is just begun.

The pale purple even
   Melts around thy flight;
Like a star of heaven
   In the broad daylight
Thou art unseen, but yet I hear thy shrill delight.

Keen as are the arrows
   Of that silver sphere,
Whose intense lamp narrows
   In the white dawn clear,
Until we hardly see, we feel that it is there.

All the earth and air
   With thy voice is loud,
As, when night is bare,
   From one lonely cloud
The moon rains out her beams, and heaven is overflowed.

What thou art we know not;
   What is most like thee?

From rainbow clouds there flow not
   Drops so bright to see,
As from thy presence showers a rain of melody.

Like a poet hidden
   In the light of thought,
Singing hymns unbidden,
   Till the world is wrought
To sympathy with hopes and fears it heeded not:

Like a high-born maiden
   In a palace tower,
Soothing her love-laden
   Soul in secret hour
With music sweet as love, which overflows her bower:

Like a glow-worm golden
   In a dell of dew,
Scattering unbeholden
   Its aerial hue
Among the flowers and grass, which screen it from the view:

Like a rose embowered
   In its own green leaves,
By warm winds deflowered,
   Till the scent it gives
Makes faint with too much sweet those heavy-winged thieves:

Sound of vernal showers
   On the twinkling grass,
Rain-awakened flowers,
   All that ever was,
Joyous, and clear, and fresh, thy music doth surpass.

Teach us, sprite or bird,
   What sweet thoughts are thine:
I have never heard
   Praise of love or wine
That panted forth a flood of rapture so divine.

Chorus hymeneal,
        Or triumphal chaunt,
Matched with thine would be all
        But an empty vaunt—
A thing wherein we feel there is some hidden want.

What objects are the fountains
        Of thy happy strain?
What fields, or waves, or mountains?
        What shapes of sky or plain?
What love of thine own kind? what ignorance of pain?

With thy clear keen joyance,
        Languor cannot be:
Shadow of annoyance
        Never came near thee:
Thou lovest, but never knew love's sad satiety.

Waking or asleep,
        Thou of death must deem
Things more true and deep
        Than we mortals dream,
Or how could thy notes flow in such a crystal stream?

We look before and after,
        And pine for what is not:
Our sincerest laughter
        With some pain is fraught;
Our sweetest songs are those that tell of saddest thought.

Yet if we could scorn
        Hate, and pride, and fear;
If we were things born
        Not to shed a tear,
I know not how thy joy we ever should come near.

Better than all measures
        Of delightful sound,
Better than all treasures
        That in books are found,
Thy skill to poet were, thou scorner of the ground!

Teach me half the gladness
    That thy brain must know,
Such harmonious madness
    From my lips would flow,
The world should listen then, as I am listening now.

PERCY BYSSHE SHELLEY

Shelley's Skylark
(The Neighborhood of Leghorn: March, 1887)

Somewhere afield here something lies
In Earth's oblivious eyeless trust
That moved a poet to prophecies—
A pinch of unseen, unguarded dust:

The dust of the lark that Shelley heard,
And made immortal through times to be;—
Though it only lived like another bird,
And knew not its immortality:

Lived its meek life; then, one day, fell—
A little ball of feather and bone;
And how it perished, when piped farewell,
And where it wastes, are alike unknown.

Maybe it rests in the loam I view,
Maybe it throbs in a myrtle's green,
Maybe it sleeps in the coming hue
Of a grape on the slopes of yon inland scene.

Go find it, faeries, go and find
That tiny pinch of priceless dust,
And bring a casket silver-lined,
And framed of gold that gems encrust;

And we will lay it safe therein,
And consecrate it to endless time;
For it inspired a bard to win
Ecstatic heights in thought and rhyme.

THOMAS HARDY

The Daffodils

I wandered lonely as a cloud
That floats on high o'er vales and hills,
When all at once I saw a crowd,
A host, of golden daffodils;
Beside the lake, beneath the trees,
Fluttering and dancing in the breeze.

Continuous as the stars that shine
And twinkle on the milky way,
They stretched in never-ending line
Along the margin of a bay:
Ten thousand saw I at a glance,
Tossing their heads in sprightly dance.

The waves beside them danced; but they
Out-did the sparkling waves in glee:
A poet could not but be gay,
In such a jocund company:
I gazed—and gazed—but little thought
What wealth the show to me had brought:

For oft, when on my couch I lie
In vacant or in pensive mood,
They flash upon that inward eye
Which is the bliss of solitude;
And then my heart with pleasure fills,
And dances with the daffodils.

WILLIAM WORDSWORTH

My Heart Leaps Up

My heart leaps up when I behold
  A rainbow in the sky:
So was it when my life began;
So is it now I am a man;
So be it when I shall grow old,
  Or let me die!

The Child is father of the Man;
And I could wish my days to be
Bound each to each by natural piety.

Kubla Khan

In Xanadu did Kubla Khan
A stately pleasure-dome decree:
Where Alph, the sacred river, ran
Through caverns measureless to man
   Down to a sunless sea.
So twice five miles of fertile ground
With walls and towers were girdled round:
And there were gardens bright with sinuous rills,
Where blossomed many an incense-bearing tree;
And here were forests ancient as the hills,
Enfolding sunny spots of greenery.

But oh! that deep romantic chasm which slanted
Down the green hill athwart a cedarn cover!
A savage place! as holy and enchanted
As e'er beneath a waning moon was haunted
By woman wailing for her demon-lover!
And from this chasm, with ceaseless turmoil seething,
As if this earth in fast thick pants were breathing,
A mighty fountain momently was forced:
Amid whose swift half-intermitted burst
Huge fragments vaulted like rebounding hail,
Or chaffy grain beneath the thresher's flail:
And 'mid these dancing rocks at once and ever
It flung up momently the sacred river.
Five miles meandering with a mazy motion
Through wood and dale the sacred river ran,
Then reached the caverns measureless to man,
And sank in tumult to a lifeless ocean:

23

And 'mid this tumult Kubla heard from far
Ancestral voices prophesying war!
    The shadow of the dome of pleasure
    Floated midway on the waves;
    Where was heard the mingled measure
    From the fountain and the caves.
It was a miracle of rare device,
A sunny pleasure-dome with caves of ice!

    A damsel with a dulcimer
    In a vision once I saw:
    It was an Abyssinian maid,
    And on her dulcimer she played,
    Singing of Mount Abora.
Could I revive within me
Her symphony and song,
To such a deep delight 'twould win me,
That with music loud and long,
I would build that dome in air,
That sunny dome! those caves of ice!
And all who heard should see them there,
And all should cry, Beware! Beware!
His flashing eyes, his floating hair!
Weave a circle round him thrice,
And close your eyes with holy dread,
For he on honey-dew hath fed,
And drunk the milk of Paradise.

SAMUEL TAYLOR COLERIDGE

To the Evening Star

Thou fair-haired angel of the evening,
Now, whilst the sun rests on the mountains, light
Thy bright torch of love; thy radiant crown
Put on, and smile upon our evening bed!
Smile on our loves, and while thou drawest the
Blue curtains of the sky, scatter thy silver dew

24

On every flower that shuts its sweet eyes
In timely sleep. Let thy west wind sleep on
The lake; speak silence with thy glimmering eyes,
And wash the dusk with silver. Soon, full soon,
Dost thou withdraw; then the wolf rages wide,
And the lion glares through the dun forest:
The fleeces of our flocks are covered with
Thy sacred dew: protect them with thine influence.

WILLIAM BLAKE

Piping Down the Valleys Wild
(FROM *Songs of Innocence*)

Piping down the valleys wild,
Piping songs of pleasant glee,
On a cloud I saw a child,
And he laughing said to me:

"Pipe a song about a Lamb!"
So I piped with merry chear.
"Piper, pipe that song again";
So I piped: he wept to hear.

"Drop thy pipe, thy happy pipe;
Sing thy songs of happy chear":
So I sung the same again,
While he wept with joy to hear.

"Piper, sit thee down and write
In a book, that all may read."
So he vanish'd from my sight,
And I pluck'd a hollow reed,

And I made a rural pen,
And I stain'd the water clear,
And I wrote my happy songs
Every child may joy to hear.

WILLIAM BLAKE

Mirth, with Thee I Mean to Live

(FROM *L'Allegro*)

Haste thee, Nymph, and bring with thee
Jest and youthful Jollity,
Quips and Cranks and wanton Wiles,
Nods and Becks and Wreathèd Smiles,
Such as hang on Hebe's cheek,
And love to live in dimple sleek;
Sport that wrinkled Care derides,
And Laughter holding both his sides.
Come, and trip it as you go
On the light fantastic toe,
And in thy right hand lead with thee,
The Mountain Nymph, sweet Liberty;
And if I give thee honor due,
Mirth, admit me of thy crew,
To live with her, and live with thee,
In unreprovèd pleasures free;
To hear the Lark begin his flight,
And, singing, startle the dull night,
From his watch-tower in the skies,
Till the dappled dawn doth rise;
Then to come, in spite of sorrow,
And at my window bid good-morrow,
Through the Sweet-Briar or the Vine,
Or the twisted Eglantine.
While the Cock, with lively din,
Scatters the rear of darkness thin;
And to the stack, or the Barn-door,
Stoutly struts his Dames before,
Oft listening how the Hounds and Horn
Cheerly rouse the slumbering morn,
From the side of some Hoar Hill,
Through the high wood echoing shrill.
Some time walking not unseen
By Hedge-row Elms, on Hillocks green,

Right against the Eastern gate,
Where the great Sun begins his state,
Robed in flames and Amber light,
The clouds in thousand Liveries dight.
While the Plowman, near at hand,
Whistles o'er the Furrowed Land,
And the Milkmaid singeth blithe,
And the Mower whets his scythe,
And every Shepherd tells his tale
Under the Hawthorn in the dale.
. . . These delights, if thou canst give,
Mirth, with thee I mean to live.

JOHN MILTON

Hark, Hark! the Lark

(FROM Cymbeline)

Hark, hark! the lark at heaven's gate sings,
    And Phoebus 'gins arise,
His steeds to water at those springs
    On chaliced flowers that lies;
And winking Mary-buds begin
    To ope their golden eyes;
With every thing that pretty is,
    My lady sweet, arise:
        Arise, arise!

WILLIAM SHAKESPEARE

Where the Bee Sucks

(FROM *The Tempest*)

Where the bee sucks, there suck I,
In a cowslip's bell I lie;
There I couch when owls do cry.
On the bat's back I do fly
After summer merrily:
Merrily, merrily, shall I live now
Under the blossom that hangs on the bough.

WILLIAM SHAKESPEARE

common with John Donne and Robert Herrick, males born in 1572 and 1591, than with Robert Browning, born in 1806. The last poems in this group reflect another pattern; a father's love for his children. Oddly, so far as I can discover, good poems of another love remain to be written. Perhaps it is natural that the male poets have failed. But Elizabeth Barrett Browning's verses to her child are not her best; and Christina Rossetti, Emily Dickinson, and Edna Millay had no children.

BOOK TWO

Of Love

Obviously, poets write love poems with love; and, equally obviously, most readers love love poems best. Even in circles which tend to distrust poetry in general there is an uneasy sense that poetry and love somehow belong together, and love is, on the whole and with exceptions, approved. There isn't much more worth saying about love poems. Except, perhaps, that the best poets write their best love poems as young poets, and a part of the joy of reading them is to share their youth.

I would urge readers of these love poems to browse like butterflies, sipping here and hovering there and fluttering, haphazard, from poem to poem. Poets have always tended to approve the butterfly's wayward way of life, and there may be something to it. Readers who, having been properly taught, insist on beginning at the beginning and plodding steadily to the end, will find these poems arranged, for the most part, according to the chronology of their authors' lives. This does not make much sense, but at least it gives an opportunity for thoughtful readers to test the rash statements, made by some psychologists, that the nature of love between men and women changes across the centuries. They may discover that Edna St. Vincent Millay, a woman born in 1892, had rather more in

*common with John Donne and Robert Herrick, males born in
1572 and 1591, than with Robert Browning, born in 1806.*

*The last poems in this group reflect another pattern: a
father's love for his children. Oddly, so far as I can discover,
good poems of mother love remain to be written. Perhaps it is
natural that the male poets have failed. But Elizabeth Barrett
Browning's verses to her child are not her best; and Christina
Rossetti, Emily Dickinson and Edna Millay had no children.*

The Face of Helen

(FROM Dr. Faustus)

Was this the face that launched a thousand ships,
And burnt the topless towers of Ilium?
Sweet Helen, make me immortal with a kiss.

(Kisses her.)

Her lips suck forth my soul: see, where it flies!
Come, Helen, come, give me my soul again.
Here will I dwell, for heaven is in these lips,
And all is dross that is not Helena.
I will be Paris, and for love of thee,
Instead of Troy, shall Wertenberg be sacked;
And I will combat with weak Menelaus,
And wear thy colors on my plumed crest;
Yes, I will wound Achilles in the heel,
And then return to Helen for a kiss.
O, thou are fairer than the evening air
Clad in the beauty of a thousand stars;
Brighter art thou than flaming Jupiter
When he appeared to hapless Semele;
More lovely than the monarch of the sky
In wanton Arethusa's azured arms;
And none but thou shalt be my paramour.

CHRISTOPHER MARLOWE

O Mistress Mine

(FROM Twelfth Night)

O Mistress mine, where are you roaming?
O stay and hear! your true love's coming
    That can sing both high and low;
Trip no further, pretty sweeting,
Journeys end in lovers' meeting,
    Every wise man's son doth know.

What is love? 'Tis not hereafter;
Present mirth hath present laughter;
   What's to come is still unsure:
In delay there lies no plenty;
Then come kiss me, Sweet-and-twenty,
   Youth's a stuff will not endure.

WILLIAM SHAKESPEARE

Shall I Compare Thee to a Summer's Day?

Shall I compare thee to a summer's day?
Thou art more lovely and more temperate:
Rough winds do shake the darling buds of May,
And summer's lease hath all too short a date:
Sometime too hot the eye of heaven shines,
And often is his gold complexion dimmed;
And every fair from fair sometime declines,
By chance, or nature's changing course, untrimmed;
But thy eternal summer shall not fade,
Nor lose possession of that fair thou owest;
Nor shall Death brag thou wanderest in his shade,
When in eternal lines to time thou growest:
   So long as men can breathe, or eyes can see,
   So long lives this, and this gives life to thee.

WILLIAM SHAKESPEARE

When in the Chronicle of Wasted Time

When in the chronicle of wasted time
I see descriptions of the fairest wights,
And beauty making beautiful old rhyme,
In praise of ladies dead, and lovely knights;
Then in the blazon of sweet beauty's best,
Of hand, of foot, of lip, of eye, of brow,
I see their antique pen would have expressed

Even such a beauty as you master now.
So all their praises are but prophecies
Of this our time, all you prefiguring;
And, for they looked but with divining eyes,
They had not skill enough your worth to sing:
   For we, which now behold these present days,
   Have eyes to wonder, but lack tongues to praise.

WILLIAM SHAKESPEARE

Let Me Not to the Marriage of True Minds

Let me not to the marriage of true minds
Admit impediments. Love is not love
Which alters when it alteration finds,
Or bends with the remover to remove:
O no! it is an ever-fixed mark
That looks on tempests and is never shaken;
It is the star to every wandering bark,
Whose worth's unknown, although his height be taken.
Love's not Time's fool, though rosy lips and cheeks
Within his bending sickle's compass come;
Love alters not with his brief hours and weeks,
But bears it out even to the edge of doom:
   If this be error, and upon me proved,
   I never writ, nor no man ever loved.

WILLIAM SHAKESPEARE

When to the Sessions of Sweet Silent Thought

When to the sessions of sweet silent thought
I summon up remembrance of things past,
I sigh the lack of many a thing I sought,
And with old woes new wail my dear time's waste:
Then can I drown an eye, unused to flow,
For precious friends hid in death's dateless night,

33

And weep afresh love's long since cancelled woe,
And moan the expense of many a vanished sight:
Then can I grieve at grievances foregone,
And heavily from woe to woe tell o'er
The sad account of fore-bemoaned moan,
Which I now pay as if not paid before:
 But if the while I think on thee, dear friend,
 All losses are restored, and sorrows end.

WILLIAM SHAKESPEARE

When in Disgrace with Fortune and Men's Eyes

When in disgrace with fortune and men's eyes
I all alone beweep my outcast state,
And trouble deaf heaven with my bootless cries,
And look upon myself and curse my fate,
Wishing me like to one more rich in hope,
Featured like him, like him with friends possessed,
Desiring this man's art and that man's scope,
With what I most enjoy contented least;
Yet in these thoughts myself almost despising,
Haply I think on thee, and then my state,
Like to the lark at break of day arising,
From sullen earth sings hymns at heaven's gate:
 For thy sweet love remembered such wealth brings
 That then I scorn to change my state with kings.

WILLIAM SHAKESPEARE

That Time of Year Thou May'st in Me Behold

That time of year thou may'st in me behold
When yellow leaves, or none, or few, do hang
Upon those boughs which shake against the cold,
Bare ruined choirs, where late the sweet birds sang.
In me thou seest the twilight of such day
As after sunset fadeth in the west,

34

Which by and by black night doth take away,
Death's second self that seals up all in rest.
In me thou seest the glowing of such fire
That on the ashes of his youth doth lie,
As the death-bed whereon it must expire,
Consumed with that which it was nourished by.
  This thou perceiv'st, which makes thy love more strong,
  To love that well which thou must leave ere long.

WILLIAM SHAKESPEARE

To Celia

Drink to me only with thine eyes,
  And I will pledge with mine;
Or leave a kiss but in the cup
  And I'll not look for wine.
The thirst that from the soul doth rise
  Doth ask a drink divine;
But might I of Jove's nectar sup,
  I would not change for thine.

I sent thee late a rosy wreath,
  Not so much honoring thee
As giving it a hope that there
  It could not withered be;
But thou thereon didst only breathe
  And sent'st it back to me;
Since when it grows, and smells, I swear,
  Not of itself but thee!

BEN JONSON

Come, My Celia

(FROM *Volpone*)

Come, my Celia, let us prove,
  While we can, the sports of love;
Time will not be ours forever,
He, at length, our good will sever.

Spend not then his gifts in vain;
Suns that set may rise again:
But if once we lose this light,
'Tis with us perpetual night.
Why should we defer our joys?
Fame and rumor are but toys.
Cannot we delude the eyes
Of a few poor household-spies?
Or his easier ears beguile,
Thus removèd, by our wile?
'Tis no sin, love's fruits to steal;
But the sweet thefts to reveal:
To be taken, to be seen,
These have crimes accounted been.

BEN JONSON

The Good-Morrow

I wonder, by my troth, what thou and I
Did, till we loved? Were we not weaned till then?
But sucked on country pleasures, childishly?
Or snored we in the Seven Sleepers' den?
'Twas so; but this, all pleasures fancies be;
If ever any beauty I did see,
Which I desired, and got, 'twas but a dream of thee.

And now good-morrow to our waking souls,
Which watch not one another out of fear;
For love all love of other sights controls,
And makes one little room an everywhere.
Let sea-discoverers to new worlds have gone,
Let maps to other worlds on worlds have shown,
Let us possess one world; each hath one, and is one.

My face in thine eye, thine in mine appears,
And true plain hearts do in the faces rest;
Where can we find two better hemispheres

Without sharp north, without declining west?
Whatever dies, was not mixed equally;
If our two loves be one, or thou and I
Love so alike that none do slacken, none can die.

JOHN DONNE

Go and Catch a Falling Star

Go and catch a falling star,
   Get with child a mandrake root,
Tell me where all past years are,
   Or who cleft the Devil's foot;
Teach me to hear mermaids singing,
Or to keep off envy's stinging,
          And find
          What wind
Serves to advance an honest mind.

If thou be'st born to strange sights,
   Things invisible to see,
Ride ten thousand days and nights,
   Till Age snow white hairs on thee;
Thou, when thou return'st, wilt tell me
All strange wonders that befell thee,
          And swear
          No where
Lives a woman true and fair.

If thou find'st one, let me know;
   Such a pilgrimage were sweet.
Yet do not; I would not go,
   Though at next door we might meet,
Though she were true when you met her,
And last till you write your letter,
          Yet she
          Will be
False, ere I come, to two or three.

JOHN DONNE

Take, O Take Those Lips Away

Take, O take those lips away
    That so sweetly were forsworn,
And those eyes, the break of day;
    Lights that do mislead the morn.
But my kisses bring again,
Seals of love, though sealed in vain.

Hide, O hide those hills of snow,
    Which thy frozen bosom bears,
On whose tops the pinks that grow
    Are of those that April wears!
But first set my poor heart free,
Bound in those icy chains by thee.

WILLIAM SHAKESPEARE (?)
and JOHN FLETCHER

The Manly Heart

Shall I, wasting in despair,
Die because a woman's fair?
Or make pale my cheeks with care
'Cause another's rosy are?
Be she fairer than the day,
Or the flowery meads in May,
    If she think not well of me,
    What care I how fair she be?

Shall my silly heart be pined
'Cause I see a woman kind?
Or a well disposèd nature
Joinèd with a lovely feature?
Be she meeker, kinder, than
Turtle-dove or pelican,
    If she be not so to me,
    What care I how kind she be?

Shall a woman's virtues move
Me to perish for her love?
Or her well-deservings known
Make me quite forget mine own?
Be she with that goodness blest
Which may merit name of Best,
   If she be not such to me,
   What care I how good she be?

'Cause her fortune seems too high,
Shall I play the fool and die?
She that bears a noble mind,
If not outward helps she find,
Thinks what with them he would do
Who without them dares her woo;
   And unless that mind I see,
   What care I how great she be?

Great, or good, or kind, or fair,
I will ne'er the more despair;
If she love me, this believe,
I will die ere she shall grieve;
If she slight me when I woo,
I can scorn and let her go;
   For if she be not for me,
   What care I for whom she be?

GEORGE WITHER

Delight in Disorder

A sweet disorder in the dress
Kindles in clothes a wantonness:
A lawn about the shoulders thrown
Into a fine distraction:
An erring lace, which here and there
Enthrals the crimson stomacher:
A cuff neglectful, and thereby

Ribbons to flow confusedly:
A winning wave, deserving note,
In the tempestuous petticoat:
A careless shoe-string, in whose tie
I see a wild civility:
Do more bewitch me than when art
Is too precise in every part.

ROBERT HERRICK

To His Mistress Objecting
to Him Neither Toying or Talking

You say I love not, 'cause I do not play
Still with your curls, and kiss the time away.
You blame me too because I can't devise
Some sport to please those babies in your eyes;
By love's religion I must here confess it,
The most I love when I the least express it.
Small griefs find tongues; full casks are ever found
To give, if any, yet but little sound.

ROBERT HERRICK

Upon Julia's Clothes

Whenas in silks my Julia goes,
Then, then, methinks, how sweetly flows
The liquefaction of her clothes.

Next, when I cast mine eyes and see
That brave vibration each way free,
O how that glittering taketh me!

ROBERT HERRICK

To the Virgins, to Make Much of Time

Gather ye rosebuds while ye may,
    Old Time is still a-flying,
And this same flower that smiles to-day,
    To-morrow will be dying.

The glorious lamp of heaven, the sun,
    The higher he's a-getting,
The sooner will his race be run,
    And nearer he's to setting.

That age is best which is the first,
    When youth and blood are warmer;
But being spent, the worse, and worst
    Times still succeed the former.

Then be not coy, but use your time,
    And while ye may, go marry;
For having lost but once your prime,
    You may for ever tarry.

ROBERT HERRICK

He That Loves a Rosy Cheek
(FROM *Unfading Beauty*)

He that loves a rosy cheek
    Or a coral lip admires,
Or from star-like eyes doth seek
    Fuel to maintain his fires:
As old Time makes these decay,
So his flames must waste away.

But a smooth and steadfast mind,
    Gentle thoughts, and calm desires,
Hearts with equal love combined
    Kindle never-dying fires:
Where these are not, I despise
Lovely cheeks, or lips, or eyes.

THOMAS CAREW

Thus Eve to Adam

(FROM *Paradise Lost*, Book IV)

"My author and disposer, what thou biddest
Unargued I obey; so God ordains,
God is thy law, thou mine: to know no more
Is woman's happiest knowledge and her praise.
With thee conversing, I forget all time,
All seasons and their change, all please alike.
Sweet is the breath of morn, her rising sweet
With charm of earliest birds; pleasant the sun
When first on this delightful land he spreads
His orient beams, on herb, tree, fruit, and flower,
Glistering with dew; fragrant the fertile earth
After soft showers; and sweet the coming on
Of grateful evening mild, then silent night
With this her solemn bird and this fair moon,
And these the gems of heaven, her starry train:
But neither breath of morn when she ascends
With charm of earliest birds, nor rising sun
On this delightful land, nor herb, fruit, flower,
Glistering with dew, nor fragrance after showers,
Nor grateful evening mild, nor silent night
With this her solemn bird, nor walk by moon,
Or glittering starlight without thee is sweet.
But wherefore all night long shine these, for whom
This glorious sight, when sleep hath shut all eyes?"

JOHN MILTON

The Constant Lover

Out upon it, I have loved
Three whole days together!
And am like to love three more,
If it prove fair weather.

Time shall moult away his wings,
    Ere he shall discover
In the whole wide world again
    Such a constant lover.

But the spite on't is, no praise
    Is due at all to me:
Love with me had made no stays,
    Had it any been but she.

Had it any been but she,
    And that very face,
There had been at least ere this
    A dozen dozen in her place.

JOHN SUCKLING

Why So Pale and Wan?

Why so pale and wan, fond lover?
    Prithee, why so pale?
Will, when looking well can't move her,
    Looking ill prevail?
    Prithee, why so pale?

Why so dull and mute, young sinner?
    Prithee, why so mute?
Will, when speaking well can't win her,
    Saying nothing do't?
    Prithee, why so mute?

Quit, quit, for shame, this will not move:
    This cannot take her.
If of herself she will not love,
    Nothing can make her:
    The devil take her!

JOHN SUCKLING

Had we but world enough, and time,
This coyness, Lady, were no crime.
We would sit down and think which way
To walk, and pass our long love's day.
Thou by the Indian Ganges' side
Shouldst rubies find: I by the tide
Of Humber would complain. I would
Love you ten years before the Flood:
And you should, if you please, refuse
Till the conversion of the Jews.
My vegetable love should grow
Vaster than empires, and more slow;
An hundred years should go to praise
Thine eyes, and on thy forehead gaze.
Two hundred to adore each breast,
But thirty thousand to the rest;
An age at least to every part,
And the last age should show your heart.
For, Lady, you deserve this state,
Nor would I love at lower rate.

But at my back I always hear
Time's wingèd chariot hurrying near;
And yonder all before us lie
Deserts of vast eternity.
Thy beauty shall no more be found,
Nor, in thy marble vault, shall sound
My echoing song: then worms shall try
That long preserved virginity,
And your quaint honor turns to dust,
And into ashes all my lust:
The grave's a fine and private place
But none, I think, do there embrace.

Now therefore, while the youthful hue
Sits on thy skin like morning dew,
And while thy willing soul transpires

At every pore with instant fires,
Now let us sport us while we may,
And now, like amorous birds of prey,
Rather at once our time devour
Than languish in his slow-chapt power.
Let us roll all our strength and all
Our sweetness up into one ball,
And tear our pleasures with rough strife
Through the iron gates of life:
Thus, though we cannot make our sun
Stand still, yet we will make him run.

ANDREW MARVELL

Annie Laurie

Maxwelton braes are bonnie
  Where early fa's the dew,
And it's there that Annie Laurie
  Gie'd me her promise true—
Gie'd me her promise true,
  Which ne'er forgot will be;
And for bonnie Annie Laurie
  I'd lay me doun and dee.

Her brow is like the snaw-drift;
  Her throat is like the swan;
Her face it is the fairest
  That e'er the sun shone on—
That e'er the sun shone on—
  And dark blue is her ee;
And for bonnie Annie Laurie
  I'd lay me doun and dee.

Like dew on the gowan lying
  Is the fa' o' her fairy feet;
And like winds in summer sighing,
  Her voice is low and sweet—

Her voice is low and sweet—
    And she's a' the world to me;
And for bonnie Annie Laurie
    I'd lay me doun and dee.

WILLIAM DOUGLAS

Never Seek to Tell Thy Love

Never seek to tell thy love
Love that never told can be;
For the gentle wind does move
Silently, invisibly.

I told my love, I told my love,
I told her all my heart,
Trembling, cold, in ghastly fears—
Ah, she doth depart.

Soon as she was gone from me
A traveller came by
Silently, invisibly—
O, was no deny.

WILLIAM BLAKE

The Clod and the Pebble

"Love seeketh not itself to please,
    Nor for itself hath any care,
But for another gives its ease,
    And builds a Heaven in Hell's despair."

So sung a little Clod of Clay
    Trodden with the cattle's feet,
But a Pebble of the brook
    Warbled out these metres meet:

"Love seeketh only Self to please,
To bind another to its delight.
Joys in another's loss of ease,
And builds a Hell in Heaven's despite."

WILLIAM BLAKE

The Garden of Love

I went to the Garden of Love
And saw what I never had seen:
A Chapel was built in the midst,
Where I used to play on the green.

And the gates of this Chapel were shut,
And "Thou shalt not" writ over the door;
So I turned to the Garden of Love
That so many sweet flowers bore;

And I saw it was fillèd with graves,
And tomb-stones where flowers should be;
And priests in black gowns were walking their rounds,
And binding with briars my joys and desires.

WILLIAM BLAKE

John Anderson My Jo

John Anderson my jo, John,
When we were first acquent
Your locks were like the raven,
Your bonnie brow was brent;
But now your brow is beld, John,
Your locks are like the snow;
But blessings on your frosty pow,
John Anderson my jo.

John Anderson, my jo, John,
We clamb the hill thegither,
And mony a canty day, John,
We've had wi' ane anither:
Now we maun totter down, John,
But hand in hand we'll go,
And sleep thegither at the foot,
John Anderson my jo.

ROBERT BURNS

A Red, Red Rose

O, my luve's like a red, red rose
    That's newly sprung in June;
O, my luve's like the melodie
    That's sweetly played in tune.

As fair thou art, my bonnie lass,
    So deep in luve am I:
And I will luve thee still, my dear,
    Till a' the seas gang dry.

Till a' the seas gang dry, my dear,
    And the rocks melt wi' the sun;
And I will luve thee still, my dear,
    While the sands o' life shall run.

And fare-thee-weel, my only luve!
    And fare-thee-weel a while!
And I will come again, my luve,
    Tho' it were ten thousand mile.

ROBERT BURNS

She was a phantom of delight
When first she gleamed upon my sight;
A lovely apparition, sent
To be a moment's ornament;
Her eyes as stars of twilight fair;
Like twilight's, too, her dusky hair;
But all things else about her drawn
From May-time and the cheerful dawn;
A dancing shape, an image gay,
To haunt, to startle and waylay.

I saw her upon nearer view,
A Spirit, yet a Woman too!
Her household motions light and free,
And steps of virgin liberty;
A countenance in which did meet
Sweet records, promises as sweet;
A creature not too bright or good
For human nature's daily food;
For transient sorrows, simple wiles,
Praise, blame, love, kisses, tears, and smiles.

And now I see with eye serene
The very pulse of the machine;
A being breathing thoughtful breath,
A traveller between life and death;
The reason firm, the temperate will,
Endurance, foresight, strength, and skill;
A perfect Woman, nobly planned,
To warn, to comfort, and command;
And yet a Spirit still, and bright
With something of angelic light.

WILLIAM WORDSWORTH

Lucy

She dwelt among the untrodden ways
Beside the springs of Dove,
A Maid whom there were none to praise
And very few to love:

A violet by the mossy stone
Half hidden from the eye!
Fair as a star, when only one
Is shining in the sky.

She lived unknown, and few could know
When Lucy ceased to be;
But she is in her grave, and oh,
The difference to me!

WILLIAM WORDSWORTH

Believe Me, If All Those Endearing Young Charms

Believe me, if all those endearing young charms,
Which I gaze on so fondly to-day,
Were to change by to-morrow, and fleet in my arms,
Like fairy-gifts fading away,
Thou wouldst still be adored, as this moment thou art,
Let thy loveliness fade as it will,
And around the dear ruin each wish of my heart
Would entwine itself verdantly still.

It is not while beauty and youth are thine own,
And thy cheeks unprofaned by a tear,
That the fervor and faith of a soul may be known,
To which time will but make thee more dear!
No, the heart that has truly loved never forgets,
But as truly loves on to the close,
As the sunflower turns to her god when he sets
The same look which she turned when he rose!

THOMAS MOORE

Rondeau

Jenny kissed me when we met,
    Jumping from the chair she sat in;
Time, you thief, who love to get
    Sweets into your list, put that in!
Say I'm weary, say I'm sad,
    Say that health and wealth have missed me,
Say I'm growing old, but add,
    Jenny kissed me.

LEIGH HUNT

Maid of Athens

Maid of Athens, ere we part,
Give, oh, give me back my heart!
Or, since that has left my breast,
Keep it now, and take the rest!
Hear my vow before I go,
Ζώη μοῦ, σὰς ἀγαπῶ.*

By those tresses unconfined,
Wooed by each Aegean wind;
By those lids whose jetty fringe
Kiss thy soft cheeks' blooming tinge;
By those wild eyes like the roe,
Ζώη μοῦ, σὰς ἀγαπῶ.

By that lip I long to taste;
By that zone-encircled waist;
By all the token-flowers that tell
What words can never speak so well;
By love's alternate joy and woe,
Ζώη μοῦ, σὰς ἀγαπῶ.

---

* For Byron the Greek language was just another medium of communication like English. His famous final line may be pronounced something like "Zoe mou, sass agapo." It means "My life, I love you."

51

Maid of Athens! I am gone:
Think of me, sweet! when alone.
Though I fly to Istambol,
Athens holds my heart and soul:
Can I cease to love thee? No!
Ζώη μοῦ, σὰς ἀγαπῶ.

GEORGE GORDON BYRON

We'll Go No More a-Roving

So, we'll go no more a-roving
  So late into the night,
Though the heart be still as loving,
  And the moon be still as bright.

For the sword outwears the sheath,
  And the soul wears out the breast,
And the heart must pause to breathe,
  And Love itself have rest.

Though the night was made for loving,
  And the day returns too soon,
Yet we'll go no more a-roving
  By the light of the moon.

GEORGE GORDON BYRON

Love's Philosophy

The fountains mingle with the river,
  And the rivers with the ocean,
The winds of heaven mix forever
  With a sweet emotion;
Nothing in the world is single;
  All things by a law divine
In one another's being mingle;
  Why not I with thine?

See the mountains kiss high heaven,
    And the waves clasp one another;
No sister flower would be forgiven
    If it disdained its brother;
And the sunlight clasps the earth,
    And the moonbeams kiss the sea;
What are all these kissings worth,
    If thou kiss not me?

PERCY BYSSHE SHELLEY

To——

One word is too often profaned
    For me to profane it,
One feeling too falsely disdained
    For thee to disdain it.
One hope is too like despair
    For prudence to smother,
And Pity from thee more dear
    Than that from another.

I can give not what men call love,
    But wilt thou accept not
The worship the heart lifts above
    And the heavens reject not:
The desire of the moth for the star,
    Of the night for the morrow,
The devotion to something afar
    From the sphere of our sorrow.

PERCY BYSSHE SHELLEY

Sonnet

Written on a Blank Page in Shakespeare's Poems, Facing "A Lover's Complaint"

Bright star! would I were steadfast as thou art—
 Not in lone splendor hung aloft the night
And watching, with eternal lids apart,
 Like nature's patient, sleepless Eremite,
The moving waters at their priest-like task
 Of pure ablution round earth's human shores,
Or gazing on the new soft fallen mask
 Of snow upon the mountains and the moors—
No—yet still steadfast, still unchangeable,
 Pillow'd upon my fair love's ripening breast,
To feel for ever its soft fall and swell,
 Awake for ever in a sweet unrest,
Still, still to hear her tender-taken breath,
And so live ever—or else swoon to death.

JOHN KEATS

Lochinvar

O, young Lochinvar is come out of the west,
Through all the wide Border his steed was the best,
And, save his good broadsword, he weapons had none,
He rode all unarmed, and he rode all alone.
So faithful in love, and so dauntless in war,
There never was knight like the young Lochinvar.

He stayed not for brake, and he stopped not for stone,
He swam the Eske River where ford there was none;
But ere he alighted at Netherby gate
The bride had consented, the gallant came late;
For a laggard in love, and a dastard in war,
Was to wed the fair Ellen of brave Lochinvar.

So boldly he entered the Netherby Hall,
Among bridesmen and kinsmen and brothers and all.
Then spoke the bride's father, his hand on his sword,

(For the poor craven bridegroom said never a word),
"O come ye in peace here, or come ye in war,
Or to dance at our bridal, young Lord Lochinvar?"

"I long wooed your daughter, my suit you denied;—
Love swells like the Solway, but ebbs like its tide,—
And now I am come, with this lost love of mine,
To lead but one measure, drink one cup of wine.
There are maidens in Scotland more lovely by far,
That would gladly be bride to the young Lochinvar."

The bride kissed the goblet; the knight took it up,
He quaffed off the wine, and he threw down the cup.
She looked down to blush, and she looked up to sigh,
With a smile on her lips, and a tear in her eye.
He took her soft hand ere her mother could bar,—
"Now tread we a measure!" said young Lochinvar.

So stately his form, and so lovely her face
That never a hall such a galliard did grace;
While her mother did fret, and her father did fume.
And the bridegroom stood dangling his bonnet and plume;
And the bridesmaids whispered, " 'Twere better by far
To have matched our fair cousin with young Lochinvar."

One touch to her hand, and one word in her ear,
When they reached the hall-door, and the charger stood near;
So light to the croupe the fair lady he swung,
So light to the saddle before her he sprung!
"She is won! we are gone, over bank, bush and scaur;
They'll have fleet steeds that follow," quoth young Lochinvar.

There was mounting 'mong Graemes of the Netherby clan;
Forsters, Fenwicks, and Musgraves, they rode and they ran:
There was racing and chasing on Cannobie Lee,
But the lost bride of Netherby ne'er did they see.
So daring in love, and so dauntless in war,
Have ye e'er heard of gallant like young Lochinvar?

WALTER SCOTT

Secret Love

I hid my love when young till I
Couldn't bear the buzzing of a fly;
I hid my life to my despite
Till I could not bear to look at light:
I dare not gaze upon her face
But left her memory in each place;
Where'er I saw a wild flower lie
I kissed and bade my love good-bye.

I met her in the greenest dells,
Where dewdrops pearl the wood bluebells;
The lost breeze kissed her bright blue eye,
The bee kissed and went singing by,
A sunbeam found a passage there,
A gold chain round her neck so fair;
As secret as the wild bee's song
She lay there all the summer long.

I hid my love in field and town
Till e'en the breeze would knock me down;
The bees seemed singing ballads o'er,
The fly's bass turned a lion's roar;
And even silence found a tongue,
To haunt me all the summer long;
The riddle nature could not prove
Was nothing else but secret love.

JOHN CLARE

She Is Not Fair

She is not fair to outward view
    As many maidens be,
Her loveliness I never knew
    Until she smiled on me;
Oh! then I saw her eye was bright,
A well of love, a spring of light.

56

But now her looks are coy and cold,
  To mine they ne'er reply,
And yet I cease not to behold
  The love-light in her eye:
Her very frowns are fairer far
Than smiles of other maidens are.

HARTLEY COLERIDGE

How Do I Love Thee?
(FROM *Sonnets from the Portuguese*)

How do I love thee? Let me count the ways.
I love thee to the depth and breadth and height
My soul can reach, when feeling out of sight
For the ends of Being and ideal Grace.
I love thee to the level of everyday's
Most quiet need, by sun and candle-light.
I love thee freely, as men strive for Right;
I love thee purely, as they turn from Praise.
I love thee with the passion put to use
In my old griefs, and with my childhood's faith.
I love thee with a love I seemed to lose
With my lost saints,—I love thee with the breath,
Smiles, tears of all my life!—and, if God choose,
I shall but love thee better after death.

ELIZABETH BARRETT BROWNING

Come into the Garden, Maud
(FROM *Maud*)

Come into the garden, Maud,
  For the black bat, night, has flown,
Come into the garden, Maud,
  I am here at the gate alone;
And the woodbine spices are wafted abroad,
  And the musk of the rose is blown.

57

For a breeze of morning moves,
    And the planet of Love is on high,
Beginning to faint in the light that she loves
    On a bed of daffodil sky,
To faint in the light of the sun she loves,
    To faint in his light, and to die.

All night have the roses heard
    The flute, violin, bassoon;
All night has the casement jessamine stirred
    To the dancers dancing in tune;
Till a silence fell with the waking bird,
    And a hush with the setting moon.

I said to the lily, "There is but one
    With whom she has heart to be gay.
When will the dancers leave her alone?
    She is weary of dance and play."
Now half to the setting moon are gone,
    And half to the rising day;
Low on the sand and loud on the stone
    The last wheel echoes away.

I said to the rose, "The brief night goes
    In babble and revel and wine.
O young lord-lover, what sights are those,
    For one that will never be thine?
But mine, but mine," so I sware to the rose,
    "For ever and ever, mine."

And the soul of the rose went into my blood,
    As the music clashed in the hall;
And long by the garden lake I stood,
    For I heard your rivulet fall
From the lake to the meadow and on to the wood,
    Our wood, that is dearer than all.

From the meadow your walks have left so sweet
    That whenever a March-wind sighs

He sets the jewel-print of your feet
    In violets blue as your eyes,
To the woody hollows in which we meet
    And the valleys of Paradise.

The slender acacia would not shake
    One long milk-bloom on the tree;
The white lake-blossom fell into the lake
    As the pimpernel dozed on the lea;
But the rose was awake all night for your sake,
    Knowing your promise to me;
The lilies and roses were all awake,
    They sighed for the dawn and thee.

Queen rose of the rosebud garden of girls,
    Come hither, the dances are done,
In gloss of satin and glimmer of pearls,
    Queen lily and rose in one;
Shine out, little head, sunning over with curls,
    To the flowers, and be their sun.

There has fallen a splendid tear
    From the passion-flower at the gate.
She is coming, my dove, my dear;
    She is coming, my life, my fate;
The red rose cries, "She is near, she is near";
    And the white rose weeps, "She is late";
The larkspur listens, "I hear, I hear";
    And the lily whispers, "I wait."

She is coming, my own, my sweet;
    Were it ever so airy a tread,
My heart would hear her and beat,
    Were it earth in an earthy bed;
My dust would hear her and beat,
    Had I lain for a century dead;
Would start and tremble under her feet,
    And blossom in purple and red.

ALFRED TENNYSON

59

Come, fill the Cup, and in the fire of Spring
Your Winter-garment of Repentance fling:
　　The Bird of Time has but a little way
To flutter—and the Bird is on the Wing.

Whether at Naishápúr or Babylon,
Whether the Cup with sweet or bitter run,
　　The Wine of Life keeps oozing drop by drop,
The Leaves of Life keep falling one by one. . . .

A Book of Verses underneath the Bough,
A Jug of Wine, a Loaf of Bread—and Thou
　　Beside me singing in the Wilderness—
Oh, Wilderness were Paradise enow!

Some for the Glories of This World; and some
Sigh for the Prophet's Paradise to come;
　　Ah, take the Cash, and let the Credit go,
Nor heed the rumble of a distant Drum!

Look to the blowing Rose about us—"Lo,
Laughing," she says, "into the world I blow,
　　At once the silken tassel of my Purse
Tear, and its Treasure on the Garden throw."

And those who husbanded the Golden grain,
And those who flung it to the winds like Rain,
　　Alike to no such aureate Earth are turned
As, buried once, Men want dug up again. . . .

Ah, my Belovèd, fill the cup that clears
To-day of past Regrets and future Fears:
　　To-morrow!—Why, To-morrow I may be
Myself with Yesterday's Sev'n thousand Years.

For some we loved, the loveliest and the best
That from his Vintage rolling Time hath prest,
　　Have drunk their Cup a Round or two before,
And one by one crept silently to rest.

And we, that now make merry in the Room
They left, and Summer dresses in new bloom,
    Ourselves must we beneath the Couch of Earth
Descend—ourselves to make a Couch—for whom?

Ah, make the most of what we yet may spend,
Before we too into the Dust descend;
    Dust into Dust, and under Dust, to lie,
Sans Wine, sans Song, sans Singer, and—sans End! . . .

The Moving Finger writes; and, having writ,
Moves on: nor all your Piety nor Wit
    Shall lure it back to cancel half a Line,
Nor all your Tears wash out a Word of it.

And that inverted Bowl they call the Sky,
Whereunder crawling coop'd we live and die,
    Lift not your hands to *It* for help—for It
As impotently rolls as you or I.

With Earth's first Clay They did the Last Man knead,
And there of the Last Harvest sowed the Seed:
    And the first Morning of Creation wrote
What the Last Dawn of Reckoning shall read.

YESTERDAY *This* Day's Madness did prepare;
To-MORROW's Silence, Triumph, or Despair:
    Drink! for you know not whence you came, nor why:
Drink! for you know not why you go, nor where. . . .

Yet Ah, that Spring should vanish with the Rose!
That Youth's sweet-scented manuscript should close!
    The Nightingale that in the branches sang,
Ah whence, and whither flown again, who knows!

Would but the Desert of the Fountain yield
One glimpse—if dimly, yet indeed, reveal'd,
    To which the fainting Traveller might spring,
As springs the trampled herbage of the field!

Would but some wingèd Angel ere too late
Arrest the yet unfolded Roll of Fate,
    And make the stern Recorder otherwise
Enregister, or quite obliterate!

Ah Love! could you and I with Him conspire
To grasp this sorry Scheme of Things entire,
    Would not we shatter it to bits—and then
Re-mould it nearer to the Heart's Desire!

EDWARD FITZGERALD

To Helen

Helen, thy beauty is to me
    Like those Nicaean barks of yore,
That gently, o'er a perfumed sea,
    The weary, wayworn wanderer bore
    To his own native shore.

On desperate seas long wont to roam,
    Thy hyacinth hair, thy classic face,
Thy Naiad airs, have brought me home
    To the glory that was Greece
    And the grandeur that was Rome.

Lo! in yon brilliant window-niche
    How statue-like I see thee stand,
The agate lamp within thy hand!
    Ah, Psyche, from the regions which
    Are Holy Land!

EDGAR ALLAN POE

Meeting at Night

The gray sea and the long black land;
And the yellow half-moon large and low;
And the startled little waves that leap

In fiery ringlets from their sleep,
As I gain the cove with pushing prow,
And quench its speed in the slushy sand.

Then a mile of warm sea-scented beach;
Three fields to cross till a farm appears;
A tap at the pane, the quick sharp scratch
And blue spurt of a lighted match,
And a voice less loud, through its joys and fears,
Than the two hearts beating each to each!

ROBERT BROWNING

Parting at Morning

Round the cape of a sudden came the sea,
And the sun looked over the mountain's rim:
And straight was a path of gold for him,
And the need of a world of men for me.

ROBERT BROWNING

Love Among the Ruins

Where the quiet-colored end of evening smiles
Miles and miles
On the solitary pastures where our sheep
Half-asleep
Tinkle homeward through the twilight, stray or stop
As they crop—
Was the sight once of a city great and gay
(So they say)
Of our country's very capital, its prince
Ages since
Held his court in, gathered councils, wielding far
Peace and war.

Now,—the country does not even boast a tree,
As you see,

To distinguish slopes of verdure, certain rills
From the hills
Intersect and give a name to (else they run
Into one),
Where the domed and daring palace shot its spires
Up like fires
O'er the hundred-gated circuit of a wall
Bounding all,
Made of marble, men might march on nor be pressed,
Twelve abreast.

And such plenty and perfection, see, of grass
Never was!
Such a carpet as, this summer-time, o'erspreads
And embeds
Every vestige of the city, guessed alone,
Stock or stone—
Where a multitude of men breathed joy and woe
Long ago;
Lust of glory pricked their hearts up, dread of shame
Struck them tame;
And that glory and that shame alike, the gold
Bought and sold.

Now,—the single little turret that remains
On the plains,
By the caper overrooted, by the gourd
Overscored,
While the patching houseleek's head of blossom winks
Thro' the chinks—
Marks the basement whence a tower in ancient time
Sprang sublime,
And a burning ring, all round, the chariots traced
As they raced,
And the monarch and his minions and his dames
Viewed the games.

And I know, while thus the quiet-colored eve
Smiles to leave

To their folding, all our many-tinkling fleece
    In such peace,
And the slopes and rills in undistinguished gray
    Melt away—
That a girl with eager eyes and yellow hair
    Waits me there
In the turret whence the charioteers caught soul
    For the goal,
When the king looked, where she looks now, breathless, dumb
    Till I come.

But he looked upon the city, every side
    Far and wide,
All the mountains topped with temples, all the glades'
    Colonnades,
All the causeys, bridges, aqueducts,—and then,
    All the men!
When I do come, she will speak not, she will stand,
    Either hand
On my shoulder, give her eyes the first embrace
    Of my face,
Ere we rush, ere we extinguish sight and speech
    Each on each.

In one year they sent a million fighters forth
    South and North,
And they built their gods a brazen pillar high
    As the sky,
Yet reserved a thousand chariots in full force—
    Gold, of course.
Oh heart! oh blood that freezes, blood that burns!
    Earth's returns
For whole centuries of folly, noise and sin!
    Shut them in,
With their triumphs and their glories and the rest!
    Love is best.

ROBERT BROWNING

The sea is calm to-night.
The tide is full, the moon lies fair
Upon the straits;—on the French coast the light
Gleams and is gone; the cliffs of England stand,
Glimmering and vast, out in the tranquil bay.
Come to the window, sweet is the night-air!
Only, from the long line of spray
Where the sea meets the moon-blanched land,
Listen! you hear the grating roar
Of pebbles which the waves draw back, and fling,
At their return, up the high strand,
Begin, and cease, and then again begin,
With tremulous cadence slow, and bring
The eternal note of sadness in.

Sophocles long ago
Heard it on the Aegean, and it brought
Into his mind the turbid ebb and flow
Of human misery; we
Find also in the sound a thought,
Hearing it by this distant northern sea.

The sea of faith
Was once, too, at the full, and round earth's shore
Lay like the folds of a bright girdle furled.
But now I only hear
Its melancholy, long, withdrawing roar,
Retreating, to the breath
Of the night-wind, down the vast edges drear
And naked shingles of the world.

Ah, love, let us be true
To one another! for the world, which seems
To lie before us like a land of dreams,
So various, so beautiful, so new,
Hath really neither joy, nor love, nor light,

Nor certitude, nor peace, nor help for pain;
And we are here as on a darkling plain
Swept with confused alarms of struggle and flight,
Where ignorant armies clash by night.

MATTHEW ARNOLD

Have You Got a Brook

Have you got a brook in your little heart,
Where bashful flowers blow,
And blushing birds go down to drink
And shadows tremble so?

And nobody knows, so still it flows,
That any brook is there;
And yet your little draught of life
Is daily drunken there.

Then look out for the little brook in March,
When the rivers overflow,
And the snows come hurrying from the hills,
And the bridges often go.

And later, in August it may be,
When the meadows parching lie,
Beware, lest this little brook of life
Some burning noon go dry!

EMILY DICKINSON

Did the Harebell

Did the harebell loose her girdle
To the lover bee,
Would the bee the harebell hallow
Much as formerly?

Did the paradise, persuaded,
Yield her moat of pearl,
Would the Eden be an Eden,
Or the earl an earl?

EMILY DICKINSON

I Gave Myself

I gave myself to him,
And took himself for pay.
The solemn contract of a life
Was ratified this way.

The wealth might disappoint,
Myself a poorer prove
Than this great purchaser suspect,
The daily own of Love.

Depreciate the vision;
But, till the merchant buy,
Still fable, in the isles of spice,
The subtle cargoes lie.

At least, 'tis mutual risk,—
Some found it mutual gain;
Sweet debt of Life,—each night to owe,
Insolvent, every noon.

EMILY DICKINSON

Remember

Remember me when I am gone away,
Gone far away into the silent land;
When you can no more hold me by the hand,
Nor I half turn to go, yet turning stay.
Remember me when no more, day by day,

You tell me of our future that you planned:
Only remember me; you understand
It will be late to counsel then or pray.
Yet if you should forget me for a while
And afterwards remember, do not grieve:
For if the darkness and corruption leave
A vestige of the thoughts that once I had,
Better by far you should forget and smile
Than that you should remember and be sad.

CHRISTINA ROSSETTI

Love Is Enough

Love is enough: though the World be a-waning,
And the woods have no voice but the voice of complaining,
  Though the skies be too dark for dim eyes to discover
The gold-cups and daisies fair blooming thereunder,
Though the hills be held shadows, and the sea a dark wonder,
  And this day draw a veil over all deeds pass'd over,
Yet their hands shall not tremble, their feet shall not falter:
The void shall not weary, the fear shall not alter
  These lips and these eyes of the loved and the lover.

WILLIAM MORRIS

So Sweet Love Seemed

So sweet love seemed that April morn,
When first we kissed beside the thorn,
So strangely sweet, it was not strange
We thought that love could never change.

But I can tell—let truth be told—
That love will change in growing old;
Though day by day is naught to see,
So delicate his motions be.

69

And in the end 'twill come to pass
Quite to forget what once he was,
Nor even in fancy to recall
The pleasure that was all in all.

His little spring, that sweet we found,
So deep in summer floods is drowned,
I wonder, bathed in joy complete,
How love so young could be so sweet.

ROBERT BRIDGES

Mandalay

By the old Moulmein Pagoda, lookin' eastward to the sea,
There's a Burma girl a-settin', and I know she thinks o' me;
For the wind is in the palm trees, an' the temple bells they say:
"Come you back, you British soldier; come you back to
    Mandalay!"
    Come you back to Mandalay,
    Where the old Flotilla lay:
    Can't you 'ear their paddles chunkin' from Rangoon to
      Mandalay!
    On the road to Mandalay,
    Where the flyin'-fishes play,
    An' the dawn comes up like thunder outer China 'crost the
      Bay!

'Er petticoat was yaller an' 'er little cap was green,
An' 'er name was Supi-yaw-let—jes' the same as Theebaw's
    Queen,
An' I seed her fust a-smokin' of a whackin' white cheroot,
An' a-wastin' Christian kisses on an 'eathen idol's foot:
    Bloomin' idol made o' mud—
    What they called the Great Gawd Budd—
    Plucky lot she cared for idols when I kissed 'er where she
      stud!
    On the road to Mandalay—

When the mist was on the rice-fields an' the sun was droppin'
    slow,
She'd git her little banjo and she'd sing "*Kulla-lo-lo!*"
With 'er arm upon my shoulder, an 'er cheek agin my cheek,
We useter watch the steamers an' the *hathis* pilin' teak.
    Elephints a-pilin' teak
    In the sludgy, squdgy creek,
    Where the silence 'ung that 'eavy you was 'arf afraid to
        speak!
    On the road to Mandalay—

But that's all shove be'ind me—long ago an' fur away,
An' there ain't no 'buses runnin' from the Bank to Mandalay;
An' I'm learnin' 'ere in London what the ten-year sodger
    tells:
"If you've 'eard the East a-callin', you won't 'eed nothin' else."
    No! you won't 'eed nothin' else
    But them spicy garlic smells,
    An' the sunshine an' the palm trees an' the tinkly temple
        bells!
    On the road to Mandalay—

I am sick o' wastin' leather on these gritty pavin'-stones,
An' the blasted Henglish drizzle wakes the fever in my bones;
Tho' I walks with fifty 'ousemaids outer Chelsea to the Strand,
An' they talks a lot of lovin', but wot do they understand?
    Beefy face an' grubby 'and—
    Law! wot *do* they understand?
    I've a neater, sweeter maiden in a cleaner, greener land!
    On the road to Mandalay—

Ship me somewheres east of Suez, where the best is like the
    worst,
Where there aren't no Ten Commandments an' a man can
    raise a thirst!
For the temple bells are callin', an' it's there that I would be—
By the old Moulmein Pagoda, lookin' lazy at the sea—
    On the road to Mandalay,

Where the old Flotilla lay,
With our sick beneath the awnings when we went to
    Mandalay!
Oh, the road to Mandalay
Where the flyin'-fishes play,
An' the dawn comes up like thunder outer China 'crost the
    Bay!

RUDYARD KIPLING

When I Was One-and-Twenty

When I was one-and-twenty
  I heard a wise man say,
"Give crowns and pounds and guineas
  But not your heart away;
Give pearls away and rubies
  But keep your fancy free."
But I was one-and-twenty,
  No use to talk to me.

When I was one-and-twenty
  I heard him say again,
"The heart out of the bosom
  Was never given in vain;
'Tis paid with sighs a plenty
  And sold for endless rue."
And I am two-and-twenty,
  And oh, 'tis true, 'tis true.

A. E. HOUSMAN

Oh, See How Thick the Goldcup Flowers

Oh see how thick the goldcup flowers
  Are lying in field and lane,
With dandelions to tell the hours
  That never are told again,

Oh may I squire you round the meads
  And pick you posies gay?
—'Twill do no harm to take my arm.
  "You may, young man, you may."

Ah, spring was sent for lass and lad,
  'Tis now the blood runs gold,
And man and maid had best be glad
  Before the world is old.
What flowers today may flower tomorrow,
  But never as good as new.
—Suppose I wound my arm right round.
  " 'Tis true, young man, 'tis true."

Some lads there are, 'tis shame to say,
  That only court to thieve,
And once they bear the bloom away
  'Tis little enough they leave.
Then keep your heart for men like me
  And safe from trustless chaps.
My love is true and all for you.
  "Perhaps, young man, perhaps."

Oh, look in my eyes then, can you doubt?
  —Why, 'tis a mile from town.
How green the grass is all about!
  We might as well sit down.
—Ah, life, what is it but a flower?
  Why must true lovers sigh?
Be kind, have pity, my own, my pretty,—
  "Good-bye, young man, good-bye."

                    A. E. HOUSMAN

          Oh, When I Was in Love

  Oh, when I was in love with you,
    Then I was clean and brave,
  And miles around the wonder grew
    How well I did behave.

                73

And now the fancy passes by,
And nothing will remain,
And miles around they'll say that I
Am quite myself again.

A . E . H O U S M A N

When You Are Old

When you are old and gray and full of sleep,
And nodding by the fire, take down this book,
And slowly read, and dream of the soft look
Your eyes had once, and of their shadows deep;

How many loved your moments of glad grace,
And loved your beauty with love false or true;
But one man loved the pilgrim soul in you,
And loved the sorrows of your changing face;

And bending down beside the glowing bars,
Murmur, a little sadly, how love fled
And paced upon the mountains overhead
And hid his face amid a crowd of stars.

W . B . Y E A T S

Lucinda Matlock

I went to the dances at Chandlerville,
And played snap-out at Winchester.
One time we changed partners,
Driving home in the moonlight of middle June,
And then I found Davis.
We were married and lived together for seventy years,
Enjoying, working, raising the twelve children,
Eight of whom we lost
Ere I had reached the age of sixty.
I spun, I wove, I kept the house, I nursed the sick,

I made the garden, and for holiday
Rambled over the fields where sang the larks,
And by Spoon River gathering many a shell,
And many a flower and medicinal weed—
Shouting to the wooded hills, singing to the green valleys.
At ninety-six I had lived enough, that is all,
And passed to a sweet repose.
What is this I hear of sorrow and weariness,
Anger, discontent and drooping hopes?
Degenerate sons and daughters,
Life is too strong for you—
It takes life to love Life.

EDGAR LEE MASTERS

The Highwayman

PART ONE

I

The wind was a torrent of darkness among the gusty trees,
The moon was a ghostly galleon tossed upon cloudy seas,
The road was a ribbon of moonlight over the purple moor,
And the highwayman came riding—
        Riding—riding—
The highwayman came riding, up to the old inn-door.

II

He'd a French cocked-hat on his forehead, a bunch of lace at
      his chin,
A coat of the claret velvet, and breeches of brown doe-skin;
They fitted with never a wrinkle: his boots were up to the
      thigh!
And he rode with a jewelled twinkle,
        His pistol butts a-twinkle,
His rapier hilt a-twinkle, under the jewelled sky.

75

III

Over the cobbles he clattered and clashed in the dark inn-yard,
And he tapped with his whip on the shutters, but all was
    locked and barred;
He whistled a tune to the window, and who should be waiting
    there
But the landlord's black-eyed daughter,
             Bess, the landlord's daughter,
Plaiting a dark red love-knot into her long black hair.

IV

And dark in the dark old inn-yard a stable-wicket creaked
Where Tim the ostler listened; his face was white and peaked;
His eyes were hollows of madness, his hair like mouldy hay,
But he loved the landlord's daughter,
             The landlord's red-lipped daughter,
Dumb as a dog he listened, and he heard the robber say—

V

"One kiss, my bonny sweetheart, I'm after a prize to-night,
But I shall be back with the yellow gold before the morning
    light;
Yet, if they press me sharply, and harry me through the day,
Then look for me by moonlight,
             Watch for me by moonlight,
I'll come to thee by moonlight, though hell should bar the
    way."

VI

He rose upright in the stirrups; he scarce could reach her
    hand,
But she loosened her hair i' the casement! His face burnt like
    a brand
As the black cascade of perfume came tumbling over his
    breast;
And he kissed its waves in the moonlight,
            (Oh, sweet black waves in the moonlight!)
Then he tugged at his rein in the moonlight, and galloped
    away to the West.

PART TWO

I

He did not come in the dawning; he did not come at noon;
And out o' the tawny sunset, before the rise o' the moon,
When the road was a gipsy's ribbon, looping the purple moor,
A red-coat troop came marching—
      Marching—marching—
King George's men came marching, up to the old inn-door.

II

They said no word to the landlord, they drank his ale instead,
But they gagged his daughter and bound her to the foot of her
      narrow bed;
Two of them knelt at her casement, with muskets at their side!
There was death at every window;
      And hell at one dark window;
For Bess could see, through her casement, the road that *he*
      would ride.

III

They had tied her up to attention, with many a sniggering jest;
They had bound a musket beside her, with the barrel beneath
      her breast!
"Now keep good watch!" and they kissed her. She heard the
      dead man say—
Look for me by moonlight;
      Watch for me by moonlight;
I'll come to thee by moonlight, though hell should bar the way!

IV

She twisted her hands behind her; but all the knots held good!
She writhed her hands till her fingers were wet with sweat or
      blood!
They stretched and strained in the darkness, and the hours
      crawled by like years,

Till, now, on the stroke of midnight,
        Cold, on the stroke of midnight,
The tip of one finger touched it! The trigger at least was hers!

V

The tip of one finger touched it; she strove no more for the rest!
Up, she stood up to attention, with the barrel beneath her breast,
She would not risk their hearing: she would not strive again;
For the road lay bare in the moonlight;
        Blank and bare in the moonlight;
And the blood of her veins in the moonlight throbbed to her love's refrain.

VI

Tlot-tlot; tlot-tlot! Had they heard it? The horse-hoofs ringing clear;
Tlot-tlot, tlot-tlot, in the distance? Were they deaf that they did not hear?
Down the ribbon of moonlight, over the brow of the hill,
The highwayman came riding,
        Riding, riding!
The red-coats looked to their priming! She stood up, straight and still!

VII

Tlot-tlot, in the frosty silence! *Tlot-tlot,* in the echoing night!
Nearer he came and nearer! Her face was like a light!
Her eyes grew wide for a moment; she drew one last deep breath,
Then her finger moved in the moonlight,
        Her musket shattered the moonlight,
Shattered her breast in the moonlight and warned him—with her death.

VIII

He turned; he spurred to the Westward; he did not know
    who stood
Bowed, with her head o'er the musket, drenched with her own
    red blood!
Not till the dawn he heard it, and slowly blanched to hear
How Bess, the landlord's daughter,
            The landlord's black-eyed daughter,
Had watched for her love in the moonlight, and died in the
    darkness there.

IX

Back, he spurred like a madman, shrieking a curse to the sky,
With the white road smoking behind him, and his rapier
    brandished high!
Blood-red were his spurs i' the golden noon; wine-red was his
    velvet coat;
When they shot him down on the highway,
            Down like a dog on the highway,
And he lay in his blood on the highway, with the bunch of
    lace at his throat.

X

*And still of a winter's night, they say, when the wind is in
    the trees,*
When the moon is a ghostly galleon tossed upon cloudy seas,
When the road is a ribbon of moonlight over the purple moor,
A highwayman comes riding—
            Riding—riding—
A highwayman comes riding, up to the old inn-door.

XI

Over the cobbles he clatters and clangs in the dark inn-yard;
*And he taps with his whip on the shutters, but all is locked
    and barred;*

He whistles a tune to the window, and who should be waiting
there
But the landlord's black-eyed daughter,
Bess, the landlord's daughter,
Plaiting a dark red love-knot into her long black hair.

ALFRED NOYES

Love on the Farm

What large, dark hands are those at the window
Grasping in the golden light
Which weaves its way through the evening wind
 At my heart's delight?

Ah, only the leaves! But in the west
I see a redness suddenly come
Into the evening's anxious breast—
 'Tis the wound of love goes home!

The woodbine creeps abroad
Calling low to her lover:
 The sunlit flirt who all the day
 Has poised above her lips in play
 And stolen kisses, shallow and gay
 Of pollen, now has gone away—
 She woos the moth with her sweet, low word;
And when above her his moth-wings hover
Then her bright breast she will uncover
And yield her honey-drop to her lover.

Into the yellow, evening glow
Saunters a man from the farm below;
Leans, and looks in at the low-built shed
Where the swallow has hung her marriage bed.
 The bird lies warm against the wall.
 She glances quick her startled eyes
 Towards him, then she turns away

Her small head, making warm display
Of red upon the throat. Her terrors sway
Her out of the nest's warm, busy ball,
Whose plaintive cry is heard as she flies
In one blue stoop from out the sties
Into the twilight's empty hall.

Oh, water-hen, beside the rushes,
Hide your quaintly scarlet blushes,
Still your quick tail, lie still as dead,
Till the distance folds over his ominous tread!
The rabbit presses back her ears,
Turns back her liquid, anguished eyes
And crouches low; then with wild spring
Spurts from the terror of his oncoming,
To be choked back, the wire ring
Her frantic effort throttling:
Piteous brown ball of quivering fears!

Ah, soon in his large, hard hands she dies,
And swings all loose from the swing of his walk!
Yet calm and kindly are his eyes
And ready to open in brown surprise
Should I not answer to his talk
Or should he my tears surmise.

I hear his hand on the latch, and rise from my chair
Watching the door open; he flashes bare
His strong teeth in a smile, and flashes his eyes
In a smile like triumph upon me; then careless-wise
He flings the rabbit soft on the table-board
And comes toward me: he! the uplifted sword
Of his hand against my bosom! and oh, the broad
Blade of his glance that asks me to applaud
His coming! With his hand he turns my face to him
And caresses me with his fingers that still smell grim
Of rabbit's fur! God, I am caught in a snare!
I know not what fine wire is round my throat;

I only know I let him finger there
My pulse of life, and let him nose like a stoat
Who sniffs with joy before he drinks the blood.

And down his mouth comes to my mouth! and down
His bright dark eyes come over me, like a hood
Upon my mind! his lips meet mine, and a flood
Of sweet fire sweeps across me, so I drown
Against him, die, and find death good.

D. H. LAWRENCE

All in Green Went My Love Riding

All in green went my love riding
on a great horse of gold
into the silver dawn.

four lean hounds crouched low and smiling
the merry deer ran before.

Fleeter be they than dappled dreams
the swift sweet deer
the red rare deer.

Four red roebuck at a white water
the cruel bugle sang before.

Horn at hip went my love riding
riding the echo down
into the silver dawn.

four lean hounds crouched low and smiling
the level meadows ran before.

Softer be they than slippered sleep
the lean lithe deer
the fleet flown deer.

Four fleet does at a gold valley
the famished arrow sang before.

Bow at belt went my love riding
riding the mountain down
into the silver dawn.

four lean hounds crouched low and smiling
the sheer peaks ran before.

Paler be they than daunting death
the sleek slim deer
the tall tense deer.

Four tall stags at a green mountain
the lucky hunter sang before.

All in green went my love riding
on a great horse of gold
into the silver dawn.

four lean hounds crouched low and smiling
my heart fell dead before.

E. E. CUMMINGS

It May Not Always Be So

it may not always be so; and i say
that if your lips, which i have loved, should touch
another's, and your dear strong fingers clutch
his heart, as mine in time not far away;
if on another's face your sweet hair lay
in such a silence as i know, or such
great writhing words as, uttering overmuch,
stand helplessly before the spirit at bay;

if this should be, i say if this should be—
you of my heart, send me a little word;
that i may go unto him, and take his hands,
saying, Accept all happiness from me.
Then shall i turn my face, and hear one bird
sing terribly afar in the lost lands.

E. E. CUMMINGS

If I Have Made, My Lady

if i have made, my lady, intricate
imperfect various things chiefly which wrong
your eyes (frailer than most deep dreams are frail)
songs less firm than your body's whitest song
upon my mind—if i have failed to snare
the glance too shy—if through my singing slips
the very skillful strangeness of your smile
the keen primeval silence of your hair
—let the world say "his most wise music stole
nothing from death"—

        you only will create
(who are so perfectly alive) my shame:
lady through whose profound and fragile lips
the sweet small clumsy feet of April came

into the ragged meadow of my soul.

E. E. CUMMINGS

Time Does Not Bring Relief

Time does not bring relief; you all have lied
Who told me time would ease me of my pain!
I miss him in the weeping of the rain;
I want him at the shrinking of the tide;
The old snows melt from every mountain-side,
And last year's leaves are smoke in every lane;
But last year's bitter loving must remain
Heaped on my heart, and my old thoughts abide.
There are a hundred places where I fear
To go,—so with his memory they brim.
And entering with relief some quiet place
Where never fell his foot or shone his face
I say, "There is no memory of him here!"
And so stand stricken, so remembering him.

EDNA ST. VINCENT MILLAY

Oh, Think Not I Am Faithful to a Vow!

Oh, think not I am faithful to a vow!
Faithless am I save to love's self alone.
Were you not lovely I would leave you now:
After the feet of beauty fly my own.
Were you not still my hunger's rarest food,
And water ever to my wildest thirst,
I would desert you—think not but I would!—
And seek another as I sought you first.
But you are mobile as the veering air,
And all your charms more changeful than the tide,
Wherefore to be inconstant is no care:
I have but to continue at your side.
So wanton, light and false, my love, are you,
I am most faithless when I am most true.

EDNA ST. VINCENT MILLAY

He's Coming

He's coming. He just called. Said he was coming,
Maybe, right away. O southern river,
Kiss that trestle sweetly,
Rub that upright gently,
And keep no train from home.

He's coming. Said all papers would be signed
By Sunday. O you honeysuckle timber,
Wrap those tulips, redbuds,
Hold those oaks from falling
Down on the right of way.

He's coming. Said expect him. There! what music
Rails already make, and pounded switches:
Wheels inside the south wind.
Where? O you the south wind,
Keep soft and strong today.

MARK VAN DOREN

Secret Laughter

There is a secret laughter
  That often comes to me,
And though I go about my work
As humble as can be,
There is no prince or prelate
  I envy—no, not one.
No evil can befall me—
  By God, I have a son.

CHRISTOPHER MORLEY

To Be Sung

If blossoms could blossom
One petal of petals
To whom all other blooms are
As leaves are to flowers,
It would be to the others
As you are, my daughter,
To all other daughters
Whom songs are adoring.
For what am I here for
If not to make love-songs
Of all the world's beauty
Whose birthday we share?

If purest of fragrance
Brewed a quintessence
Too delicate-lonely
To ever be breathed,
It would be to the others
As you are, my daughter,
To all other daughters
Whom songs are encircling.
For what am I here for

If not to weave lassos
Of songs for the lonely
To tug them to love?

Say yes to the breezes.
If any dishevels
One curl of a ringlet,
I'll know and be with you.
The grace-notes that feather
The wing-beats of longing
Are lead till they heal with
Their singing your crying.
For what is a song for
If not to smooth ringlets
Of daughters too hurt by
The prose of the world?

When storms replace breezes,
No hurt can have healing.
Then the love I now sing you
Can pillow your fading.
For what am I here for
If not to link fingers
With daughters whose wistfulness
Worlds never answer?
For what is a song for
If not to stretch hands out
To signal the falling,
"You're never alone"?

PETER VIERECK

BOOK THREE

The Mysteries

Able men have written stout books about the great mysteries of the Universe—life, death and God. Their prose sometimes soars and more often stumbles. It attempts to define the undefinable, to express the inexpressible. The poet has advantages. He does not need to define. He is free to indulge, to use Wordsworth's phrase, in "intimations."

This section, after a few familiar lines from Shakespeare, Donne and Milton, moves on to gentle George Herbert and Henry Vaughan, and to that genius of intimation, William Blake. It includes Wordsworth's great ode, Coleridge's cryptic "Rime," Tennyson and Browning on death, and some of Emily Dickinson's most evocative whisperings. It concludes with an American Negro folk-sermon on The Creation—and where has the Bible story found a finer echo?

The Stuff of Dreams

(FROM PROSPERO'S SPEECH, *The Tempest*, Act IV, Scene I)

Our revels now are ended. These our actors,
As I foretold you, were all spirits, and
Are melted into air, into thin air.
And, like the baseless fabric of this vision,
The cloud-capped towers, the gorgeous palaces,
The solemn temples, the great globe itself—
Yea, all which it inherit—shall dissolve
And, like this insubstantial pageant faded,
Leave not a rack behind. We are such stuff
As dreams are made on, and our little life
Is rounded with a sleep.

WILLIAM SHAKESPEARE

Death, Be Not Proud

Death, be not proud, though some have called thee
Mighty and dreadful, for thou art not so;
For those whom thou think'st thou dost overthrow
Die not, poor death, nor yet canst thou kill me.
From rest and sleep, which but thy pictures be,
Much pleasure; then from thee much more must flow,
And soonest our best men with thee do go,
Rest of their bones, and soul's delivery.
Thou art slave to fate, chance, kings, and desperate men,
And dost with poison, war, and sickness dwell,
And poppy or charms can make us sleep as well
And better than thy stroke; why swell'st thou then?
One short sleep past, we wake eternally,
And death shall be no more; Death, thou shalt die.

JOHN DONNE

On His Blindness

When I consider how my light is spent
Ere half my days in this dark world and wide,
And that one talent, which is death to hide,
Lodged with me useless, though my soul more bent
To serve therewith my Maker, and present
My true account, lest He returning chide;
"Doth God exact day-labor, light denied?"
I fondly ask. But Patience, to prevent
That murmur, soon replies, "God doth not need
Either man's work or his own gifts; who best
Bear his mild yoke, they serve him best; his state
Is kingly; thousands at his bidding speed,
And post o'er land and ocean without rest;
They also serve who only stand and wait."

JOHN MILTON

Love

Love bade me welcome, yet my soul drew back,
    Guilty of dust and sin.
But quick-eyed Love, observing me grow slack
    From my first entrance in,
Drew nearer to me, sweetly questioning
    If I lacked any thing.

"A guest," I answered, "worthy to be here":
    Love said, "You shall be he."
"I, the unkind, ungrateful? Ah, my dear,
    I cannot look on Thee."
Love took my hand, and smiling did reply,
    "Who made the eyes but I?"

"Truth, Lord; but I have marred them: let my shame
    Go where it doth deserve."

92

"And know you not," says Love, "Who bore the blame?"
  "My dear, then I will serve."
"You must sit down," says Love, "and taste my meat."
  So I did sit and eat.

GEORGE HERBERT

The World

I saw Eternity the other night,
Like a great ring of pure and endless light,
  All calm, as it was bright;
And round beneath it, time in hours, days, years,
  Driven by the spheres
Like a vast shadow moved; in which the world
  And all her train were hurled:
The doting lover in his quaintest strain
  Did there complain;
Near him, his lute, his fancy, and his flights,
  Wit's sour delights,
With gloves and knots, the silly snares of pleasure,
  Yet his dear treasure,
All scattered lay, while he his eyes did pour
  Upon a flower.

The darksome statesman, hung with weights and woe,
Like a thick midnight-fog, moved there so slow,
  He did not stay, nor go;
Condemning thoughts, like sad eclipses, scowl
  Upon his soul,
And clouds of crying witnesses without
  Pursued him with one shout;
Yet digged the mole, and lest his ways be found
  Worked underground,
Where he did clutch his prey, but One did see
  That policy;

Churches and altars fed him; perjuries
    Were gnats and flies;
It rained about him blood and tears, but he
    Drank them as free.

The fearful miser on a heap of rust
Sat pining all his life there, did scarce trust
    His own hands with the dust,
Yet would not place one piece above, but lives
    In fear of thieves.
Thousands there were as frantic as himself,
    And hugged each one his pelf:
The downright epicure placed heav'n in sense,
    And scorned pretense;
While others, slipped into a wide excess,
    Said little less;
The weaker sort slight trivial wares enslave,
    Who think them brave;
And poor, despised Truth sat counting by
    Their victory.

Yet some, who all this while did weep and sing,
And sing and weep, soared up into the ring;
    But most would use no wing.
O fools, said I, thus to prefer dark night
    Before true light!
To live in grots and caves, and hate the day
    Because it shows the way;
The way which from this dead and dark abode
    Leads up to God;
A way where you might tread the sun, and be
    More bright than he!
But as I did their madness so discuss,
    One whispered thus:
This ring the Bridegroom did for none provide
    But for His bride.

HENRY VAUGHAN

Huswifery

Make me, O Lord, thy spinning wheel complete;
  Thy holy word my distaff make for me.
Make mine affections thy swift flyers neat,
  And make my soul thy holy spool to be.
  My conversation make to be thy reel,
  And reel the yarn thereon spun of thy wheel.

Make me thy loom, then, knit therein this twine:
  And make thy holy spirit, Lord, wind quills:
Then weave the web thyself. The yarn is fine.
  Thine ordinances make my fulling mills.
  Then dye the same in heavenly colors choice,
  All pinked with varnished flowers of paradise.

Then clothe therewith mine understanding, will,
  Affections, judgment, conscience, memory;
My words and actions, that their shine may fill
  My ways with glory and thee glorify.
  Then mine apparel shall display before ye
  That I am clothed in holy robes for glory.

EDWARD TAYLOR

The Tyger

Tyger! Tyger! burning bright,
In the forests of the night,
What immortal hand or eye
Could frame thy fearful symmetry?

In what distant deeps or skies
Burnt the fire of thine eyes?
On what wings dare he aspire?
What the hand dare seize the fire?

And what shoulder, and what art,
Could twist the sinews of thy heart?

And when thy heart began to beat,
What dread hand and what dread feet?

What the hammer? what the chain?
In what furnace was thy brain?
What the anvil? what dread grasp
Dare its deadly terrors clasp?

When the stars threw down their spears,
And watered heaven with their tears,
Did He smile His work to see?
Did He who made the Lamb make thee?

Tyger! Tyger! burning bright
In the forests of the night,
What immortal hand or eye
Dare frame thy fearful symmetry?

WILLIAM BLAKE

Auguries of Innocence

To see a World in a Grain of Sand,
And a Heaven in a Wild Flower,
Hold Infinity in the palm of your hand,
And Eternity in an hour.
A Robin Redbreast in a Cage
Puts all Heaven in a Rage.
A dove-house fill'd with Doves and Pigeons
Shudders Hell thro' all its regions.
A dog starv'd at his Master's Gate
Predicts the ruin of the State.
A Horse misus'd upon the Road
Calls to Heaven for Human blood.
Each outcry of the hunted Hare
A fibre from the Brain does tear.
A Skylark wounded in the wing,
A Cherubim does cease to sing.
The Game Cock clip'd and arm'd for fight

Does the Rising Sun affright.
Every Wolf's and Lion's howl
Raises from Hell a Human Soul.
The wild Deer, wand'ring here and there,
Keeps the Human Soul from Care.
The Lamb misus'd breeds Public Strife
And yet forgives the Butcher's knife.
The Bat that flits at close of Eve
Has left the Brain that won't Believe.
The Owl that calls upon the Night
Speaks the Unbeliever's fright.
He who shall hurt the little Wren
Shall never be belov'd by Men.
He who the Ox to wrath has mov'd
Shall never be by Woman lov'd.
The wanton Boy that kills the Fly
Shall feel the Spider's enmity.
He who torments the Chafer's Sprite
Weaves a Bower in endless Night.
The Catterpiller on the Leaf
Repeats to thee thy Mother's grief.
Kill not the Moth nor Butterfly,
For the Last Judgment draweth nigh.
He who shall train the Horse to war
Shall never pass the Polar Bar.
The Beggar's Dog and Widow's Cat,
Feed them and thou wilt grow fat.
The Gnat that sings his Summer's Song
Poison gets from Slander's tongue.
The poison of the Snake and Newt
Is the sweat of Envy's Foot.
The poison of the Honey Bee
Is the Artist's Jealousy.
The Prince's Robes and Beggar's Rags
Are Toadstools on the Miser's Bags.
A Truth that's told with bad intent
Beats all the Lies you can invent.

It is right it should be so;
Man was made for Joy and Woe;
And when this we rightly know,
Thro' the World we safely go,
Joy and Woe are woven fine,
A Clothing for the soul divine.
Under every grief and pine
Runs a joy with silken twine.
The Babe is more than swadling Bands;
Throughout all these Human Lands
Tools were made, and Born were hands,
Every Farmer Understands.
Every Tear from Every Eye
Becomes a Babe in Eternity;
This is caught by Females bright
And return'd to its own delight.
The Bleat, the Bark, Bellow and Roar,
Are Waves that Beat on Heaven's Shore.
The Babe that weeps the Rod beneath
Writes Revenge in realms of Death.
The Beggar's Rags, fluttering in Air,
Does to Rags the Heavens tear.
The Soldier, arm'd with Sword and Gun,
Palsied strikes the Summer's Sun.
The poor Man's Farthing is worth more
Than all the Gold on Afric's shore.
One Mite wrung from the Lab'rer's hands
Shall buy and sell the Miser's Lands;
Or, if protected from on high,
Does that whole Nation sell and buy.
He who mocks the Infant's Faith
Shall be mock'd in Age and Death.
He who shall teach the Child to Doubt
The rotting Grave shall ne'er get out.
He who respects the Infant's faith
Triumphs over Hell and Death.
The Child's Toys and the Old Man's Reasons

Are the Fruits of the Two seasons.
The Questioner, who sits so sly,
Shall never know how to Reply.
He who replies to words of Doubt
Doth put the Light of Knowledge out.
The Strongest Poison ever known
Came from Caesar's Laurel Crown.
Nought can Deform the Human Race
Like to the Armour's iron brace.
When Gold and Gems adorn the Plow
To Peaceful Arts shall Envy Bow.
A Riddle, or the Cricket's Cry,
Is to Doubt a fit Reply.
The Emmet's Inch and Eagle's Mile
Make Lame Philosophy to smile.
He who Doubts from what he sees
Will ne'er Believe, do what you Please.
If the Sun and Moon should Doubt,
They'd immediately Go Out.
To be in a Passion you Good may do,
But no Good if a Passion is in you.
The Whore and Gambler, by the State
Licensed, build that Nation's Fate.
The Harlot's cry from Street to Street
Shall weave Old England's winding Sheet.
The Winner's Shout, the Loser's Curse,
Dance before dead England's Hearse.
Every Night and every Morn
Some to Misery are Born.
Every Morn and every Night
Some are Born to Sweet Delight.
Some are Born to Sweet Delight,
Some are Born to Endless Night.
We are led to Believe a Lie
When we see not Thro' the Eye,
Which was Born in a Night to perish in a Night,
When the Soul Slept in Beams of Light.

God Appears, and God is Light,
To those poor souls who dwell in Night;
But does a Human Form Display
To those who Dwell in Realms of Day.

WILLIAM BLAKE

On Another's Sorrow

Can I see another's woe,
And not be in sorrow too?
Can I see another's grief,
And not seek for kind relief?

Can I see a falling tear,
And not feel my sorrow's share?
Can a father see his child
Weep, nor be with sorrow fill'd?

Can a mother sit and hear
An infant groan an infant fear?
No, no! never can it be!
Never, never can it be!

And can he who smiles on all
Hear the wren with sorrows small,
Hear the small bird's grief and care,
Hear the woes that infants bear,

And not sit beside the nest,
Pouring pity in their breast;
And not sit the cradle near,
Weeping tear on infant's tear;

And not sit both night and day,
Wiping all our tears away?
O, no! never can it be!
Never, never can it be!

He doth give his joy to all;
He becomes an infant small;
He becomes a man of woe;
He doth feel the sorrow too.

Think not thou canst sigh a sigh
And thy maker is not by;
Think not thou canst weep a tear
And thy maker is not near.

O! he gives to us his joy
That our grief he may destroy;
Till our grief is fled and gone
He doth sit by us and moan.

WILLIAM BLAKE

Our Birth Is But a Sleep

(FROM *Ode on Intimations of Immortality from Recollections of Early Childhood*)

Our birth is but a sleep and a forgetting:
The Soul that rises with us, our life's Star,
    Hath had elsewhere its setting,
        And cometh from afar:
    Not in entire forgetfulness,
    And not in utter nakedness,
But trailing clouds of glory do we come
        From God, who is our home:
Heaven lies about us in our infancy!
Shades of the prison-house begin to close
        Upon the growing Boy,
But He beholds the light, and whence it flows,
        He sees it in his joy;
The Youth, who daily farther from the east
        Must travel, still is Nature's Priest,
        And by the vision splendid
        Is on his way attended;

At length the Man perceives it die away,
And fade into the light of common day.

Earth fills her lap with pleasures of her own;
Yearnings she hath in her own natural kind,
And, even with something of a Mother's mind,
      And no unworthy aim,
        The homely Nurse doth all she can
To make her Foster-child, her Inmate Man,
      Forget the glories he hath known,
And that imperial palace whence he came.
Behold the Child among his new-born blisses,
A six years' Darling of a pigmy size!
See, where 'mid work of his own hand he lies,
Fretted by sallies of his mother's kisses,
With light upon him from his father's eyes!
See, at his feet, some little plan or chart,
Some fragment from his dream of human life,
Shaped by himself with newly-learned art;
      A wedding or a festival,
      A mourning or a funeral;
        And this hath now his heart,
      And unto this he frames his song:
        Then will he fit his tongue
To dialogues of business, love, or strife;
        But it will not be long
        Ere this be thrown aside,
        And with new joy and pride
The little Actor cons another part;
Filling from time to time his "humorous stage"
With all the Persons, down to palsied Age,
That Life brings with her in her equipage;
        As if his whole vocation
        Were endless imitation.

Thou, whose exterior semblance doth belie
      Thy Soul's immensity;
Thou best Philosopher, who yet dost keep

Thy heritage, thou Eye among the blind,
That, deaf and silent, read'st the eternal deep,
Haunted for ever by the eternal mind,—
        Mighty Prophet! Seer blest!
        On whom those truths do rest,
Which we are toiling all our lives to find,
In darkness lost, the darkness of the grave;
Thou, over whom thy Immortality
Broods like the Day, a Master o'er a Slave,
A Presence which is not to be put by;
Thou little Child, yet glorious in the might
Of heaven-born freedom on thy being's height,
Why with such earnest pains dost thou provoke
The years to bring the inevitable yoke,
Thus blindly with thy blessedness at strife?
Full soon thy Soul shall have her earthly freight,
And custom lie upon thee with a weight,
Heavy as frost, and deep almost as life!

        O joy! that in our embers
        Is something that doth live,
        That nature yet remembers
        What was so fugitive!
The thought of our past years in me doth breed
Perpetual benediction: not indeed
For that which is most worthy to be blest;
Delight and liberty, the simple creed
Of Childhood, whether busy or at rest,
With new-fledged hope still fluttering in his breast:—
        Not for these I raise
        The song of thanks and praise;
        But for those obstinate questionings
        Of sense and outward things,
        Fallings from us, vanishings;
        Blank misgivings of a Creature
Moving about in worlds not realised,
High instincts before which our mortal Nature

103

Did tremble like a guilty Thing surprised:
     But for those first affections,
     Those shadowy recollections,
     Which, be they what they may,
Are yet the fountain-light of all our day,
Are yet a master-light of all our seeing;
     Uphold us, cherish, and have power to make
Our noisy years seem moments in the being
Of the eternal Silence: truths that wake,
     To perish never:
Which neither listlessness, nor mad endeavour,
     Nor Man nor Boy,
Nor all that is at enmity with joy,
Can utterly abolish or destroy.
     Hence in a season of calm weather
     Though inland far we be,
Our Souls have sight of that immortal sea
     Which brought us hither,
     Can in a moment travel thither,
And see the Children sport upon the shore,
And hear the mighty waters rolling evermore.

Then sing, ye Birds, sing, sing a joyous song!
     And let the young Lambs bound
     As to the tabor's sound!
We in thought will join your throng,
     Ye that pipe and ye that play,
     Ye that through your hearts to-day
     Feel the gladness of the May!
What though the radiance which was once so bright
Be now for ever taken from my sight,
     Though nothing can bring back the hour
Of splendour in the grass, of glory in the flower;
     We will grieve not, rather find
     Strength in what remains behind;
     In the primal sympathy
     Which having been must ever be;

In the soothing thoughts that spring
Out of human suffering;
In the faith that looks through death,
In years that bring the philosophic mind.

And O, ye Fountains, Meadows, Hills, and Groves,
Forebode not any severing of our loves!
Yet in my heart of hearts I feel your might;
I only have relinquished one delight
To live beneath your more habitual sway.
I love the Brooks which down their channels fret,
Even more than when I tripped lightly as they;
The innocent brightness of a new-born Day
          Is lovely yet;
The Clouds that gather round the setting sun
Do take a sober colouring from an eye
That hath kept watch o'er man's mortality;
Another race hath been, and other palms are won.
Thanks to the human heart by which we live,
Thanks to its tenderness, its joys, and fears,
To me the meanest flower that blows can give
Thoughts that do often lie too deep for tears.

WILLIAM WORDSWORTH

The Rime of the Ancient Mariner

PART THE FIRST

*An ancient
Mariner meet-
eth three Gal-
lants bidden to
a wedding-feast,
and detaineth
one.*

It is an ancient Mariner
And he stoppeth one of three.
"By thy long grey beard and glittering eye,
Now wherefore stopp'st thou me?

The Bridegroom's doors are opened wide,
And I am next of kin;
The guests are met, the feast is set:
May'st hear the merry din."

He holds him with his skinny hand,
"There was a ship," quoth he.
"Hold off! unhand me, grey-beard loon!"
Eftsoons his hand dropt he.

The Wedding-Guest is spell-bound by the eye of the old seafaring man, and constrained to hear his tale.

He holds him with his glittering eye—
The Wedding-Guest stood still,
And listens like a three years' child:
The Mariner hath his will.

The Wedding-Guest sat on a stone:
He cannot choose but hear;
And thus spake on that ancient man,
The bright-eyed Mariner.

The ship was cheered, the harbor cleared,
Merrily did we drop
Below the kirk, below the hill,
Below the lighthouse top.

The Mariner tells how the ship sailed southward with a good wind and fair weather, till it reached the Line.

The Sun came up upon the left,
Out of the sea came he!
And he shone bright, and on the right
Went down into the sea.

Higher and higher every day,
Till over the mast at noon—
The Wedding-Guest here beat his breast,
For he heard the loud bassoon.

The Wedding-Guest heareth the bridal music; but the Mariner continueth his tale.

The bride hath paced into the hall,
Red as a rose is she;
Nodding their heads before her goes
The merry minstrelsy.

The Wedding-Guest he beat his breast,
Yet he cannot choose but hear;
And thus spake on that ancient man,
The bright-eyed Mariner.

And now the storm-blast came, and he
Was tyrannous and strong:
He struck with his o'ertaking wings,
And chased us south along.

With sloping masts and dipping prow,
As who pursued with yell and blow
Still treads the shadow of his foe
And forward bends his head,
The ship drove fast, loud roared the blast,
And southward aye we fled.

And now there came both mist and snow,
And it grew wondrous cold:
And ice, mast-high, came floating by,
As green as emerald.

And through the drifts the snowy clifts
Did send a dismal sheen:
Nor shapes of men nor beasts we ken—
The ice was all between.

The ice was here, the ice was there,
The ice was all around:
It cracked and growled, and roared and howled,
Like noises in a swound!

At length did cross an Albatross:
Through the fog it came;
As if it had been a Christian soul,
We hailed it in God's name.

It ate the food it ne'er had eat,
And round and round it flew.
The ice did split with a thunder-fit;
The helmsman steered us through!

And a good south wind sprung up behind;
The Albatross did follow,
And every day, for food or play,
Came to the mariners' hollo!

In mist or cloud, on mast or shroud,
It perched for vespers nine;
Whiles all the night, through fog-smoke white,
Glimmered the white Moon-shine.

"God save thee, ancient Mariner!
From the fiends, that plague thee thus!—
Why look'st thou so?"—With my crossbow
I shot the Albatross.

PART THE SECOND

The Sun now rose upon the right:
Out of the sea came he,
Still hid in mist, and on the left
Went down into the sea.

And the good south wind still blew behind,
But no sweet bird did follow,
Nor any day for food or play
Came to the mariners' hollo!

And I had done a hellish thing,
And it would work 'em woe:
For all averred, I had killed the bird
That made the breeze to blow.

"Ah, wretch!" said they, "the bird to slay,
That made the breeze to blow!"

Nor dim nor red, like God's own head,
The glorious Sun uprist:
Then all averred, I had killed the bird
That brought the fog and mist.
" 'Twas right," said they, "such birds to slay,
That bring the fog and mist."

The fair breeze blew, the white foam flew,
The furrow followed free;
We were the first that ever burst
Into that silent sea.

Down dropt the breeze, the sails dropt down,

The ship hath been suddenly becalmed.
'Twas sad as sad could be;
And we did speak only to break
The silence of the sea!

All in a hot and copper sky,
The bloody Sun, at noon,
Right up above the mast did stand,
No bigger than the Moon.

Day after day, day after day,
We stuck, nor breath nor motion;
As idle as a painted ship
Upon a painted ocean.

And the Alba-tross begins to be avenged.
Water, water, every where,
And all the boards did shrink;
Water, water, every where,
Nor any drop to drink.

The very deep did rot: O Christ!
That ever this should be!
Yea, slimy things did crawl with legs
Upon the slimy sea.

About, about, in reel and rout
The death-fires danced at night;
The water, like a witch's oils,
Burnt green, and blue, and white.

A Spirit had fol-lowed them; one of the invis-ible inhabitants of this planet, neither de-
And some in dreams assurèd were
Of the Spirit that plagued us so;
Nine fathom deep he had followed us
From the land of mist and snow.

parted souls nor angels; concerning whom the learned Jew, Josephus, and the Platonic Constantinopolitan, Michael Psellus, may be consulted. They are very numerous, and there is no climate or element without one or more.

And every tongue, through utter drought,
Was withered at the root;
We could not speak, no more than if
We had been choked with soot.

The shipmates,
in their sore
distress, would
fain throw the
whole guilt on
the ancient
Ah! well-a-day! what evil looks
Had I from old and young!
Instead of the cross, the Albatross
About my neck was hung.

whereof they hang the dead sea-bird round his neck.

PART THE THIRD

The ancient
Mariner be-
holdeth a sign
in the element
afar off.

There passed a weary time. Each throat
Was parched, and glazed each eye.
A weary time! a weary time!
How glazed each weary eye,
When looking westward, I beheld
A something in the sky.

At first it seemed a little speck,
And then it seemed a mist;
It moved and moved, and took at last
A certain shape, I wist.

A speck, a mist, a shape, I wist!
And still it neared and neared:
As if it dodged a water-sprite,
It plunged and tacked and veered.

At its nearer ap-
proach, it seem-
eth him to be a
ship; and at a
dear ransom he
freeth his
speech from the
bonds of thirst.

With throats unslaked, with black lips baked,
We could nor laugh nor wail;
Through utter drought all dumb we stood!
I bit my arm, I sucked the blood,
And cried, A sail! a sail!

With throats unslaked, with black lips baked,
Agape they heard me call:
Gramercy! they for joy did grin,
And all at once their breath drew in,
As they were drinking all.

And horror fol-
lows. For can it
be a ship that
comes onward
without wind
or tide?

See! see! (I cried) she tacks no more!
Hither to work us weal;
Without a breeze, without a tide,
She steadies with upright keel!

The western wave was all a-flame.
The day was well-nigh done!
Almost upon the western wave
Rested the broad bright Sun;
When that strange shape drove suddenly
Betwixt us and the Sun.

*It seemeth him
but the skeleton
of a ship.*

And straight the Sun was flecked with bars,
(Heaven's Mother send us grace!)
As if through a dungeon-grate he peered
With broad and burning face.

Alas! (thought I, and my heart beat loud)
How fast she nears and nears!
Are those *her* sails that glance in the Sun,
Like restless gossameres?

*And its ribs are
seen as bars on
the face of the
setting Sun. The
Spectre-Woman
and her Death-
mate, and no
other on board
the skeleton-
ship.*

Are those *her* ribs through which the Sun
Did peer, as through a grate?
And is that Woman all her crew?
Is that a Death? and are there two?
Is Death that woman's mate?

*Like vessel, like
crew!*

Her lips were red, *her* looks were free,
Her locks were yellow as gold:
Her skin was as white as leprosy,
The Night-mare Life-in-Death was she,
Who thicks man's blood with cold.

*Death and Life-
in-Death have
diced for the
ship's crew, and
she (the latter)
winneth the an-
cient Mariner.*

The naked hulk alongside came,
And the twain were casting dice;
"The game is done! I've won! I've won!"
Quoth she, and whistles thrice.

*No twilight
within the
courts of the
Sun.*

The Sun's rim dips; the stars rush out:
At one stride comes the dark;
With far-heard whisper, o'er the sea,
Off shot the spectre-bark.

We listened and looked sideways up!
Fear at my heart, as at a cup,
My life-blood seemed to sip!
The stars were dim, and thick the night,
The steersman's face by his lamp gleamed white;
From the sails the dew did drip—
Till clomb above the eastern bar
The hornèd Moon, with one bright star
Within the nether tip.

One after one, by the star-dogged Moon,
Too quick for groan or sigh,
Each turned his face with a ghastly pang,
And cursed me with his eye.

Four times fifty living men,
(And I heard nor sigh nor groan)
With heavy thump, a lifeless lump,
They dropped down one by one.

The souls did from their bodies fly,—
They fled to bliss or woe!
And every soul, it passed me by,
Like the whizz of my cross-bow!

PART THE FOURTH

"I fear thee, ancient Mariner!
I fear thy skinny hand!
And thou art long, and lank, and brown,
As is the ribbed sea-sand.

I fear thee and thy glittering eye,
And thy skinny hand, so brown."—

Fear not, fear not, thou Wedding-Guest!
This body dropt not down.

Alone, alone, all, all alone,
Alone on a wide wide sea!
And never a saint took pity on
My soul in agony.

The many men, so beautiful!
And they all dead did lie:
And a thousand thousand slimy things
Lived on; and so did I.

*And envieth
that they should
live, and so
many lie dead.*
I looked upon the rotting sea,
And drew my eyes away;
I looked upon the rotting deck,
And there the dead men lay.

I looked to heaven, and tried to pray;
But or ever a prayer had gusht,
A wicked whisper came, and made
My heart as dry as dust.

I closed my lids, and kept them close,
And the balls like pulses beat;
For the sky and the sea, and the sea and the sky
Lay like a load on my weary eye,
And the dead were at my feet.

*But the curse
liveth for him
in the eye of
the dead men.*
The cold sweat melted from their limbs,
Nor rot nor reek did they:
The look with which they looked on me
Had never passed away.

An orphan's curse would drag to hell
A spirit from on high;
But oh! more horrible than that
Is the curse in a dead man's eye!
Seven days, seven nights, I saw that curse,
And yet I could not die.

*In his loneliness
and fixedness he
yearneth to-
wards the jour-
neying Moon,
and the stars*
The moving Moon went up the sky
And no where did abide:
Softly she was going up,
And a star or two beside—

*that still sojourn, yet still move onward; and everywhere the blue sky be-
longs to them, and is their appointed rest, and their native country and
their own natural homes, which they enter unannounced, as lords that are
certainly expected and yet there is a silent joy at their arrival.*

Her beams bemocked the sultry main,
Like April hoar-frost spread;
But where the ship's huge shadow lay,
The charmèd water burnt alway
A still and awful red.

By the light of the Moon he beholdeth God's creatures of the great calm.

Beyond the shadow of the ship,
I watched the water-snakes:
They moved in tracks of shining white,
And when they reared, the elfish light
Fell off in hoary flakes.

Within the shadow of the ship
I watched their rich attire:
Blue, glossy green, and velvet black,
They coiled and swam; and every track
Was a flash of golden fire.

Their beauty and their happiness.

O happy living things! no tongue
Their beauty might declare:
A spring of love gushed from my heart,

He blesseth them in his heart.

And I blessed them unaware:
Sure my kind saint took pity on me,
And I blessed them unaware.

The spell begins to break.

The self-same moment I could pray;
And from my neck so free
The Albatross fell off, and sank
Like lead into the sea.

PART THE FIFTH

O sleep! it is a gentle thing,
Beloved from pole to pole!
To Mary Queen the praise be given!
She sent the gentle sleep from Heaven,
That slid into my soul.

By grace of the holy Mother, the ancient Mariner is refreshed with rain.

The silly buckets on the deck,
That had so long remained,
I dreamt that they were filled with dew;
And when I awoke, it rained.

My lips were wet, my throat was cold,
My garments all were dank;
Sure I had drunken in my dreams,
And still my body drank.

I moved, and could not feel my limbs:
I was so light—almost
I thought that I had died in sleep,
And was a blessèd ghost.

He heareth sounds and seeth strange sights and commotions in the sky and the element.

And soon I heard a roaring wind:
It did not come anear;
But with its sound it shook the sails,
That were so thin and sere.

The upper air burst into life!
And a hundred fire-flags sheen,
To and fro they were hurried about!
And to and fro, and in and out,
The wan stars danced between.

And the coming wind did roar more loud,
And the sails did sigh like sedge;
And the rain poured down from one black
    cloud;
The Moon was at its edge.

The thick black cloud was cleft, and still
The Moon was at its side:
Like waters shot from some high crag,
The lightning fell with never a jag,
A river steep and wide.

The bodies of the ship's crew are inspired and the ship moves on;

The loud wind never reached the ship,
Yet now the ship moved on!
Beneath the lightning and the Moon
The dead men gave a groan.

They groaned, they stirred, they all uprose,
Nor spake, nor moved their eyes;
It had been strange, even in a dream,
To have seen those dead men rise.

The helmsman steered, the ship moved on;
Yet never a breeze up-blew;
The mariners all 'gan work the ropes,
Where they were wont to do;
They raised their limbs like lifeless tools—
We were a ghastly crew.

The body of my brother's son
Stood by me, knee to knee:
The body and I pulled at one rope,
But he said nought to me.

"I fear thee, ancient Mariner!"
Be calm, thou Wedding-Guest!
'Twas not those souls that fled in pain,
Which to their corses came again,
But a troop of spirits blest:

For when it dawned—they dropped their arms,
And clustered round the mast;
Sweet sounds rose slowly through their mouths,
And from their bodies passed.

But not by the
souls of the
men, nor by
dæmons of earth
or middle air,
but by a blessed
troop of angelic
spirits, sent
down by the in-
vocation of the
guardian saint.

Around, around, flew each sweet sound,
Then darted to the Sun;
Slowly the sounds came back again,
Now mixed, now one by one.

Sometimes a-dropping from the sky
I heard the sky-lark sing;
Sometimes all little birds that are,
How they seemed to fill the sea and air
With their sweet jargoning!

And now 'twas like all instruments,
Now like a lonely flute;
And now it is an angel's song,
That makes the heavens be mute.

It ceased; yet still the sails made on
A pleasant noise till noon,
A noise like of a hidden brook
In the leafy month of June,

That to the sleeping woods all night
Singeth a quiet tune.

Till noon we quietly sailed on,
Yet never a breeze did breathe:
Slowly and smoothly went the ship,
Moved onward from beneath.

Under the keel nine fathom deep,
From the land of mist and snow,
The spirit slid: and it was he
That made the ship to go.
The sails at noon left off their tune,
And the ship stood still also.

The Sun, right up above the mast,
Had fixed her to the ocean:
But in a minute she 'gan stir,
With a short uneasy motion—
Backwards and forwards half her length
With a short uneasy motion.

Then like a pawing horse let go,
She made a sudden bound:
It flung the blood into my head,
And I fell down in a swound.

How long in that same fit I lay,
I have not to declare;
But ere my living life returned,
I heard and in my soul discerned
Two voices in the air.

"Is it he?" quoth one, "Is this the man?
By him who died on cross,
With his cruel bow he laid full low
The harmless Albatross.

The spirit who bideth by himself
In the land of mist and snow,
He loved the bird that loved the man
Who shot him with his bow."

The other was a softer voice,
As soft as honey-dew:
Quoth he, "The man hath penance done,
And penance more will do."

PART THE SIXTH

First Voice:

"But tell me, tell me! speak again,
Thy soft response renewing—
What makes that ship drive on so fast?
What is the ocean doing?"

Second Voice:

"Still as a slave before his lord,
The ocean hath no blast;
His great bright eye most silently
Up to the Moon is cast—

If he may know which way to go;
For she guides him smooth or grim.
See, brother, see! how graciously
She looketh down on him."

First Voice:

*The Mariner
hath been cast
into a trance;
for the angelic
power causeth
the vessel to
drive north-
ward faster
than human life
could endure.*

"But why drives on that ship so fast,
Without or wave or wind?"

Second Voice:

"The air is cut away before,
And closes from behind.

Fly, brother, fly! more high, more high!
Or we shall be belated:
For slow and slow that ship will go,
When the Mariner's trance is abated."

*The supernat-
ural motion is
retarded; the
Mariner
awakes, and his
penance begins
anew.*

I woke, and we were sailing on
As in a gentle weather:
'Twas night, calm night, the Moon was high;
The dead men stood together.

All stood together on the deck,
For a charnel-dungeon fitter:
All fixed on me their stony eyes,
That in the Moon did glitter.

The pang, the curse, with which they died,
Had never passed away:
I could not draw my eyes from theirs,
Nor turn them up to pray.

*The curse is fi-
nally expiated.*

And now this spell was snapt: once more
I viewed the ocean green,
And looked far forth, yet little saw
Of what had else been seen—

Like one, that on a lonesome road
Doth walk in fear and dread,
And having once turned round walks on
And turns no more his head;
Because he knows, a frightful fiend
Doth close behind him tread.

But soon there breathed a wind on me,
Nor sound nor motion made:
Its path was not upon the sea,
In ripple or in shade.

It raised my hair, it fanned my cheek
Like a meadow-gale of spring—
It mingled strangely with my fears,
Yet it felt like a welcoming.

Swiftly, swiftly flew the ship,
Yet she sailed softly too:
Sweetly, sweetly blew the breeze—
On me alone it blew.

Oh! dream of joy! is this indeed
The light-house top I see?
Is this the hill? is this the kirk?
Is this mine own countree?

We drifted o'er the harbor-bar,
And I with sobs did pray—
O let me be awake, my God!
Or let me sleep alway.

The harbor-bay was clear as glass,
So smoothly it was strewn!
And on the bay the moonlight lay,
And the shadow of the Moon.

The rock shone bright, the kirk no less,
That stands above the rock:
The moonlight steeped in silentness
The steady weathercock.

The angelic spirits leave the dead bodies,

And the bay was white with silent light,
Till rising from the same,
Full many shapes, that shadows were,
In crimson colors came.

And appear in their own forms of light.

A little distance from the prow
Those crimson shadows were:
I turned my eyes upon the deck—
Oh, Christ! what saw I there!

Each corse lay flat, lifeless and flat,
And, by the holy rood!
A man all light, a seraph-man,
On every corse there stood.

This seraph-band, each waved his hand:
It was a heavenly sight!
They stood as signals to the land,
Each one a lovely light;

This seraph-band, each waved his hand,
No voice did they impart—
No voice; but oh! the silence sank
Like music on my heart.

But soon I heard the dash of oars,
I heard the Pilot's cheer;
My head was turned perforce away,
And I saw a boat appear.

The Pilot, and the Pilot's boy.
I heard them coming fast:
Dear Lord in Heaven! it was a joy
The dead men could not blast.

I saw a third—I heard his voice:
It is the Hermit good!
He singeth loud his godly hymns
That he makes in the wood.
He'll shrieve my soul, he'll wash away
The Albatross's blood.

PART THE SEVENTH

The Hermit of the Wood

This Hermit good lives in that wood
Which slopes down to the sea.
How loudly his sweet voice he rears!
He loves to talk with marineres
That come from a far countree.

He kneels at morn, and noon, and eve—
He hath a cushion plump:
It is the moss that wholly hides
The rotted old oak-stump.

The skiff-boat neared: I heard them talk,
"Why this is strange, I trow!
Where are those lights so many and fair,
That signal made but now?"

121

Approacheth the ship with wonder.

"Strange, by my faith!" the Hermit said—
"And they answered not our cheer!
The planks looked warped! and see those sails
How thin they are and sere!
I never saw aught like to them,
Unless perchance it were

Brown skeletons of leaves that lag
My forest-brook along;
When the ivy-tod is heavy with snow,
And the owlet whoops to the wolf below,
That eats the she-wolf's young."

"Dear Lord! it hath a fiendish look—
(The Pilot made reply)
I am a-feared"—"Push on, push on!"
Said the Hermit cheerily.

The boat came closer to the ship,
But I nor spake nor stirred;
The boat came close beneath the ship,
And straight a sound was heard.

The ship suddenly sinketh.

Under the water it rumbled on,
Still louder and more dread:
It reached the ship, it split the bay;
The ship went down like lead.

The ancient Mariner is saved in the Pilot's boat.

Stunned by that loud and dreadful sound,
Which sky and ocean smote,
Like one that hath been seven days drowned
My body lay afloat;
But swift as dreams, myself I found
Within the Pilot's boat.

Upon the whirl, where sank the ship,
The boat spun round and round;
And all was still, save that the hill
Was telling of the sound.

I moved my lips—the Pilot shrieked
And fell down in a fit;
The holy Hermit raised his eyes,
And prayed where he did sit.

I took the oars: the Pilot's boy,
Who now doth crazy go,
Laughed loud and long, and all the while
His eyes went to and fro.
"Ha! ha!" quoth he, "full plain I see,
The Devil knows how to row."

And now, all in my own countree,
I stood on the firm land!
The Hermit stepped forth from the boat,
And scarcely he could stand.

The ancient Mariner earnestly entreateth the Hermit to shrieve him; and the penance of life falls on him.

"O shrieve me, shrieve me, holy man!"
The Hermit crossed his brow.
"Say quick," quoth he, "I bid thee say—
What manner of man art thou?"

Forthwith this frame of mine was wrenched
With a woeful agony,
Which forced me to begin my tale;
And then it left me free.

And ever and anon throughout his future life an agony constraineth him to travel from land to land;

Since then, at an uncertain hour,
That agony returns:
And till my ghastly tale is told,
This heart within me burns.

I pass, like night, from land to land;
I have strange power of speech;
That moment that his face I see,
I know the man that must hear me:
To him my tale I teach.

What loud uproar bursts from that door!
The wedding-guests are there:

123

But in the garden-bower the bride
And bride-maids singing are:
And hark the little vesper bell,
Which biddeth me to prayer!

O Wedding-Guest! this soul hath been
Alone on a wide wide sea:
So lonely 'twas, that God himself
Scarce seemèd there to be.

O sweeter than the marriage-feast,
'Tis sweeter far to me,
To walk together to the kirk
With a goodly company!—

To walk together to the kirk,
And all together pray,
While each to his great Father bends,
Old men, and babes, and loving friends,
And youths and maidens gay!

Farewell, farewell! but this I tell
To thee, thou Wedding-Guest!
He prayeth well, who loveth well
Both man and bird and beast.

*And to teach,
by his own ex-
ample, love and
reverence to all
things that God
made and lov-
eth.*

He prayeth best, who loveth best
All things both great and small;
For the dear God who loveth us,
He made and loveth all.

The Mariner, whose eye is bright,
Whose beard with age is hoar,
Is gone: and now the Wedding-Guest
Turned from the bridegroom's door.

He went like one that hath been stunned,
And is of sense forlorn:
A sadder and a wiser man,
He rose the morrow morn.

SAMUEL TAYLOR COLERIDGE

Death

Death stands above me, whispering low
I know not what into my ear;
Of his strange language all I know
Is, there is not a word of fear.

WALTER SAVAGE LANDOR

Stanzas Written in Dejection Near Naples

The sun is warm, the sky is clear,
    The waves are dancing fast and bright;
Blue isles and snowy mountains wear
    The purple noon's transparent might:
    The breath of the moist earth is light
Around its unexpanded buds;
    Like many a voice of one delight—
The winds', the birds', the ocean-floods',
The City's voice itself is soft like Solitude's.

I see the Deep's untrampled floor
    With green and purple sea-weeds strown;
I see the waves upon the shore,
    Like light dissolved in star-showers thrown;
    I sit upon the sands alone;
The lightning of the noon-tide ocean
    Is flashing round me, and a tone
Arises from its measured motion—
How sweet! did any heart now share in my emotion.

Alas! I have not hope nor health,
    Nor peace within nor calm around,
Nor that Content surpassing wealth
    The sage in meditation found,
    And walked with inward glory crowned—
Nor fame, nor power, nor love, nor leisure;
    Others I see whom these surround—
Smiling they live, and call life pleasure;
To me that cup has been dealt in another measure.

Yet now despair itself is mild,
    Even as the winds and waters are;
I could lie down like a tired child,
    And weep away the life of care
    Which I have borne and yet must bear,
Till death like sleep might steal on me,
    And I might feel in the warm air
My cheek grow cold, and hear the sea
Breathe o'er my dying brain its last monotony.

Some might lament that I were cold,
    As I, when this sweet day is gone,
Which my lost heart, too soon grown old,
    Insults with his untimely moan;
They might lament—for I am one
    Whom men love not,—and yet regret,
    Unlike this day, which, when the sun
Shall on its stainless glory set,
Will linger, though enjoyed, like joy in memory yet.

PERCY BYSSHE SHELLEY

Music, When Soft Voices Die

Music, when soft voices die,
Vibrates in the memory—
Odors, when sweet violets sicken,
Live within the sense they quicken.

Rose leaves, when the rose is dead,
Are heaped for the beloved's bed;
And so thy thoughts, when Thou art gone,
Love itself shall slumber on.

PERCY BYSSHE SHELLEY

Abou Ben Adhem

Abou Ben Adhem (may his tribe increase!)
Awoke one night from a deep dream of peace,
And saw, within the moonlight in his room,
Making it rich, and like a lily in bloom,
An angel writing in a book of gold:—
Exceeding peace had made Ben Adhem bold,
And to the Presence in the room he said,
"What writest thou?"—The vision raised its head,
And with a look made of all sweet accord,
Answered, "The names of those who love the Lord."
"And is mine one?" said Abou. "Nay, not so,"
Replied the Angel. Abou spoke more low,
But cheerly still; and said, "I pray thee, then,
Write me as one who loves his fellow-men."

The angel wrote and vanished. The next night
It came again, with a great wakening light,
And showed the names whom love of God had blessed,
And lo! Ben Adhem's name led all the rest.

LEIGH HUNT

Crossing the Bar

Sunset and evening star,
    And one clear call for me!
And may there be no moaning of the bar,
    When I put out to sea,

But such a tide as moving seems asleep,
    Too full for sound and foam,
When that which drew from out the boundless deep
    Turns again home.

Twilight and evening bell,
    And after that the dark!
And may there be no sadness of farewell,
    When I embark;

For though from out our bourne of Time and Place
  The flood may bear me far,
I hope to see my Pilot face to face,
  When I have crossed the bar.

ALFRED TENNYSON

Break, Break, Break

Break, break, break,
  On thy cold gray stones, O Sea!
And I would that my tongue could utter
  The thoughts that arise in me.

O well for the fisherman's boy,
  That he shouts with his sister at play!
O well for the sailor lad,
  That he sings in his boat on the bay!

And the stately ships go on
  To their haven under the hill;
But O for the touch of a vanished hand,
  And the sound of a voice that is still!

Break, break, break,
  At the foot of thy crags, O Sea!
But the tender grace of a day that is dead
  Will never come back to me.

ALFRED TENNYSON

Flower in the Crannied Wall

Flower in the crannied wall,
I pluck you out of the crannies,
I hold you here, root and all, in my hand,
Little flower—but *if* I could understand
What you are, root and all, and all in all,
I should know what God and man is.

ALFRED TENNYSON

Grow Old Along with Me

(FROM *Rabbi Ben Ezra*)

Grow old along with me!
The best is yet to be,
The last of life, for which the first was made:
Our times are in his hand
Who saith, "A whole I planned,
Youth shows but half; trust God: see all, nor be afraid!"

ROBERT BROWNING

Prospice

Fear death?—to feel the fog in my throat,
    The mist in my face,
When the snows begin, and the blasts denote
    I am nearing the place,
The power of the night, the press of the storm,
    The post of the foe;
Where he stands, the Arch Fear in a visible form,
    Yet the strong man must go:
For the journey is done and the summit attained,
    And the barriers fall,
Though a battle's to fight ere the guerdon be gained,
    The reward of it all.
I was ever a fighter, so—one fight more,
    The best and the last!
I would hate that death bandaged my eyes, and forbore,
    And bade me creep past.
No! let me taste the whole of it, fare like my peers
    The heroes of old,
Bear the brunt, in a minute pay glad life's arrears
    Of pain, darkness and cold.
For sudden the worst turns the best to the brave,
    The black minute's at end,
And the elements' rage, the fiend-voices that rave,
    Shall dwindle, shall blend,

Shall change, shall become first a peace out of pain,
  Then a light, then thy breast,
O thou soul of my soul! I shall clasp thee again,
  And with God be the rest!

ROBERT BROWNING

Belief and Unbelief
(FROM *Bishop Blougram's Apology*)

. . . Belief,
As unbelief before, shakes us by fits,
Confounds us like its predecessor. Where's
The gain? how can we guard our unbelief,
Make it bear fruit to us?—the problem here.
Just when we are safest, there's a sunset-touch,
A fancy from a flower-bell, some one's death,
A chorus-ending from Euripides,—
And that's enough for fifty hopes and fears
As old and new at once as nature's self,
To rap and knock and enter in our soul,
Take hands and dance there, a fantastic ring,
Round the ancient idol, on his base again,—
The grand Perhaps! we look on helplessly.
There the old misgivings, crooked questions are—
This good God,—what he could do, if he would,
Would, if he could—then must have done long since:
If so, when, where, and how? some way must be,—
Once feel about, and soon or late you hit
Some sense, in which it might be, after all.
Why not, "The Way, the Truth, the Life?"

                                    —That way
Over the mountain, which who stands upon
Is apt to doubt if it be meant for a road;
While, if he views it from the waste itself,
Up goes the line there, plain from base to brow,
Not vague, mistakable! what's a break or two

Seen from the unbroken desert either side?
And then (to bring in fresh philosophy)
What if the breaks themselves should prove at last
The most consummate of contrivances
To train a man's eye, teach him what is faith?
And so we stumble at truth's very test!
All we have gained then by our unbelief
Is a life of doubt diversified by faith,
For one of faith diversified by doubt:
We called the chess-board white,—we call it black.

ROBERT BROWNING

Epilogue

(TO *Asolando*)

At the midnight in the silence of the sleep-time
    When you set your fancies free,
Will they pass to where—by death, fools think, imprisoned—
Low he lies who once so loved you, whom you loved so,
        —Pity me?

Oh to love so, be so loved, yet so mistaken!
    What had I on earth to do
With the slothful, with the mawkish, the unmanly?
Like the aimless, helpless, hopeless, did I drivel
        —Being—who?

One who never turned his back but marched breast forward,
    Never doubted clouds would break,
Never dreamed, though right were worsted, wrong would
      triumph,
Held we fall to rise, are baffled to fight better,
        Sleep to wake.

No, at noonday in the bustle of man's worktime
    Greet the unseen with a cheer!

Bid him forward, breast and back as either should be,
"Strive and thrive!" cry "Speed,—fight on, fare ever
There as here!"

ROBERT BROWNING

Say Not

Say not, the struggle naught availeth,
    The labor and the wounds are vain,
The enemy faints not, nor faileth,
    And as things have been they remain.

If hopes were dupes, fears may be liars;
    It may be, in yon smoke concealed,
Your comrades chase e'en now the fliers,
    And, but for you, possess the field.

For while the tired waves, vainly breaking,
    Seem here no painful inch to gain,
Far back, through creeks and inlets making,
    Comes silent, flooding in, the main.

And not by eastern windows only,
    When daylight comes, comes in the light;
In front, the sun climbs slow, how slowly,
    But westward, look, the land is bright.

ARTHUR HUGH CLOUGH

Invictus

Out of the night that covers me,
    Black as the pit from pole to pole,
I thank whatever gods there be
    For my unconquerable soul.

In the fell clutch of circumstance
    I have not winced nor cried aloud.

Under the bludgeonings of fate
My head is bloody, but unbowed.

Beyond this space of wrath and tears
Looms but the Horror of the shade,
And yet the menace of the years
Finds and shall find me unafraid.

It matters not how strait the gate,
How charged with punishments the scroll,
I am the master of my fate:
I am the captain of my soul.

WILLIAM ERNEST HENLEY

The Music Makers

We are the music-makers,
And we are the dreamers of dreams,
Wandering by lone sea-breakers,
And sitting by desolate streams;
World-losers and world-forsakers,
On whom the pale moon gleams:
Yet we are the movers and shakers
Of the world forever, it seems.

With wonderful deathless ditties
We build up the world's great cities,
And out of a fabulous story
We fashion an empire's glory:
One man with a dream, at pleasure,
Shall go forth and conquer a crown;
And three with a new song's measure
Can trample an empire down.

We, in the ages lying
In the buried past of the earth,
Built Nineveh with our sighing,
And Babel itself with our mirth;

And o'erthrew them with prophesying
To the old of the new world's worth;
For each age is a dream that is dying,
Or one that is coming to birth.

ARTHUR O'SHAUGHNESSY

The Raven

Once upon a midnight dreary, while I pondered, weak and
weary,
Over many a quaint and curious volume of forgotten lore,—
While I nodded, nearly napping, suddenly there came a
tapping,
As of someone gently rapping, rapping at my chamber door.
" 'Tis some visitor," I muttered, "tapping at my chamber door:
Only this and nothing more."

Ah, distinctly I remember it was in the bleak December,
And each separate dying ember wrought its ghost upon the
floor.
Eagerly I wished the morrow;—vainly I had sought to borrow
From my books surcease of sorrow—sorrow for the lost
Lenore,
For the rare and radiant maiden whom the angels name
Lenore:
Nameless here for evermore.

And the silken sad uncertain rustling of each purple curtain
Thrilled me—filled me with fantastic terrors never felt before;
So that now, to still the beating of my heart, I stood repeating,
" 'Tis some visitor entreating entrance at my chamber door:
Some late visitor entreating entrance at my chamber door:
This it is and nothing more."

Presently my soul grew stronger; hesitating then no longer,
"Sir," said I, "or Madam, truly your forgiveness I implore;
But the fact is I was napping, and so gently you came rapping,
And so faintly you came tapping, tapping at my chamber door,

That I scarce was sure I heard you"—here I opened wide the
    door:—
        Darkness there and nothing more.

Deep into that darkness peering, long I stood there wondering,
    fearing,
Doubting, dreaming dreams no mortals ever dared to dream
    before;
But the silence was unbroken, and the stillness gave no token,
And the only word there spoken was the whispered word,
    "Lenore!"
This I whispered, and an echo murmured back the word,
    "Lenore!"
        Merely this and nothing more.

Back into the chamber turning, all my soul within me burning,
Soon again I heard a tapping somewhat louder than before.
"Surely," said I, "surely that is something at my window
    lattice;
Let me see, then, what thereat is, and this mystery explore;
Let my heart be still a moment and this mystery explore;
        'Tis the wind and nothing more."

Open here I flung the shutter, when, with many a flirt and
    flutter,
In there stepped a stately Raven of the saintly days of yore.
Not the least obeisance made he; not a minute stopped or
    stayed he;
But, with mien of lord or lady, perched above my chamber
    door,
Perched upon a bust of Pallas just above my chamber door:
        Perched and sat, and nothing more.

Then this ebony bird beguiling my sad fancy into smiling
By the grave and stern decorum of the countenance it wore,—
"Though thy crest be shorn and shaven, thou," I said, "art
    sure no craven,
Ghastly grim and ancient Raven wandering from the Nightly
    shore:

Tell me what thy lordly name is on the Night's Plutonian
    shore!"
            Quoth the Raven, "Nevermore."

Much I marvelled this ungainly fowl to hear discourse so
    plainly,
Though its answer little meaning—little relevancy bore;
For we cannot help agreeing that no living human being
Ever yet was blessed with seeing bird above his chamber door,
Bird or beast upon the sculptured bust above his chamber door,
            With such name as "Nevermore."

But the Raven, sitting lonely on the placid bust, spoke only
That one word, as if his soul in that one word he did outpour.
Nothing further then he uttered, not a feather then he
    fluttered,
Till I scarcely more than muttered,—"Other friends have
    flown before;
On the morrow *he* will leave me, as my Hopes have flown
    before."
            Then the bird said, "Nevermore."

Startled by the stillness broken by reply so aptly spoken,
"Doubtless," said I, "what it utters is its only stock and store,
Caught from some unhappy master whom unmerciful Disaster
Followed fast and followed faster till his songs one burden
    bore:
Till the dirges of his Hope that melancholy burden bore
            Of 'Never—nevermore.' "

But the Raven still beguiling all my fancy into smiling,
Straight I wheeled a cushioned seat in front of bird and bust
    and door;
Then, upon the velvet sinking, I betook myself to linking
Fancy unto fancy, thinking what this ominous bird of yore,
What this grim, ungainly, ghastly, gaunt, and ominous bird of
    yore
            Meant in croaking "Nevermore."

This I sat engaged in guessing, but no syllable expressing
To the fowl whose fiery eyes now burned into my bosom's
    core;
This and more I sat divining, with my head at ease reclining
On the cushion's velvet lining that the lamp-light gloated o'er,
But whose velvet violet lining with the lamp-light gloating o'er
    She shall press, ah, nevermore!

Then, methought, the air grew denser, perfumed from an
    unseen censer
Swung by seraphim whose foot-falls tinkled on the tufted
    floor.
"Wretch," I cried, "thy God hath lent thee—by these angels
    he hath sent thee
Respite—respite and nepenthe from thy memories of Lenore!
Quaff, oh quaff this kind nepenthe, and forget this lost
    Lenore!"
        Quoth the Raven, "Nevermore."

"Prophet!" said I, "thing of evil! prophet still, if bird or devil!
Whether Tempter sent, or whether tempest tossed thee here
    ashore,
Desolate, yet all undaunted, on this desert land enchanted—
On this home by Horror haunted—tell me truly, I implore:
Is there—*is* there balm in Gilead?—tell me—tell me, I implore!"
        Quoth the Raven, "Nevermore."

"Prophet!" said I, "thing of evil! prophet still, if bird or devil!
By that Heaven that bends above us, by that God we both
    adore,
Tell this soul with sorrow laden if, within the distant Aidenn,
It shall clasp a sainted maiden whom the angels name Lenore:
Clasp a rare and radiant maiden whom the angels name
    Lenore!"
        Quoth the Raven, "Nevermore."

"Be that word our sign of parting, bird or fiend!" I shrieked,
    upstarting:

"Get thee back into the tempest and the Night's Plutonian
    shore!
Leave no black plume of that lie thy soul hath spoken!
Leave my loneliness unbroken! quit the bust above my door!
Take thy beak from out my heart, and take thy form from off
    my door!"
           Quoth the Raven, "Nevermore."

And the Raven, never flitting, still is sitting, still is sitting,
On the pallid bust of Pallas just above my chamber door;
And his eyes have all the seeming of a demon's that is
    dreaming,
And the lamp-light o'er him streaming throws his shadow on
    the floor;
And my soul from out that shadow that lies floating on the
    floor
           Shall be lifted—nevermore!

EDGAR ALLAN POE

The Garden of Proserpine

Here, where the world is quiet;
  Here, where all trouble seems
Dead winds' and spent waves' riot
  In doubtful dreams of dreams;
I watch the green field growing
For reaping folk and sowing,
For harvest-time and mowing,
  A sleepy world of streams.

I am tired of tears and laughter,
  And men that laugh and weep;
Of what may come hereafter
  For men that sow to reap:
I am weary of days and hours,
Blown buds of barren flowers,
Desires and dreams and powers
  And everything but sleep.

Here life has death for neighbour,
　And far from eye or ear
Wan waves and wet winds labour,
　Weak ships and spirits steer;
They drive adrift, and whither
They wot not who make thither;
But no such winds blow hither,
　And no such things grow here.

No growth of moor or coppice,
　No heather-flower or vine,
But bloomless buds of poppies,
　Green grapes of Proserpine,
Pale beds of blowing rushes
Where no leaf blooms or blushes
Save this whereout she crushes
　For dead men deadly wine.

Pale, without name or number,
　In fruitless fields of corn,
They bow themselves and slumber
　All night till light is born;
And like a soul belated,
In hell and heaven unmated,
By cloud and mist abated
　Comes out of darkness morn.

Though one were strong as seven,
　He too with death shall dwell,
Nor wake with wings in heaven,
　Nor weep for pains in hell;
Though one were fair as roses,
His beauty clouds and closes;
And well though love reposes,
　In the end it is not well.

Pale, beyond porch and portal,
　Crowned with calm leaves, she stands
Who gathers all things mortal
　With cold immortal hands;

Her languid lips are sweeter
Than love's who fears to greet her
To men that mix and meet her
   From many times and lands.

She waits for each and other,
   She waits for all men born;
Forgets the earth her mother,
   The life of fruits and corn;
And spring and seed and swallow
Take wing for her and follow
Where summer song rings hollow
   And flowers are put to scorn.

There go the loves that wither,
   The old loves with wearier wings;
And all dead years draw thither,
   And all disastrous things;
Dead dreams of days forsaken,
Blind buds that snows have shaken,
Wild leaves that winds have taken
   Red strays of ruined springs.

We are not sure of sorrow,
   And joy was never sure;
To-day will die to-morrow;
   Time stoops to no man's lure;
And love, grown faint and fretful,
With lips but half regretful
Sighs, and with eyes forgetful
   Weeps that no loves endure.

From too much love of living,
   From hope and fear set free,
We thank with brief thanksgiving
   Whatever gods may be
That no life lives for ever;
That dead men rise up never;
That even the weariest river
   Winds somewhere safe to sea.

Then star nor sun shall waken,
  Nor any change of light:
Nor sound of waters shaken,
  Nor any sound or sight:
Nor wintry leaves nor vernal,
Nor days nor things diurnal;
Only the sleep eternal
  In an eternal night.

ALGERNON CHARLES SWINBURNE

The Hound of Heaven

I fled Him, down the nights and down the days;
  I fled Him, down the arches of the years;
I fled Him, down the labyrinthine ways
  Of my own mind; and in the mist of tears
I hid from Him, and under running laughter.
        Up vistaed hopes I sped;
        And shot, precipitated
Adown Titanic glooms of chasmed fears,
  From those strong Feet that followed, followed after.
        But with unhurrying chase,
        And unperturbèd pace,
Deliberate speed, majestic instancy,
        They beat—and a Voice beat
        More instant than the Feet—
"All things betray thee, who betrayest Me."

        I pleaded, outlaw-wise,
By many a hearted casement, curtained red,
  Trellised with intertwining charities;
(For, though I knew His love Who followèd,
        Yet was I sore adread
Lest, having Him, I must have naught beside)
But, if one little casement parted wide,
  The gust of His approach would clash it to.
  Fear wist not to evade, as Love wist to pursue.

Across the margent of the world I fled,
  And troubled the gold gateways of the stars,
  Smiting for shelter on their clangèd bars;
      Fretted to dulcet jars
And silvern chatter the pale ports o' the moon.
I said to dawn: Be sudden—to eve: Be soon;
  With thy young skiey blossoms heap me over
      From this tremendous Lover!
Float thy vague veil about me, lest He see!
  I tempted all His servitors, but to find
My own betrayal in their constancy,
In faith to Him their fickleness to me,
  Their traitorous trueness, and their loyal deceit.
To all swift things for swiftness did I sue;
  Clung to the whistling mane of every wind.
      But whether they swept, smoothly fleet,
      The long savannahs of the blue;
          Or whether, Thunder-driven,
      They clanged his chariot 'thwart a heaven
Plashy with flying lightnings round the spurn o' their feet:—
  Fear wist not to evade as Love wist to pursue.
          Still with unhurrying chase,
          And unperturbèd pace,
      Deliberate speed, majestic instancy,
          Come on the following Feet,
          And a Voice above their beat—
      "Naught shelters thee, who wilt not shelter Me."

I sought no more that, after which I strayed,
      In face of man or maid;
But still within the little children's eyes
      Seems something, something that replies,
They at least are for me, surely for me!
I turned me to them very wistfully;
But just as their young eyes grew sudden fair
      With dawning answers there,

Their angel plucked them from me by the hair.
"Come then, ye other children, Nature's—share
With me" (said I) "your delicate fellowship;
  Let me greet you lip to lip,
  Let me twine with you caresses,
      Wantoning
  With our Lady-Mother's vagrant tresses,
      Banqueting
  With her in her wind-walled palace,
  Underneath her azured daïs,
  Quaffing, as your taintless way is,
      From a chalice
Lucent-weeping out of the dayspring."
      So it was done:
I in their delicate fellowship was one—
Drew the bolt of Nature's secrecies.
  I knew all the swift importings
  On the willful face of skies;
  I knew how the clouds arise
  Spumèd of the wild sea-snortings;
      All that's born or dies
  Rose and drooped with; made them shapers
Of mine own moods, or wailful or divine—
  With them joyed and was bereaven.
  I was heavy with the even,
  When she lit her glimmering tapers
  Round the day's dead sanctities.
  I laughed in the morning's eyes.
I triumphed and I saddened with all weather,
  Heaven and I wept together,
And its sweet tears were salt with mortal mine;
Against the red throb of its sunset-heart
  I laid my own to beat,
  And share commingling heat;
But not by that, by that, was eased my human smart.
In vain my tears were wet on Heaven's gray cheek.

For ah! we know not what each other says,
    These things and I; in sound *I* speak—
Their sound is but their stir, they speak by silences.
Nature, poor stepdame, cannot slake my drouth;
    Let her, if she would owe me,
Drop yon blue bosom-veil of sky, and show me
    The breasts o' her tenderness:
Never did any milk of hers once bless
        My thirsting mouth.
        Nigh and nigh draws the chase,
        With unperturbèd pace,
    Deliberate speed, majestic instancy;
        And past those noisèd Feet
        A Voice comes yet more fleet—
"Lo! naught contents thee, who content'st not Me."

Naked I wait Thy love's uplifted stroke!
My harness piece by piece Thou hast hewn from me,
        And smitten me to my knee;
    I am defenseless utterly.
    I slept, methinks, and woke,
And, slowly gazing, find me stripped in sleep.
In the rash lustihead of my young powers,
    I shook the pillaring hours
And pulled my life upon me; grimed with smears,
I stand amid the dust o' the mounded years—
My mangled youth lies dead beneath the heap.
My days have crackled and gone up in smoke,
Have puffed and burst as sun-starts on a stream.
    Yea, faileth now even dream
The dreamer, and the lute the lutanist;
Even the linked fantasies, in whose blossomy twist
I swung the earth a trinket at my wrist,
Are yielding; cords of all too weak account
For earth with heavy griefs so overplussed.
    Ah! is Thy love indeed
A weed, albeit an amaranthine weed,

Suffering no flowers except its own to mount?
　　Ah! must—
　　Designer infinite!—
Ah! must Thou char the wood ere Thou canst limn with it?
My freshness spent its wavering shower i' the dust;
And now my heart is as a broken fount,
Wherein tear-dripping stagnate, spilt down ever
　　From the dank thoughts that shiver
Upon the sighful branches of my mind.
　　Such is; what is to be?
The pulp so bitter, how shall taste the rind?
I dimly guess what Time in mists confounds;
Yet ever and anon a trumpet sounds
From the hid battlements of Eternity,
Those shaken mists a space unsettle, then
Round the half-glimpsèd turrets slowly wash again;
　　But not ere him who summoneth
　　I first have seen, enwound
With glooming robes purpureal, cypress-crowned;
His name I know, and what his trumpet saith.
Whether man's heart or life it be which yields
　　Thee harvest, must Thy harvest-fields
　　Be dunged with rotten death?
　　　　　Now of that long pursuit
　　　　　Comes on at hand the bruit;
　　That Voice is round me like a bursting sea:
　　　　"And is thy earth so marred,
　　　　Shattered in shard on shard?
　　Lo, all things fly thee, for thou fliest Me!
　　"Strange, piteous, futile thing!
Wherefore should any set thee love apart?
Seeing none but I makes much of naught" (He said),
"And human love needs human meriting:
　　How hast thou merited—
Of all man's clotted clay the dingiest clot?
　　Alack, thou knowest not
How little worthy of any love thou art!

145

Whom wilt thou find to love ignoble thee
    Save Me, save only Me?
All which I took from thee I did but take,
    Not for thy harms,
But just that thou might'st seek it in My arms.
    All which thy child's mistake
Fancies as lost, I have stored for thee at home:
    Rise, clasp My hand, and come."

        Halts by me that footfall:
        Is my gloom, after all,
Shade of His hand, outstretched caressingly?
        "Ah, fondest, blindest, weakest,
        I am He Whom thou seekest!
Thou dravest love from thee, who dravest Me."

FRANCIS THOMPSON

To a Snowflake

What heart could have thought you?—
Past our devisal
  (O filigree petal!)
Fashioned so purely,
Fragilely, surely,
From what Paradisal
  Imagineless metal,
Too costly for cost?
Who hammered you, wrought you,
From argentine vapor?—
  "God was my shaper.
Passing surmisal,
He hammered, He wrought me,
From curled silver vapor,
To lust of His mind:—
  Thou couldst not have thought me!
So purely, so palely,

146

Tinily, surely,
Mightily, frailly,
Insculped and embossed,
With His hammer of wind,
And His graver of frost."

FRANCIS THOMPSON

Ex Ore Infantium

Little Jesus, wast Thou shy
Once, and just so small as I?
And what did it feel like to be
Out of Heaven, and just like me?
Didst Thou sometimes think of *there*,
And ask where all the angels were?
I should think that I would cry
For my house all made of sky;
I would look about the air,
And wonder where my angels were;
And at waking 'twould distress me—
Not an angel there to dress me!

Hadst Thou ever any toys,
Like us little girls and boys?
And didst Thou play in Heaven with all
The angels, that were not too tall,
With stars for marbles? Did the things
Play *Can you see me?* through their wings?

Didst Thou kneel at night to pray,
And didst Thou join Thy hands, this way?
And did they tire sometimes, being young,
And make the prayer seem very long?
And dost Thou like it best, that we
Should join our hands to pray to Thee?
I used to think, before I knew,

The prayer not said unless we do.
And did Thy Mother at the night
Kiss Thee, and fold the clothes in right?
And didst Thou feel quite good in bed,
Kissed, and sweet, and Thy prayers said?

Thou canst not have forgotten all
That it feels like to be small:
And Thou know'st I cannot pray
To Thee in my father's way—
When Thou wast so little, say,
Couldst Thou talk Thy Father's way?—
So, a little Child, come down
And hear a child's tongue like Thy own;
Take me by the hand and walk,
And listen to my baby-talk.
To Thy Father show my prayer
(He will look, Thou art so fair),
And say: "O Father, I, Thy Son,
Bring the prayer of a little one."

And He will smile, that children's tongue
Has not changed since Thou wast young!

FRANCIS THOMPSON

Arcturus Is His Other Name

Arcturus is his other name,—
I'd rather call him star!
It's so unkind of science
To go and interfere!

I pull a flower from the woods,—
A monster with a glass
Computes the stamens in a breath,
And has her in a class.

Whereas I took the butterfly
Aforetime in my hat,
He sits erect in cabinets,
The clover-bells forgot.

What once was heaven, is zenith now.
Where I proposed to go
When time's brief masquerade was done,
Is mapped, and charted too!

What if the poles should frisk about
And stand upon their heads!
I hope I'm ready for the worst,
Whatever prank betides!

Perhaps the kingdom of Heaven's changed!
I hope the children there
Won't be new-fashioned when I come,
And laugh at me, and stare!

I hope the father in the skies
Will lift his little girl,—
Old-fashioned, naughty, everything,—
Over the stile of pearl!

EMILY DICKINSON

I Went to Heaven

I went to heaven,—
'Twas a small town,
Lit with a ruby,
Lathed with down.
Stiller than the fields
At the full dew,
Beautiful as pictures
No man drew.
People like the moth,
Of mechlin frames,

Duties of gossamer,
And eider names.
Almost contented
I could be
'Mong such unique
Society.

EMILY DICKINSON

The Bustle in a House

The bustle in a house
The morning after death
Is solemnest of industries
Enacted upon earth,—

The sweeping up the heart,
And putting love away
We shall not want to use again
Until eternity.

EMILY DICKINSON

Faith Is a Fine Invention

Faith is a fine invention
For gentlemen who see;
But microscopes are prudent
In an emergency!

EMILY DICKINSON

I Never Shall Love the Snow Again

I never shall love the snow again
    Since Maurice died:
With corniced drift it blocked the lane
And sheeted in a desolate plain
    The country side.

The trees with silvery rime bedight
    Their branches bare.
By day no sun appeared; by night
The hidden moon shed thievish light
    In the misty air.

We fed the birds that flew around
    In flocks to be fed:
No shelter in holly or brake they found.
The speckled thrush on the frozen ground
    Lay frozen and dead.

We skated on stream and pond; we cut
    The crinching snow
To Doric temple or Arctic hut;
We laughed and sang at nightfall, shut
    By the fireside glow.

Yet grudged we our keen delights before
    Maurice should come.
We said, In-door or out-of-door
We shall love life for a month or more,
    When he is home.

They brought him home; 'twas two days late
    For Christmas day:
Wrapped in white, in solemn state,
A flower in his hand, all still and straight
    Our Maurice lay.

And two days ere the year outgave
    We laid him low.
The best of us truly were not brave,
When we laid Maurice down in his grave,
    Under the snow.

ROBERT BRIDGES

Requiem

Under the wide and starry sky
Dig the grave and let me lie.
Glad did I live and gladly die,
    And I laid me down with a will.

This be the verse you grave for me:
Here he lies where he longed to be;
Home is the sailor, home from the sea,
    And the hunter home from the hill.

ROBERT LOUIS STEVENSON

The Creation

And God stepped out on space,
And he looked around and said:
I'm lonely—
I'll make me a world.

And far as the eye of God could see
Darkness covered everything,
Blacker than a hundred midnights
Down in a cypress swamp.

Then God smiled,
And the light broke,
And the darkness rolled up on one side,
And the light stood shining on the other,
And God said: That's good!

Then God reached out and took the light in his hands,
And God rolled the light around in his hands
Until he made the sun;
And he set that sun a-blazing in the heavens.
And the light that was left from making the sun
God gathered it up in a shining ball
And flung it against the darkness,

152

Spangling the night with the moon and stars.
Then down between
The darkness and the light
He hurled the world;
And God said: That's good!

Then God himself stepped down—
And the sun was on his right hand,
And the moon was on his left;
The stars were clustered about his head,
And the earth was under his feet.
And God walked, and where he trod
His footsteps hollowed the valleys out
And bulged the mountains up.

Then he stopped and looked and saw
That the earth was hot and barren.
So God stepped over to the edge of the world
And he spat out the seven seas—
He batted his eyes, and the lightnings flashed—
He clapped his hands, and the thunders rolled—
And the waters above the earth came down,
The cooling waters came down.

Then the green grass sprouted,
And the little red flowers blossomed,
The pine tree pointed his finger to the sky,
And the oak spread out his arms,
The lakes cuddled down in the hollows of the ground,
And the rivers ran down to the sea;
And God smiled again,
And the rainbow appeared,
And curled itself around his shoulder.

Then God raised his arm and he waved his hand
Over the sea and over the land,
And he said: Bring forth! Bring forth!
And quicker than God could drop his hand,

Fishes and fowls
And beasts and birds
Swam the rivers and the seas,
Roamed the forests and the woods,
And split the air with their wings.
And God said: That's good!

Then God walked around,
And God looked around
On all that he had made.
He looked at his sun,
And he looked at his moon,
And he looked at his little stars;
He looked on his world
With all its living things,
And God said: I'm lonely still.

Then God sat down—
On the side of a hill where he could think,
By a deep, wide river he sat down;
With his head in his hands,
God thought and thought,
Till he thought: I'll make me a man!

Up from the bed of the river
God scooped the clay;
And by the bank of the river
He kneeled him down;
And there the great God Almighty
Who lit the sun and fixed it in the sky,
Who flung the stars to the most far corner of the night,
Who rounded the earth in the middle of his hand;
This Great God,
Like a mammy bending over her baby,
Kneeled down in the dust
Toiling over a lump of clay
Till he shaped it in his own image;

Then into it he blew the breath of life,
And man became a living soul.
Amen. Amen.

JAMES WELDON JOHNSON

This great poem can stand of itself—better, to my ear, than most of Milton today. Yet its origin has a special significance. It first appeared in 1927 in a book called *God's Trombones: Seven Negro Sermons in Verse*, in a foreword to which the author remarked that "A good deal has been written on the folk creations of the American Negro: his music, sacred and secular; his plantation tales, and his dances; but that there are folk sermons, as well, is a fact that has passed unnoticed. . . .

"The old-time Negro preacher of parts was above all an orator, and in good measure an actor. He knew the secret of oratory, that at bottom it is a progression of rhythmic words more than it is anything else. . . . He often possessed a voice that was a marvelous instrument, a voice he could modulate from a sepulchral whisper to a crashing thunder clap. . . . He had the power to sweep his hearers before him; and so himself was often swept away. At such times his language was not prose but poetry. It was from memories of such preachers there grew the idea of this book of poems."

BOOK FOUR

Memories of Childhood

Some of the poems in this section were written about children, or in grown-up memory of, and often nostalgia for, the poet's own childhood. Others were written for children—sometimes, as with the Milne verses, for a particular child. And there's the rub. Children are different.

People constantly talk about "what children like." They usually mean what they themselves liked as children. Most of us forget that when we were children ourselves, we intensely disagreed with other children—liked different games, different books, different poems. Some children love Alice in Wonderland; *others don't at all. (Some of these, when they are grown up, reread* Alice *and insist that it is a book for grownups. Which certainly is true—for some adults.) Grownups and children are alike at least in this: that they differ, one from another.*

And children also, as they grow up, differ from themselves. I have known a child at one age to go hopping madly about a room, chanting "Christopher Robin goes hoppity-hop" in sheer ecstasy—and, a year or two later, to insist that he had always hated "that hoppity song."

Some of the verses in the tenth section of this book were probably written for children. Some of them are funny; and it is common folklore that children have a better sense of humor than grownups. I doubt it. Sometimes, perhaps. Sometimes not. Perhaps it is not safe even to lay down a law that children have more imagination than grownups, or more capacity for surprise, which is one of the talents that children sometimes share with poets. The only generalization that is safe is this: children are different, one from another.

I Remember, I Remember

I remember, I remember,
The house where I was born,
The little window where the sun
Came peeping in at morn;
He never came a wink too soon,
Nor brought too long a day,
But now, I often wish the night
Had borne my breath away!

I remember, I remember,
The roses, red and white,
The vi'lets, and the lily-cups,
Those flowers made of light!
The lilacs where the robin built,
And where my brother set
The laburnum on his birthday,—
The tree is living yet!

I remember, I remember,
Where I was used to swing,
And thought the air must rush as fresh
To swallows on the wing;
My spirit flew in feathers then,
That is so heavy now,
And summer pools could hardly cool
The fever on my brow!

I remember, I remember,
The fir trees dark and high;
I used to think their slender tops
Were close against the sky:
It was a childish ignorance,
But now 'tis little joy
To know I'm farther off from heav'n
Than when I was a boy.

THOMAS HOOD

Often I think of the beautiful town
   That is seated by the sea;
Often in thought go up and down
The pleasant streets of that dear old town,
   And my youth comes back to me.
      And a verse of a Lapland song
      Is haunting my memory still:
      "A boy's will is the wind's will,
And the thoughts of youth are long, long thoughts."

I can see the shadowy lines of its trees,
   And catch, in sudden gleams,
The sheen of the far-surrounding seas,
And islands that were the Hesperides
   Of all my boyish dreams.
      And the burden of that old song,
      It murmurs and whispers still:
      "A boy's will is the wind's will,
And the thoughts of youth are long, long thoughts."

I remember the black wharves and the slips,
   And the sea-tides tossing free;
And Spanish sailors with bearded lips,
And the beauty and mystery of the ships,
   And the magic of the sea.
      And the voice of that wayward song
      Is singing and saying still:
      "A boy's will is the wind's will,
And the thoughts of youth are long, long thoughts."

I remember the bulwarks by the shore,
   And the fort upon the hill;
The sunrise gun, with its hollow roar,
The drum-beat repeated o'er and o'er,
   And the bugle wild and shrill.
      And the music of that old song

Throbs in my memory still:
"A boy's will is the wind's will,
And the thoughts of youth are long, long thoughts."

I remember the sea-fight far away,
How it thundered o'er the tide!
And the dead captains, as they lay
In their graves, o'erlooking the tranquil bay,
Where they in battle died.
And the sound of that mournful song
Goes through me with a thrill:
"A boy's will is the wind's will,
And the thoughts of youth are long, long thoughts."

I can see the breezy dome of groves,
The shadows of Deering's Woods;
And the friendships old and the early loves
Come back with a Sabbath sound, as of doves
In quiet neighborhoods.
And the verse of that sweet old song,
It flutters and murmurs still:
"A boy's will is the wind's will,
And the thoughts of youth are long, long thoughts."

I remember the gleams and glooms that dart
Across the school-boy's brain;
The song and the silence in the heart,
That in part are prophecies, and in part
Are longings wild and vain.
And the voice of that fitful song
Sings on, and is never still:
"A boy's will is the wind's will,
And the thoughts of youth are long, long thoughts."

There are things of which I may not speak;
There are dreams that cannot die;
There are thoughts that make the strong heart weak,
And bring a pallor into the cheek,
And a mist before the eye,

And the words of that fatal song
Come over me like a chill:
"A boy's will is the wind's will,
And the thoughts of youth are long, long thoughts."

Strange to me now are the forms I meet
When I visit the dear old town;
But the native air is pure and sweet,
And the trees that o'ershadow each well-known street,
As they balance up and down,
Are singing the beautiful song,
Are sighing and whispering still:
"A boy's will is the wind's will,
And the thoughts of youth are long, long thoughts."

And Deering's Woods are fresh and fair,
And with joy that is almost pain
My heart goes back to wander there,
And among the dreams of the days that were,
I find my lost youth again.
And the strange and beautiful song,
The groves are repeating it still:
"A boy's will is the wind's will,
And the thoughts of youth are long, long thoughts."

HENRY WADSWORTH LONGFELLOW

The Children's Hour

Between the dark and the daylight,
When the night is beginning to lower,
Comes a pause in the day's occupations,
That is known as the Children's Hour.

I hear in the chamber above me
The patter of little feet,
The sound of a door that is opened,
And voices soft and sweet.

From my study I see in the lamplight,
  Descending the broad hall stair,
Grave Alice, and laughing Allegra,
  And Edith with golden hair.

A whisper, and then a silence:
  Yet I know by their merry eyes
They are plotting and planning together
  To take me by surprise.

A sudden rush from the stairway,
  A sudden raid from the hall!
By three doors left unguarded
  They enter my castle wall!

They climb up into my turret
  O'er the arms and back of my chair;
If I try to escape, they surround me;
  They seem to be everywhere.

They almost devour me with kisses,
  Their arms about me entwine,
Till I think of the Bishop of Bingen
  In his Mouse-Tower on the Rhine!

Do you think, O blue-eyed banditti,
  Because you have scaled the wall,
Such an old mustache as I am
  Is not a match for you all!

I have you fast in my fortress,
  And will not let you depart,
But put you down into the dungeon
  In the round-tower of my heart.

And there I will keep you forever,
  Yes, forever and a day,
Till the walls shall crumble to ruin,
  And moulder in dust away.

HENRY WADSWORTH LONGFELLOW

Daisy

Where the thistle lifts a purple crown
    Six foot out of the turf,
And the harebell shakes on the windy hill—
    O the breath of the distant surf!—

The hills look over on the South,
    And southward dreams the sea;
And, with the sea-breeze hand in hand,
    Came innocence and she.

Where 'mid the gorse the raspberry
    Red for the gatherer springs,
Two children did we stray and talk
    Wise, idle, childish things.

She listened with big-lipped surprise,
    Breast-deep 'mid flower and spine:
Her skin was like a grape, whose veins
    Run snow instead of wine.

She knew not those sweet words she spake,
    Nor knew her own sweet way;
But there's never a bird, so sweet a song
    Thronged in whose throat that day!

Oh, there were flowers in Storrington
    On the turf and on the spray;
But the sweetest flower on Sussex hills
    Was the Daisy-flower that day!

Her beauty smoothed earth's furrowed face!
    She gave me tokens three:—
A look, a word of her winsome mouth,
    And a wild raspberry.

A berry red, a guileless look,
    A still word,—strings of sand!
And yet they made my wild, wild heart
    Fly down to her little hand.

For, standing artless as the air,
    And candid as the skies,
She took the berries with her hand,
    And the love with her sweet eyes.

The fairest things have fleetest end:
    Their scent survives their close,
But the rose's scent is bitterness
    To him that loved the rose!

She looked a little wistfully,
    Then went her sunshine way:—
The sea's eye had a mist on it,
    And the leaves fell from the day.

She went her unremembering way,
    She went, and left in me
The pang of all the partings gone,
    And partings yet to be.

She left me marveling why my soul
    Was sad that she was glad;
At all the sadness in the sweet,
    The sweetness in the sad.

Still, still I seemed to see her, still
    Look up with soft replies,
And take the berries with her hand,
    And the love with her lovely eyes.

Nothing begins, and nothing ends,
    That is not paid with moan;
For we are born in others' pain,
    And perish in our own.

FRANCIS THOMPSON

Fern Hill

Now as I was young and easy under the apple boughs
About the lilting house and happy as the grass was green,
  The night above the dingle starry,
    Time let me hail and climb
  Golden in the heydays of his eyes,
And honoured among wagons I was prince of the apple towns
And once below a time I lordly had the trees and leaves
    Trail with daisies and barley
  Down the rivers of the windfall light.

And as I was green and carefree, famous among the barns
About the happy yard and singing as the farm was home,
  In the sun that is young once only,
    Time let me play and be
  Golden in the mercy of his means,
And green and golden I was huntsman and herdsman, the calves
Sang to my horn, the foxes on the hills barked clear and cold,
    And the sabbath rang slowly
  In the pebbles of the holy streams.

All the sun long it was running, it was lovely, the hay
Fields high as the house, the tunes from the chimneys, it was air
  And playing, lovely and watery
    And fire green as grass.
  And nightly under the simple stars
As I rode to sleep the owls were bearing the farm away,
All the moon long I heard, blessed among stables, the nightjars
  Flying with the ricks, and the horses
    Flashing into the dark.

And then to awake, and the farm, like a wanderer white
With the dew, come back, the cock on his shoulder: it was all
  Shining, it was Adam and maiden,
    The sky gathered again
  And the sun grew round that very day.
So it must have been after the birth of the simple light

In the first, spinning place, the spellbound horses walking warm
   Out of the whinnying green stable
     On to the fields of praise.

And honoured among foxes and pheasants by the gay house
Under the new made clouds and happy as the heart was long,
   In the sun born over and over,
     I ran my heedless ways,
   My wishes raced through the house high hay
And nothing I cared, at my sky blue trades, that time allows
In all his tuneful turning so few and such morning songs
   Before the children green and golden
     Follow him out of grace,

Nothing I cared, in the lamb white days, that time would take me
Up to the swallow thronged loft by the shadow of my hand,
   In the moon that is always rising,
     Nor that riding to sleep
   I should hear him fly with the high fields
And wake to the farm forever fled from the childless land.
     Time held me green and dying
   Though I sang in my chains like the sea.

DYLAN THOMAS

My Shadow

I have a little shadow that goes in and out with me,
And what can be the use of him is more than I can see.
He is very, very like me from the heels up to the head;
And I see him jump before me, when I jump into my bed.

The funniest thing about him is the way he likes to grow—
Not at all like proper children, which is always very slow;
For he sometimes shoots up taller than an India-rubber ball,
And he sometimes gets so little that there's none of him at all.

He hasn't got a notion of how children ought to play,
And can only make a fool of me in every sort of way,

He stays so close beside me, he's a coward you can see;
I'd think shame to stick to nurse as that shadow sticks to me!

One morning, very early, before the sun was up,
I rose and found the shining dew on every buttercup;
But my lazy little shadow, like an arrant sleepy-head,
Had stayed at home behind me and was fast asleep in bed.

ROBERT LOUIS STEVENSON

Mud

Mud is very nice to feel
    All squishy-squash between the toes!
I'd rather wade in wiggly mud
    Than smell a yellow rose.

POLLY CHASE BOYDEN

Sam

When Sam goes back in memory,
    It is to where the sea
Breaks on the shingle, emerald-green
    In white foam, endlessly;
He says—with small brown eye on mine—
    "I used to keep awake,
And lean from my window in the moon,
    Watching those billows break.
And half a million tiny hands,
    And eyes, like sparks of frost,
Would dance and come tumbling into the moon,
    On every breaker tossed.
And all across from star to star,
    I've seen the watery sea,
With not a single ship in sight,
    Just ocean there, and me;

And heard my father snore. . . . And once,
 As sure as I'm alive,
Out of those wallowing, moon-flecked waves
 I saw a mermaid dive;
Head and shoulders above the wave,
 Plain as I now see you,
Combing her hair, now back, now front,
 Her two eyes peeping through;
Calling me, 'Sam!'—quietlike—'Sam!' . . .
 But me . . . I never went
Making believe I kind of thought
 'Twas someone else she meant . . .
Wonderful lovely there she sat,
 Singing the night away,
All in the solitudinous sea
 Of that there lonely bay.
P'raps, and he'd smooth his hairless mouth,
 "P'raps if 'twere now, my son,
P'raps, if I heard a voice say, 'Sam!' . . .
 Morning would find me gone."

WALTER DE LA MARE

Many a Mickle

 A little sound—
 Only a little, a little—
 The breath in a reed,
 A trembling fiddle;
 The trumpet's ring,
 The shuddering drum;
 So all the glory, bravery, hush
 Of music come.

 A little sound—
 Only a stir and a sigh
 Of each green leaf
 Its fluttering neighbor by;

169

Oak on to oak,
The wide dark forest through—
So o'er the watery wheeling world
The night winds go.

A little sound,
Only a little, a little—
The thin high drone
Of the simmering kettle,
The gathering frost,
The click of needle and thread;
Mother, the fading wall, the dream,
The drowsy bed.

WALTER DE LA MARE

Ann and the Fairy Song

(FROM *A Child's Day*)

When she was in her garden,
And playing with her ball,
Ann heard a distant music
On the other side of the wall—
A far-off singing, shrill and sweet,
In the still and sunshine day,
And these the words were of the song
The voice did sing and say:—

"Happy, happy it is to be
Where the greenwood hangs o'er the dark blue sea;
To roam in the moonbeams clear and still
And dance with the elves
Over dale and hill;
To taste their cups, and with them roam
The fields for dewdrops and honeycomb.
Climb then, and come, as quick as you can,
And dwell with the fairies, Elizabeth Ann!"

Ann held her ball, and listened;
The faint song died away;
And it seemed it was a dream she'd dreamed
In the hot and sunshine day;
She heard the whistling of the birds,
The droning of the bees;
And then once more the singing came,
And now the words were these:—

"Never, never, comes tear or sorrow,
In the mansions old where the fairies dwell;
But only the harping of their sweet harp-strings,
And the lonesome stroke of a distant bell,
Where upon hills of thyme and heather,
The shepherd sits with his wandering sheep;
And the curlew wails, and the skylark hovers
Over the sand where the conies creep;
Climb then, and come, as quick as you can,
And dwell with the fairies, Elizabeth Ann!"

And just as Ann a-tiptoe crept,
Under the old green wall,
To where a stooping cherry tree
Grew shadowy and tall;
Above the fairy's singing
Hollow and shrill and sweet,
That seemed to make her heart stand still,
And then more wildly beat,
Came Susan's voice a-calling "Ann!
Come quick as you are able;
And wash your grubby hands, my dear,
For dinner's on the table!"

WALTER DE LA MARE

171

Up the airy mountain,
　Down the rushy glen,
We daren't go a-hunting
　For fear of little men;
Wee folk, good folk,
　Trooping all together;
Green jacket, red cap,
　　And white owl's feather!

Down along the rocky shore
　Some make their home,
They live on crispy pancakes
　Of yellow tide-foam;
Some in the reeds
　Of the black mountain lake,
With frogs for their watch-dogs,
　All night awake.

High on the hilltop
　The old King sits;
He is now so old and gray
　He's nigh lost his wits.
With a bridge of white mist
　Columbkill he crosses,
On his stately journeys
　From Slieveleague to Rosses;
Or going up with music
　On cold starry nights,
To sup with the Queen
　Of the gay Northern Lights.

They stole little Bridget
　For seven years long;
When she came down again
　Her friends were all gone.
They took her lightly back
　Between the night and morrow,

They thought that she was fast asleep,
But she was dead with sorrow.
They have kept her ever since
Deep within the lake,
On a bed of flag-leaves,
Watching till she wake.

By the craggy hill-side,
Through the mosses bare,
They have planted thorn-trees
For pleasure here and there.
If any man so daring
As dig them up in spite,
He shall find their sharpest thorns
In his bed at night.

Up the airy mountain,
Down the rushy glen,
We daren't go a-hunting
For fear of little men;
Wee folk, good folk,
Trooping all together;
Green jacket, red cap,
And white owl's feather.

WILLIAM ALLINGHAM

Hoppity

Christopher Robin goes
Hoppity, hoppity,
Hoppity, hoppity, hop.
Whenever I tell him
Politely to stop it, he
Says he can't possibly stop.
If he stopped hopping, he couldn't go anywhere,
Poor little Christopher
Couldn't go anywhere . . .

That's why he *always* goes
Hoppity, hoppity,
Hoppity,
Hoppity,
Hop.

A. A. MILNE

Oh Come, Little Children

What man of ignorance undefiled
First praised the prattle of a child
Or called its stumbling accents gentle?
He was a fraud, and sentimental,
Some lout whose premise I deplore—
A hermit or a bachelor.

No babes of my acquaintance speak
In syllables below a shriek.
This golden boy, this dimpled bouncer,
Studies to be a train announcer.
That rose-lipped girl with tresses flaxen
Outdoes, by any odds, the klaxon.
In the bright lexicon of lispers
There's no such word as "whispers."

Calliopes chant soft and formally
Compared to tots conversing normally,
While in the wails of urchins crossed,
The riveter's refrain is lost.
Articulate, they come and go,
But never pianissimo.

I'll wager—coming to the heart of this—
That fellow mentioned at the start of this
Had no experience, even cursory,
With pretty babblings from a nursery,
Or his fine lines had died aborning
At six o'clock some Christmas morning.

PHYLLIS MCGINLEY

When Father Carves the Duck

We all look on with anxious eyes
  When father carves the duck,
And mother almost always sighs
  When father carves the duck;
Then all of us prepare to rise,
And hold our bibs before our eyes,
And be prepared for some surprise,
  When father carves the duck.

He braces up and grabs a fork
  Whene'er he carves a duck,
And won't allow a soul to talk
  Until he's carved the duck.
The fork is jabbed into the sides,
Across the breast the knife he slides,
While every careful person hides
  From flying chips of duck.

The platter's almost sure to slip
  When father carves a duck,
And how it makes the dishes skip!
  Potatoes fly amuck!
The squash and cabbage leap in space,
We get some gravy in our face
And father mutters Hindoo grace
  When father carves the duck.

We then have learned to walk around
  The dining-room and pluck
From off the window-sills and walls
  Our share of father's duck.
While father growls and blows and jaws
And swears the knife was full of flaws,
And mother laughs at him because
  He couldn't carve a duck.

ERNEST VINCENT WRIGHT

Father calls me William, sister calls me Will,
Mother calls me Willie, but the fellers call me Bill!
Mighty glad I ain't a girl—ruther be a boy,
Without them sashes, curls an' things that's worn by Fauntle-
      roy!
Love to chawnk green apples an' go swimmin' in the lake—
Hate to take the castor-ile they give for belly-ache!
'Most all the time, the whole year round, there ain't no flies
      on me,
But jest 'fore Christmas I'm as good as I kin be!

Got a yeller dog named Sport, sick him on the cat;
First thing she knows she doesn't know where she is at!
Got a clipper sled, an' when us kids goes out to slide,
'Long comes the grocery cart, an' we all hook a ride!
But sometimes when the grocery man is worrited an' cross,
He reaches at us with his whip, an' larrups up his hoss,
An' then I laff an' holler, "Oh, ye never teched *me!*"
But jest 'fore Christmas I'm as good as I kin be!

Gran'ma says she hopes that when I git to be a man,
I'll be a missionarer like her oldest brother, Dan,
As was et up by the cannibuls that lives in Ceylon's Isle,
Where every prospeck pleases, an' only man is vile!
But gran'ma she has never been to see a Wild West show,
Nor read the Life of Daniel Boone, or else I guess she'd know
That Buff'lo Bill an' cow-boys is good enough for me!
Excep' jest 'fore Christmas, when I'm good as I kin be!

And then old Sport he hangs around, so solemn-like an' still
His eyes they seem a-sayin': "What's the matter, little Bill?"
The old cat sneaks down off her perch an' wonders what's
      become
Of them two enemies of hern that used to make things hum!
But I am so perlite an' 'tend so earnestly to biz,
That mother says to father: "How improved our Willie is!"
But father, havin' been a boy hisself, suspicions me
When jest 'fore Christmas, I'm as good as I kin be!

For Christmas, with its lots an' lots of candles, cakes an' toys,
Was made, they say, for proper kids an' not for naughty boys;
So wash yer face an' bresh yer hair, an' mind yer p's and q's,
An' don't bust out yer pantaloons, and don't wear out yer
    shoes;
Say "Yessum" to the ladies, an' "Yessur" to the men,
And when they's company, don't pass yer plate for pie again;
But, thinkin' of the things yer'd like to see upon that tree,
Jes 'fore Christmas be as good as yer kin be!

EUGENE FIELD

A Visit from St. Nicholas

'Twas the night before Christmas, when all through the house
Not a creature was stirring, not even a mouse;
The stockings were hung by the chimney with care,
In hopes that St. Nicholas would be there.
The children were nestled all snug in their beds,
While visions of sugar-plums danced in their heads;
And mamma in her 'kerchief, and I in my cap,
Had just settled our brains for a long winter's nap,
When out on the lawn there arose such a clatter,
I sprang from the bed to see what was the matter.
Away to the window I flew like a flash,
Tore open the shutters and threw up the sash.
The moon on the breast of the new-fallen snow
Gave the lustre of mid-day to objects below,
When, what to my wondering eyes should appear,
But a miniature sleigh, and eight tiny reindeer,
With a little old driver, so lively and quick,
I knew in a moment it must be St. Nick.
More rapid than eagles his coursers they came,
And he whistled, and shouted, and called them by name;
"Now, *Dasher!* now, *Dancer!* now, *Prancer* and *Vixen!*
On, *Comet!* on, *Cupid!* on, *Donder* and *Blitzen!*
To the top of the porch! to the top of the wall!
Now dash away! dash away! dash away all!"

As dry leaves before the wild hurricane fly,
When they meet with an obstacle, mount to the sky,
So up to the house-top the coursers they flew,
With the sleigh full of toys, and St. Nicholas too.
And then, in a twinkling, I heard on the roof
The prancing and pawing of each little hoof.
As I drew in my head, and was turning around,
Down the chimney St. Nicholas came with a bound.
He was dressed all in fur, from his head to his foot,
And his clothes were all tarnished with ashes and soot;
A bundle of toys he had flung on his back,
And he looked like a peddler just opening his pack.
His eyes—how they twinkled! his dimples how merry!
His cheeks were like roses, his nose like a cherry!
His droll little mouth was drawn up like a bow,
And the beard of his chin was as white as the snow;
The stump of a pipe he held tight in his teeth,
And the smoke it encircled his head like a wreath;
He had a broad face and a little round belly,
That shook, when he laughed, like a bowlful of jelly.
He was chubby and plump, a right jolly old elf,
And I laughed when I saw him, in spite of myself.
A wink of his eye and a twist of his head,
Soon gave me to know I had nothing to dread;
He spoke not a word, but went straight to his work,
And filled all the stockings; then turned with a jerk,
And laying his finger aside of his nose,
And giving a nod, up the chimney he rose;
He sprang to his sleigh, to his team gave a whistle,
And away they all flew like the down of a thistle.
But I heard him exclaim, ere he drove out of sight,
"Happy Christmas to all, and to all a good night."

CLEMENT CLARKE MOORE

178

BOOK FIVE

Sounds of the Sea

It's odd that there are so few good sea poems. The English language waited until the twentieth century for its supreme sea poet, John Masefield. Kipling and Stevenson also had a deep feeling for the sea, but not many others. There is a sea-surge in some of Byron's rolling stanzas, but only in a few. Some of the others are pretty hoity-toity, and Byron was perhaps most sincere when he wrote of seasickness. His way of describing storm on the Black Sea was to write:

> There's not a sea the passenger e'er pukes in
> Turns up more eloquent breakers than the Euxine.

Most poets who have attempted to put the sea in English verse are distressingly fond of words like "opaline." Swinburne on the sea was at his silliest:

> I will go back to the great sweet mother,
>   Mother and lover of men, the sea,
> I will go down to her, I and none other,
>   Close with her, kiss her and mix her with me.

The lines have a lilt, but where's either the sense or the salt spray?

The Ocean

(FROM *Childe Harold*)

There is a pleasure in the pathless woods,
There is a rapture on the lonely shore,
There is society, where none intrudes,
By the deep Sea, and music in its roar:
I love not Man the less, but Nature more,
From these our interviews, in which I steal
From all I may be, or have been before,
To mingle with the Universe, and feel
What I can ne'er express, yet cannot all conceal.

Roll on, thou deep and dark blue Ocean—roll!
Ten thousand fleets sweep over thee in vain;
Man marks the earth with ruin—his control
Stops with the shore; upon the watery plain
The wrecks are all thy deed, nor doth remain
A shadow of man's ravage, save his own,
When, for a moment, like a drop of rain,
He sinks into thy depths with bubbling groan,
Without a grave, unknelled, uncoffined and unknown. . . .

Thy shores are empires, changed in all save thee—
Assyria, Greece, Rome, Carthage, what are they?
Thy waters washed them power while they were free,
And many a tyrant since; their shores obey
The stranger, slave or savage; their decay
Has dried up realms to deserts:—not so thou,
Unchangeable save to thy wild waves' play,
Time writes no wrinkle on thine azure brow:
Such as creation's dawn beheld, thou rollest now.

And I have loved thee, Ocean! and my joy
Of youthful sports was on thy breast to be
Borne, like thy bubbles, onward: from a boy
I wanton'd with thy breakers—they to me
Were a delight; and if the freshening sea
Made them a terror—'twas a pleasing fear,

For I was as it were a child of thee,
And trusted to thy billows far and near,
And laid my hand upon thy mane—as I do here.

GEORGE GORDON BYRON

Sea-Fever

I must down to the seas again, to the lonely sea and the sky,
And all I ask is a tall ship and a star to steer her by,
And the wheel's kick and the wind's song and the white sail's
     shaking,
And a gray mist on the sea's face and a gray dawn breaking.

I must down to the seas again, for the call of the running tide
Is a wild call and a clear call that may not be denied;
And all I ask is a windy day with the white clouds flying,
And the flung spray and the blown spume, and the sea-gulls
     crying.

I must down to the seas again to the vagrant gypsy life,
To the gull's way and the whale's way where the wind's like
     a whetted knife;
And all I ask is a merry yarn from a laughing fellow-rover,
And quiet sleep and a sweet dream when the long trick's over.

JOHN MASEFIELD

Cargoes

Quinquireme of Nineveh from distant Ophir,
Rowing home to haven in sunny Palestine,
With a cargo of ivory,
And apes and peacocks,
Sandalwood, cedarwood, and sweet white wine.

Stately Spanish galleon coming from the Isthmus,
Dipping through the Tropics by the palm-green shores,
With a cargo of diamonds,

182

Emeralds, amethysts,
Topazes, and cinnamon, and gold moidores.

Dirty British coaster with a salt-caked smoke-stack,
Butting through the Channel in the mad March days,
With a cargo of Tyne coal,
Road-rails, pig-lead,
Firewood, iron-ware and cheap tin trays.

JOHN MASEFIELD

Christmas at Sea

The sheets were frozen hard, and they cut the naked hand;
The decks were like a slide, where a seaman scarce could stand;
The wind was a nor'-wester, blowing squally off the sea;
And cliffs and spouting breakers were the only things a-lee.

They heard the surf a-roaring before the break of day;
But 'twas only with the peep of light we saw how ill we lay.
We tumbled every hand on deck instanter, with a shout,
And we gave her the maintops'l, and stood to go about.

All day we tacked and tacked between the South Head and
     the North;
All day we hauled the frozen sheets and got no further forth;
All day as cold as charity, in bitter pain and dread,
For very life and nature we tacked from head to head.

We gave the South a wider berth, for there the tide-race
     roared;
But every tack we made brought the North Head close aboard;
So's we saw the cliffs and houses, and the breakers running high,
And the coastguard in his garden, with his glass against his eye.

The frost was on the village roofs as white as ocean foam;
The good red fires were burning bright in every 'longshore
     home;
The windows sparkled clear, and the chimneys volleyed out;
And I vow we sniffed the victuals as the vessel went about.

The bells upon the church were rung with a mighty jovial
      cheer;
For it's just that I should tell you (of all days in the year)
This day of our adversity was blessèd Christmas morn
And the house above the coastguard's was the house where I
      was born.

O well I saw the pleasant room, the pleasant faces there,
My mother's silver spectacles, my father's silver hair;
And well I saw the firelight, like a flight of homely elves,
Go dancing round the china-plates that stand upon the shelves.

And well I knew the talk they had, the talk that was of me,
Of the shadow on the household and the son that went to sea;
And O the wicked fool I seemed, in every kind of way,
To be here and hauling frozen ropes on blessèd Christmas Day.

They lit the high sea-light, and the dark began to fall.
"All hands to loose topgallant sails," I heard the captain call.
"By the Lord, she'll never stand it," our first mate, Jackson,
      cried.
"It's the one way or the other, Mr. Jackson," he replied.

She staggered to her bearings, but the sails were new and good,
And the ship smelt up to windward, just as though she under-
      stood.
As the winter's day was ending, in the entry of the night,
We cleared the weary headland, and passed below the light.

And they heaved a mighty breath, every soul on board but me,
As they saw her nose again pointing handsome out to sea;
But all that I could think of, in the darkness and the cold,
Was just that I was leaving home and my folks were growing
      old.

ROBERT LOUIS STEVENSON

The Long Trail

There's a whisper down the field where the year has shot her
    yield,
  And the ricks stand gray to the sun,
Singing: "Over then, come over, for the bee has quit the clover,
  And your English summer's done."
        You have heard the beat of the off-shore wind,
        And the thresh of the deep-sea rain;
        You have heard the song—how long? how long?
        Pull out on the trail again!

Ha' done with the Tents of Shem, dear lass,
We've seen the seasons through,
And it's time to turn on the old trail, our own trail, the out trail,
Pull out, pull out, on the Long Trail—the trail that is always
    new!

It's North you may run to the rime-ringed sun
  Or South to the blind Horn's hate;
Or East all the way into Mississippi Bay,
  Or West to the Golden Gate;
        Where the blindest bluffs hold good, dear lass,
        And the wildest tales are true,
        And the men bulk big on the old trail, our own trail,
          the out trail,
        And life runs large on the Long Trail—the trail that is
          always new.

The days are sick and cold, and the skies are gray and old,
  And the twice-breathed airs blow damp;
And I'd sell my tired soul for the bucking beam-sea roll
  Of a black Bilbao tramp;
        With her load-line over her hatch, dear lass,
        And a drunken Dago crew,
        And her nose held down on the old trail, our own trail,
          the out trail
        From Cadiz south on the Long Trail—the trail that is
          always new.

There be triple ways to take, of the eagle or the snake,
  Or the way of a man with a maid;
But the sweetest way to me is a ship's upon the sea
  In the heel of the North-East Trade.
        Can you hear the crash on her bows, dear lass,
        And the drum of the racing screw,
        As she ships it green on the old trail, our own trail, the
          out trail,
        As she lifts and 'scends on the Long Trail—the trail
          that is always new?

See the shaking funnels roar, with the Peter at the fore,
  And the fenders grind and heave,
And the derricks clack and grate, as the tackle hooks the crate,
  And the fall-rope whines through the sheave;
        It's "Gang-plank up and in," dear lass,
        It's "Hawsers warp her through!"
        And it's "All clear aft" on the old trail, our own trail,
          the out trail,
        We're backing down on the Long Trail—the trail that
          is always new.

O the mutter overside, when the port-fog holds us tied,
  And the sirens hoot their dread!
When foot by foot we creep o'er the hueless, viewless deep
  To the sob of the questing lead!
        It's down by the Lower Hope, dear lass,
        With the Gunfleet Sands in view,
        Till the Mouse swings green on the old trail, our own
          trail, the out trail,
        And the Gull Light lifts on the Long Trail—the trail
          that is always new.

O the blazing tropic night, when the wake's a welt of light
  That holds the hot sky tame,
And the steady fore-foot snores through the planet-powdered
  floors

186

Where the scared whale flukes in flame!
    Her plates are flaked by the sun, dear lass,
    And her ropes are taut with the dew,
    For we're booming down on the old trail, our own
        trail, the out trail,
    We're sagging south on the Long Trail—the trail that
        is always new.

Then home, get her home, where the drunken rollers comb,
  And the shouting seas drive by,
And the engines stamp and ring, and the wet bows reel and
      swing,
  And the Southern Cross rides high!
    Yes, the old lost stars wheel back, dear lass,
    That blaze in the velvet blue.
    They're all old friends on the old trail, our own trail,
        the out trail,
    They're God's own guides on the Long Trail—the trail
        that is always new.

Fly forward, O my heart, from the Foreland to the Start—
  We're steaming all too slow,
And it's twenty thousand mile to our little lazy isle
  Where the trumpet-orchids blow!
    You have heard the call of the off-shore wind
    And the voice of the deep-sea rain;
    You have heard the song—how long?—how long?
    Pull out on the trail again!

The Lord knows what we may find, dear lass,
And the Deuce knows what we may do—
But we're back once more on the old trail, our own trail, the
    out trail,
We're down, hull down, on the Long Trail—the trail that is
    always new!

RUDYARD KIPLING

Who hath desired the Sea?—the sight of salt water unbounded—
The heave and the halt and the hurl and the crash of the
comber wind-hounded?
The sleek-barrelled swell before storm, grey, foamless, enor-
mous, and growing—
Stark calm on the lap of the Line or the crazy-eyed hurricane
blowing—
His Sea in no showing the same—his Sea and the same 'neath
each showing:
His Sea as she slackens or thrills?
So and no otherwise—so and no otherwise—hillmen desire their
Hills!

Who hath desired the Sea?—the immense and contemptuous
surges?
The shudder, the stumble, the swerve, as the star-stabbing
bowsprit emerges?
The orderly clouds of the Trades, the ridged, roaring sapphire
thereunder—
Unheralded cliff-haunting flaws and the headsail's low-volley-
ing thunder—
His Sea in no wonder the same—his Sea and the same through
each wonder:
His Sea as she rages or stills?
So and no otherwise—so and no otherwise—hillmen desire their
Hills.

Who hath desired the Sea? Her menaces swift as her mercies?
The in-rolling walls of the fog and the silver-winged breeze
that disperses?
The unstable mined berg going South and the calvings and
groans that declare it—
White water half-guessed overside and the moon breaking
timely to bare it;
His Sea as his fathers have dared—his Sea as his children shall
dare it:
His Sea as she serves him or kills?

So and no otherwise—so and no otherwise—hillmen desire their
    Hills.

Who hath desired the Sea? Her excellent loneliness rather
Than forecourts of kings, and her outermost pits than the
    streets where men gather
Inland, among dust, under trees—inland where the slayer may
    slay him—
Inland, out of reach of her arms, and the bosom whereon he
    must lay him—
His Sea from the first that betrayed—at the last that shall never
    betray him:
        His Sea that his being fulfils?
So and no otherwise—so and no otherwise—hillmen desire their
    Hills.

RUDYARD KIPLING

The Liner She's a Lady

The Liner she's a lady, an' she never looks nor 'eeds—
The Man-o'-War's 'er 'usband, an' 'e gives 'er all she needs;
But, oh, the little cargo-boats, that sail the wet seas roun',
They're just the same as you an' me a-plying up an' down!

    Plyin' up an' down, Jenny, 'angin' round the Yard,
    All the way by Fratton tram down to Portsmouth 'Ard;
    Anythin' for business, an' we're growin' old—
    Plyin' up an' down, Jenny, waitin' in the cold!

The Liner she's a lady by the paint upon 'er face,
An' if she meets an accident they count it sore disgrace.
The Man-o'-War's 'er 'usband, and 'e's always 'andy by,
But, oh, the little cargo-boats, they've got to load or die!

The Liner she's a lady, and 'er route is cut an' dried;
The Man-o'-War's 'er 'usband, an' 'e always keeps beside;
But, oh, the little cargo-boats that 'aven't any man,
They've got to do their business first, and make the most they
    can!

The Liner she's a lady, and if a war should come,
The Man-o'-War's 'er 'usband, and 'e'd bid 'er stay at home;
But, oh, the little cargo-boats that fill with every tide!
'E'd 'ave to go up an' fight for them, for they are England's
       pride.

The Liner she's a lady, but if she wasn't made,
There still would be the cargo-boats for 'ome an' foreign trade.
The Man-o'-War's 'er 'usband, but if we wasn't 'ere,
'E wouldn't have to fight at all for 'ome an' friends so dear.

'Ome an' friends so dear, Jenny, 'angin' round the Yard,
All the way by Fratton tram down to Portsmouth 'Ard;
Anythin' for business, an' we're growin' old—
'Ome an' friends so dear, Jenny, waitin' in the cold!

RUDYARD KIPLING

BOOK SIX

Echoes of War

*Next to love, perhaps, war stirs men and poets most deeply.
But whether or not the nature of love changes, the nature of
war assuredly does, and also the ways in which poets, repre-
sentative men, echo the wars they know. It is a far cry from
Shakespeare's Henry V on the field of Agincourt to Wilfred
Owen, killed in the mud of the Sambre five days before the
Armistice of 1918.*

*One may wonder, however, whether these changes in moods
and minds mirror much more than the variety in human nature.
Rupert Brooke and Alan Seeger, who died in the same war
with Wilfred Owen, wrote closer to the mood of Shakespeare
than to Owen, their fellow soldier in what we so grandilo-
quently term the First World War. Southey, writing during
the Napoleonic wars, was closer to Owen than to his contemporaries, Macaulay or Tennyson. And Ts'ao Sung, a thousand years earlier, told almost the same story as Siegfried
Sassoon.*

Echoes of War

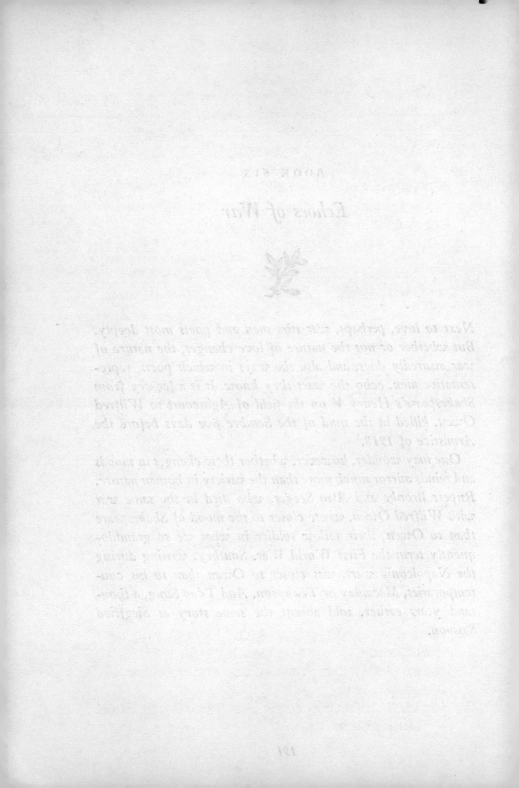

Next to love, perhaps, war stirs men and pours most deeply;
But whether or not the nature of love changes, the nature of
war certainly does; and also the way in which poets represented men, who sang the wars they knew. It is a far cry from
Shakespeare's *Henry V* on the field of Agincourt to Wilfred
Owen, killed in the mud of the Sambre just days before the
Armistice of 1918.

One may wonder, however, whether their elegy is much
and whose mirror would more than the curiosity in human nature.
Rupert Brooke and Alan Seeger, who died in the same war
with Wilfred Owen, were closer to the mood of Shakespeare
than to Owen. Their elegy reddens in what we so grimly
quaintly term the First World War. Sassoon's showing during
the Napoleonic wars, are closer to Owen than to his contemporaries, Macaulay or Tennyson. And *The Last Stand*, a poem
read years earlier, told almost the same story of Siegfried
Sassoon.

A Protest in the Sixth Year of Ch'ien Fu
(A.D. 879)

The hills and rivers of the lowland country
    You have made your battle-ground.
How do you suppose the people who live there
    Will procure "firewood and hay"?[1]
Do not let me hear you talking together
    About titles and promotions;
For a single general's reputation
    Is made out of ten thousand corpses.

TS'AO SUNG

TRANSLATED BY ARTHUR WALEY

[1] The necessaries of life.

War Song of the Saracens

We are they who come faster than fate: we are they who ride
    early or late:
We storm at your ivory gate: Pale Kings of the Sunset,
    beware!
Not on silk nor in samet we lie, not in curtained solemnity die
Among women who chatter and cry, and children who mumble
    a prayer.
But we sleep by the ropes of the camp, and we rise with a
    shout, and we tramp
With the sun or the moon for a lamp, and the spray of the wind
    in our hair.

From the lands, where the elephants are, to the forts of Merou
    and Balghar,
Our steel we have brought and our star to shine on the ruins
    of Rum.
We have marched from the Indus to Spain, and by God we will
    go there again;
We have stood on the shore of the plain where the Waters of
    Destiny boom.

A mart of destruction we made at Jalula where men were
   afraid,
For death was a difficult trade, and the sword was a broker
   of doom;

And the Spear was a Desert Physician who cured not a few
   of ambition,
And drave not a few to perdition with medicine bitter and
   strong:
And the shield was a grief to the fool and as bright as a desolate pool,
And as straight as the rock of Stamboul when their cavalry
   thundered along:
For the coward was drowned with the brave when our battle
   sheered up like a wave,
And the dead to the desert we gave, and the glory to God in
   our song.

JAMES ELROY FLECKER

To Lucasta, Going to the Wars

Tell me not, Sweet, I am unkind,
   That from the nunnery
Of thy chaste breast and quiet mind
   To war and arms I fly.

True, a new mistress now I chase,
   The first foe in the field;
And with a truer faith embrace
   A sword, a horse, a shield.

Yet this inconstancy is such
   As thou too shalt adore;
I could not love thee, Dear, so much,
   Loved I not Honor more.

RICHARD LOVELACE

Once More Unto the Breach

(FROM *King Henry V*, Act III, Scene I)

Once more unto the breach, dear friends, once more,
Or close the wall up with our English dead.
In peace there's nothing so becomes a man
As modest stillness, and humility.
But when the blast of war blows in our ears,
Then imitate the action of the tiger,
Stiffen the sinews, summon up the blood.
Disguise fair nature with hard-favored rage.
Then lend the eye a terrible aspect;
Let it pry through the portage of the head
Like the brass cannon. Let the brow o'erwhelm it,
As fearfully as doth a gallèd rock
O'erhang and jutty his confounded base,
Swilled with the wild and wasteful ocean.
Now set the teeth, and stretch the nostril wide,
Hold hard the breath, and bend up every spirit
To his full height. On, on, you noblest English,
Whose blood is fetched from fathers of war proof!
Fathers, that like so many Alexanders,
Have in these parts from morn till even fought,
And sheathed their swords for lack of argument.
Dishonor not your mothers. Now attest
That those whom you called fathers did beget you.
Be copy now to men of grosser blood,
And teach them how to war. And you, good yeomen,
Whose limbs were made in England, show us here
The mettle of your pasture; let us swear
That you are worth your breeding; which I doubt not,
For there is none of you so mean and base
That hath not noble luster in your eyes.
I see you stand like greyhounds in the slips,
Straining upon the start. The game's afoot.
Follow your spirit, and upon this charge
Cry "God for Harry, England, and Saint George!"

WILLIAM SHAKESPEARE

White founts falling in the Courts of the sun,
And the Soldan of Byzantium is smiling as they run;
There is laughter like the fountains in that face of all men
    feared,
It stirs the forest darkness, the darkness of his beard,
It curls the blood-red crescent, the crescent of his lips;
For the inmost sea of all the earth is shaken with his ships.
They have dared the white republics up the capes of Italy,
They have dashed the Adriatic round the Lion of the Sea,
And the Pope has cast his arms abroad for agony and loss,
And called the kings of Christendom for swords about the
    Cross.
The cold queen of England is looking in the glass;
The shadow of the Valois is yawning at the Mass;
From evening isles fantastical rings faint the Spanish gun,
And the Lord upon the Golden Horn is laughing in the sun.

Dim drums throbbing, in the hills half heard,
Where only on a nameless throne a crownless prince has stirred,
Where, risen from a doubtful seat and half-attainted stall,
The last knight of Europe takes weapons from the wall,
The last and lingering troubadour to whom the bird has sung,
That once went singing southward when all the world was
    young.
In that enormous silence, tiny and unafraid,
Comes up along a winding road the noise of the Crusade.
Strong gongs groaning as the guns boom far,
Don John of Austria is going to the war,
Stiff flags straining in the night-blasts cold
In the gloom black-purple, in the glint old-gold,
Torchlight crimson on the copper kettle-drums,
Then the tuckets, then the trumpets, then the cannon, and he
    comes.
Don John laughing in the brave beard curled,
Spurning of his stirrups like the thrones of all the world,
Holding his head up for a flag of all the free.

Love-light of Spain—hurrah!
Death-light of Africa!
Don John of Austria
Is riding to the sea.

Mahound is in his paradise above the evening star,
(*Don John of Austria is going to the war.*)
He moves a mighty turban on the timeless houri's knees,
His turban that is woven of the sunset and the seas.
He shakes the peacock gardens as he rises from his ease,
And he strides among the tree-tops and is taller than the trees;
And his voice through all the garden is a thunder sent to bring
Black Azrael and Ariel and Ammon on the wing.
Giants and the Genii,
Multiplex of wing and eye,
Whose strong obedience broke the sky
When Solomon was king.

They rush in red and purple from the red clouds of the morn,
From temples where the yellow gods shut up their eyes in
            scorn;
They rise in green robes roaring from the green hells of the sea
Where fallen skies and evil hues and eyeless creatures be,
On them the sea-valves cluster and the gray sea-forests curl,
Splashed with a splendid sickness, the sickness of the pearl;
They swell in sapphire smoke out of the blue cracks of the
            ground,—
They gather and they wonder and give worship to Mahound.
And he saith, "Break up the mountains where the hermit-folk
            may hide,
And sift the red and silver sands lest bone of saint abide,
And chase the Giaours flying night and day, not giving rest,
For that which was our trouble comes again out of the west.
We have set the seal of Solomon on all things under sun,
Of knowledge and of sorrow and endurance of things done.
But a noise is in the mountains, in the mountains, and I know
The voice that shook our palaces—four hundred years ago:
It is he that saith not 'Kismet'; it is he that knows not Fate;

It is Richard, it is Raymond, it is Godfrey in the gate!
It is he whose loss is laughter when he counts the wager worth,
Put down your feet upon him, that our peace be on the earth."
For he heard drums groaning, and he heard guns jar,
(*Don John of Austria is going to the war.*)
Sudden and still—hurrah!
Bolt from Iberia!
Don John of Austria
Is gone by Alcalar.

St. Michael's on his Mountain in the sea-roads of the north
(*Don John of Austria is girt and going forth.*)
Where the gray seas glitter and the sharp tides shift
And the sea folk labor and the red sails lift.
He shakes his lance of iron and he claps his wings of stone;
The noise is gone through Normandy; the noise is gone alone;
The North is full of tangled things and texts and aching eyes
And dead is all the innocence of anger and surprise,
And Christian killeth Christian in a narrow dusty room,
And Christian dreadeth Christ that hath a newer face of doom,
And Christian hateth Mary that God kissed in Galilee,—
But Don John of Austria is riding to the sea.
Don John calling through the blast and the eclipse
Crying with the trumpet, with the trumpet of his lips,
Trumpet that sayeth *ha!*
    Domino Gloria!
Don John of Austria
Is shouting to the ships.

King Philip's in his closet with the Fleece about his neck
(*Don John of Austria is armed upon the deck.*)
The walls are hung with velvet that is black and soft as sin,
And little dwarfs creep out of it and little dwarfs creep in.
He holds a crystal phial that has colors like the moon,
He touches, and it tingles, and he trembles very soon,
And his face is as a fungus of a leprous white and gray
Like plants in the high houses that are shuttered from the day,
And death is in the phial, and the end of noble work,

But Don John of Austria has fired upon the Turk.
Don John's hunting, and his hounds have bayed—
Booms away past Italy the rumor of his raid.
Gun upon gun, ha! ha!
Gun upon gun, hurrah!
Don John of Austria
Has loosed the cannonade.

The Pope was in his chapel before day or battle broke,
(*Don John of Austria is hidden in the smoke.*)
The hidden room in man's house where God sits all the year,
The secret window whence the world looks small and very
    dear.
He sees as in a mirror on the monstrous twilight sea
The crescent of his cruel ships whose name is mystery;
They fling great shadows foe-wards, making Cross and Castle
    dark,
They veil the plumèd lions on the galleys of St. Mark;
And above the ships are palaces of brown, black-bearded
    chiefs,
And below the ships are prisons, where with multitudinous
    griefs,
Christian captives sick and sunless, all a laboring race repines
Like a race in sunken cities, like a nation in the mines.
They are lost like slaves that swat, and in the skies of morning
    hung
The stairways of the tallest gods when tyranny was young.
They are countless, voiceless, hopeless as those fallen or flee-
    ing on
Before the high Kings' horses in the granite of Babylon.
And many a one grows witless in his quiet room in hell
Where a yellow face looks inward through the lattice of his
    cell,
And he finds his God forgotten, and he seeks no more a sign—
(*But Don John of Austria has burst the battle-line!*)
Don John pounding from the slaughter-painted poop,
Purpling all the ocean like a bloody pirate's sloop,

Scarlet running over on the silvers and the golds,
Breaking of the hatches up and bursting of the holds,
Thronging of the thousands up that labor under sea
White for bliss and blind for sun and stunned for liberty.
Vivat Hispania!
Domino Gloria!
Don John of Austria
Has set his people free!

Cervantes on his galley sets the sword back in the sheath
(*Don John of Austria rides homeward with a wreath.*)
And he sees across a weary land a straggling road in Spain,
Up which a lean and foolish knight forever rides in vain,
And he smiles, but not as Sultans smile, and settles back the
    blade. . . .
(*But Don John of Austria rides home from the Crusade.*)

G. K. CHESTERTON

Ivry

(March 14, 1590)

Now glory to the Lord of Hosts, from whom all glories are!
And glory to our Sovereign Liege, King Henry of Navarre!
Now let there be the merry sound of music and of dance,
Through thy corn-fields green, and sunny vines, oh pleasant
    land of France!
And thou, Rochelle, our own Rochelle, proud city of the
    waters,
Again let rapture light the eyes of all thy mourning daughters.
As thou wert constant in our ills, be joyous in our joy;
For cold, and stiff, and still are they who wrought thy walls
    annoy.
Hurrah! hurrah! a single field hath turned the chance of war,
Hurrah! hurrah! for Ivry and Henry of Navarre.

Oh! how our hearts were beating when, at the dawn of day,
We saw the army of the League drawn out in long array;
With all its priest-led citizens, and all its rebel peers,
And Appenzel's stout infantry, and Egmont's Flemish spears.

There rode the brood of false Lorraine, the curses of our land;
And dark Mayenne was in the midst, a truncheon in his hand;
And, as we looked on them, we thought of Seine's empurpled
    flood,
And good Coligny's hoary hair all dabbled with his blood;
And we cried unto the living God, who rules the fate of war,
To fight for His own holy name, and Henry of Navarre.

The King is come to marshal us, in all his armor dressed;
And he has bound a snow-white plume upon his gallant crest.
He looked upon his people, and a tear was in his eye;
He looked upon the traitors, and his glance was stern and high.
Right graciously he smiled on us, as rolled from wing to wing,
Down all our line, a deafening shout: "God save our Lord the
    King!"
"And if my standard-bearer fall, as fall full well he may,
For never saw I promise yet of such a bloody fray,
Press where ye see my white plume shine, amidst the ranks
    of war,
And be your oriflamme today the helmet of Navarre."

Hurrah! The foes are moving. Hark to the mingled din,
Of fife, and steed, and trump, and drum, and roaring culverin.
The fiery Duke is pricking fast across Saint André's plain,
With all the hireling chivalry of Guelders and Almayne.
Now by the lips of those ye love, fair gentlemen of France,
Charge for the golden lilies,—upon them with the lance!
A thousand spurs are striking deep, a thousand spears in rest,
A thousand knights are pressing close behind the snow-white
    crest;
And in they burst, and on they rushed, while like a guiding
    star,
Amidst the thickest carnage blazed the helmet of Navarre.

Now, God be praised, the day is ours. Mayenne hath turned
    his rein;
D'Aumale hath cried for quarter; the Flemish count is slain.
Their ranks are breaking like thin clouds before a Biscay gale;

The field is heaped with bleeding steeds, and flags, and cloven
mail.
And then we thought on vengeance, and, all along our van,
"Remember Saint Bartholomew" was passed from man to man.
But out spake gentle Henry, "No Frenchman is my foe:
Down, down, with every foreigner, but let your brethren go."
Oh! was there ever such a knight, in friendship or in war,
As our Sovereign Lord, King Henry, the soldier of Navarre?

Right well fought all the Frenchmen who fought for France
to-day;
And many a lordly banner God gave them for a prey.
But we of the religion have borne us best in fight;
And the good Lord of Rosny hath ta'en the cornet white.
Our own true Maximilian the cornet white hath ta'en,
The cornet white with crosses black, the flag of false Lorraine.
Up with it high; unfurl it wide; that all the host may know
How God hath humbled the proud house which wrought His
Church such woe.
Then on the ground, while trumpets sound their loudest point
of war,
Fling the red shreds, a footcloth meet for Henry of Navarre.

Ho! maidens of Vienna; ho! matrons of Lucerne;
Weep, weep, and rend your hair for those who never shall
return.
Ho! Philip, send, for charity, thy Mexican pistoles,
That Antwerp monks may sing a mass for thy poor spearmen's
souls.
Ho! gallant nobles of the League, look that your arms be
bright;
Ho! burghers of St. Genevieve, keep watch and ward tonight;
For our God hath crushed the tyrant, our God hath raised
the slave,
And mocked the counsel of the wise, and the valor of the brave.
Then glory to His holy name, from whom all glories are;
And glory to our Sovereign Lord, King Henry of Navarre!

THOMAS BABINGTON MACAULAY

The Battle of Blenheim

(August 13, 1704)

It was a summer evening;
　Old Kaspar's work was done,
And he before his cottage-door
　Was sitting in the sun;
And by him sported on the green
His little grandchild, Wilhelmine.

She saw her brother Peterkin
　Roll something large and round,
That he beside the rivulet,
　In playing there, had found:
She ran to ask what he had found,
That was so large and smooth and round.

Old Kaspar took it from the boy,
　Who stood expectant by;
And then the old man shook his head,
　And with a natural sigh,
" 'T is some poor fellow's skull," said he,
"Who fell in the great victory.

"I find them in my garden,
　For there's many here about;
And often, when I go to plough,
　The ploughshare turns them out;
For many thousand men," said he,
"Were slain in that great victory."

"Now tell us what 'twas all about,"
　Young Peterkin, he cries;
And little Wilhelmine looks up
　With wonder-waiting eyes;
"Now tell us all about the war,
And what they fought each other for."

"It was the English," Kaspar cried,
　"Who put the French to rout;
But what they fought each other for

I could not well make out;
But everybody said," quoth he,
"That 'twas a famous victory.

"My father lived at Blenheim then,
    Yon little stream hard by;
They burned his dwelling to the ground,
    And he was forced to fly;
So with his wife and child he fled,
Nor had he where to rest his head.

"With fire and sword the country round
    Was wasted far and wide,
And many a childing mother then,
    And new-born baby, died;
But things like that, you know, must be
At every famous victory.

"They say it was a shocking sight
    After the field was won;
For many thousand bodies here
    Lay rotting in the sun:
But things like that, you know, must be
After a famous victory.

"Great praise the Duke of Marlborough won
    And our good Prince Eugene."
"Why, 'twas a very wicked thing!"
    Said little Wilhelmine.
"Nay, nay, my little girl," quoth he,
"It was a famous victory.

"And everybody praised the Duke
    Who this great fight did win."
"But what good came of it at last?"
    Quoth little Peterkin.
"Why, that I cannot tell," said he;
"But 'twas a famous victory."

ROBERT SOUTHEY

204

The Eve of Waterloo

(June 18, 1815)

(FROM *Childe Harold's Pilgrimage*)

There was a sound of revelry by night,
And Belgium's capital had gathered then
Her Beauty and her Chivalry, and bright
The lamps shone o'er fair women and brave men;
A thousand hearts beat happily; and when
Music arose with its voluptuous swell,
Soft eyes looked love to eyes which spake again,
And all went merry as a marriage bell;—
But hush! hark! a deep sound strikes like a rising knell!

Did ye not hear it?—No; 'twas but the wind,
Or the car rattling o'er the stony street;
On with the dance! let joy be unconfined;
No sleep till morn, when Youth and Pleasure meet
To chase the glowing Hours with flying feet—
But hark!—that heavy sound breaks in once more,
As if the clouds its echo would repeat;
And nearer, nearer, deadlier than before!
Arm! Arm! it is—it is—the cannon's opening roar!

Within a windowed niche of that high wall
Sate Brunswick's fated chieftain; he did hear
That sound the first amid the festival,
And caught its tone with Death's prophetic ear;
And when they smiled because he deemed it near,
His heart more truly knew that peal too well
Which stretched his father on a bloody bier,
And roused the vengeance blood alone could quell:
He rushed into the field, and, foremost fighting, fell.

Ah! then and there was hurrying to and fro,
And gathering tears, and tremblings of distress,
And cheeks all pale, which but an hour ago
Blushed at the praise of their own loveliness;
And there were sudden partings, such as press

The life from out young hearts, and choking sighs
Which ne'er might be repeated; who could guess
If ever more should meet those mutual eyes,
Since upon night so sweet such awful morn could rise!

And there was mounting in hot haste: the steed,
The mustering squadron, and the clattering car,
Went pouring forward with impetuous speed,
And swiftly forming in the ranks of war;
And the deep thunder peal on peal afar;
And, near, the beat of the alarming drum
Roused up the soldier ere the morning star;
While thronged the citizens with terror dumb,
Or whispering, with white lips—"The foe! they come! they
    come!"

GEORGE GORDON BYRON

The Charge of the Light Brigade

(Balaclava, October 25, 1852)

Half a league, half a league,
  Half a league onward,
All in the valley of Death
  Rode the six hundred.
"Forward, the Light Brigade!
Charge for the guns!" he said:
Into the valley of Death
  Rode the six hundred.

"Forward, the Light Brigade!"
Was there a man dismayed?
Not though the soldier knew
  Some one had blundered:
Theirs not to make reply,
Theirs not to reason why,

Theirs but to do and die:
Into the valley of Death
  Rode the six hundred.

Cannon to right of them,
Cannon to left of them,
Cannon in front of them
  Volleyed and thundered;
Stormed at with shot and shell,
Boldly they rode and well,
Into the jaws of Death,
Into the mouth of Hell
  Rode the six hundred.

Flashed all their sabres bare,
Flashed as they turned in air
Sabring the gunners there,
Charging an army, while
  All the world wondered:
Plunged in the battery-smoke
Right through the line they broke;
Cossack and Russian
Reeled from the sabre-stroke
  Shattered and sundered.
Then they rode back, but not,
  Not the six hundred.

Cannon to right of them,
Cannon to left of them,
Cannon behind them
  Volleyed and thundered;
Storm'd at with shot and shell,
While horse and hero fell,
They that had fought so well
Came through the jaws of Death,
Back from the mouth of Hell,
All that was left of them,
  Left of six hundred.

When can their glory fade?
O the wild charge they made!
   All the world wondered.
Honor the charge they made!
Honor the Light Brigade,
   Noble six hundred.

ALFRED TENNYSON

Beat! Beat! Drums!

Beat! beat! drums!—blow! bugles! blow!
Through the windows—through doors—burst like a ruthless
      force,
Into the solemn church, and scatter the congregation,
Into the school where the scholar is studying;
Leave not the bridegroom quiet—no happiness must he have
      now with his bride,
Nor the peaceful farmer any peace, ploughing his field or
      gathering his grain,
So fierce you whirr and pound you drums—so shrill you bugles
      blow.

Beat! beat! drums!—blow! bugles! blow!
Over the traffic of cities—over the rumble of wheels in the
      streets;
Are beds prepared for sleepers at night in the houses? no
      sleepers must sleep in those beds,
No bargainers' bargains by day—no brokers or speculators—
      would they continue?
Would the talkers be talking? would the singer attempt to sing?
Would the lawyer rise in the court to state his case before the
      judge?
Then rattle quicker, heavier drums—you bugles wilder blow.

Beat! beat! drums!—blow! bugles! blow!
Make no parley—stop for no expostulation,

Mind not the timid—mind not the weeper or prayer,
Mind not the old man beseeching the young man,
Let not the child's voice be heard, nor the mother's entreaties,
Make even the trestles to shake the dead where they lie awaiting
　　　the hearses,
So strong you thump O terrible drums—so loud you bugles
　　　blow.

WALT WHITMAN

Tommy

I went into a public-'ouse to get a pint o' beer,
The publican 'e up and sez, "We serve no red-coats here."
The girls be'ind the bar they laughed an' giggled fit to die,
I outs into the street again an' to myself sez I:
　　　O it's Tommy this, an' Tommy that, an' "Tommy, go
　　　　　away";
　　　But it's "Thank you, Mister Atkins," when the band be-
　　　　　gins to play,
　　　The band begins to play, my boys, the band begins to play,
　　　O it's "Thank you, Mister Atkins," when the band begins
　　　　　to play.

I went into a theater as sober as could be,
They gave a drunk civilian room, but 'adn't none for me;
They sent me to the gallery or round the music-'alls,
But when it comes to fightin', Lord! they'll shove me in the
　　　stalls!
　　　For it's Tommy this, an' Tommy that, an' "Tommy, wait
　　　　　outside";
　　　But it's "Special train for Atkins" when the trooper's on
　　　　　the tide,
　　　The troopship's on the tide, my boys, the troopship's on
　　　　　the tide,
　　O it's "Special train for Atkins" when the trooper's on the tide.

O makin' mock o' uniforms that guard you while you sleep
Is cheaper than them uniforms, an' they're starvation cheap;
An' hustlin' drunken sodjers when they're goin' large a bit
Is five times better business than paradin' in full kit.
> Then it's Tommy this, an' Tommy that, an' "Tommy,
> 'ow's yer soul?"
> But it's "Thin red line of 'eroes" when the drums begin
> to roll,
> The drums begin to roll, my boys, the drums begin to roll,
> O it's "Thin red line of 'eroes" when the drums begin to
> roll.

We aren't no thin red 'eroes, nor we aren't no blackguards too,
But single men in barricks, most remarkable like you;
An' if sometimes our conduck isn't all your fancy paints,
Why, single men in barricks don't grow into plaster saints;
> While it's Tommy this, an' Tommy that, an' "Tommy,
> fall be'ind,"
> But it's "Please to walk in front, sir," when there's trouble
> in the wind,
> There's trouble in the wind, my boys, there's trouble in
> the wind,
> O it's "Please to walk in front, sir," when there's trouble
> in the wind.

You talk o' better food for us, an' schools, an' fires, an' all:
We'll wait for extry rations if you'll treat us rational,
Don't mess about the cook-room slops, but prove it to our face
The Widow's uniform is not the soldier-man's disgrace.
> For it's Tommy this, an' Tommy that, an' "Chuck him
> out, the brute!"
> But it's "Savior of 'is country" when the guns begin to
> shoot;
> An' it's Tommy this, an' Tommy that, an' anything you
> please;
> An' Tommy ain't a bloomin' fool—you bet that Tommy
> sees!

RUDYARD KIPLING

The Ballad of East and West

*Oh, East is East, and West is West, and never the twain shall
        meet,*
*Till Earth and Sky stand presently at God's great Judgment
        Seat:*
*But there is neither East nor West, Border, nor Breed, nor
        Birth,*
*When two strong men stand face to face, though they come
        from the ends of the earth!*

Kamal is out with twenty men to raise the Border-side,
And he has lifted the Colonel's mare that is the Colonel's pride:
He has lifted her out of the stable-door between the dawn and
        the day,
And turned the calkins upon her feet, and ridden her far away.
Then up and spoke the Colonel's son that led a troop of the
        Guides:
"Is there never a man of all my men can say where Kamal
        hides?"
Then up and spoke Mohammed Khan, the son of the Ressaldar:
"If ye know the track of the morning-mist, ye know where his
        pickets are.
At dusk he harries the Abazai—at dawn he is into Bonair,
But he must go by Fort Bukloh to his own place to fare.
So if ye gallop to Fort Bukloh as fast as a bird can fly,
By the favor of God ye may cut him off ere he win to the
        Tongue of Jagai.
But if he be past the Tongue of Jagai, right swiftly turn ye
        then,
For the length and breadth of that grisly plain is sown with
        Kamal's men.
There is rock to the left, and rock to the right, and low lean
        thorn between,
And ye may hear a breech-bolt snick where never a man is
        seen."
The Colonel's son has taken a horse, and a raw rough dun
        was he,

211

With the mouth of a bell and the heart of Hell and the head
of a gallows-tree.
The Colonel's son to the Fort has won, they bid him stay to
eat—
Who rides at the tail of a Border thief, he sits not long at his
meat.
He's up and away from Fort Bukloh as fast as he can fly,
Till he was aware of his father's mare in the gut of the Tongue
of Jagai,
Till he was aware of his father's mare with Kamal upon her
back,
And when he could spy the white of her eye, he made the pistol
crack.
He has fired once, he has fired twice, but the whistling ball
went wide.
"Ye shoot like a soldier," Kamal said. "Show now if ye can
ride!"
It's up and over the Tongue of Jagai, as blown dust-devils go,
The dun he fled like a stag of ten, but the mare like a barren
doe.
The dun he leaned against the bit and slugged his head above,
But the red mare played with the snaffle-bars, as a maiden plays
with a glove.
There was rock to the left and rock to the right, and low lean
thorn between,
And thrice he heard a breech-bolt snick though never a man
was seen.
They have ridden the low moon out of the sky, their hoofs
drum up the dawn,
The dun he went like a wounded bull, but the mare like a new-
roused fawn.
The dun he fell at a water-course—in a woeful heap fell he,
And Kamal has turned the red mare back, and pulled the rider
free.
He has knocked the pistol out of his hand—small room was
there to strive,

" 'Twas only by favor of mine," quoth he, "ye rode so long
    alive:
There was not a rock for twenty mile, there was not a clump
    of tree,
But covered a man of my own men with his rifle cocked on
    his knee.
If I had raised my bridle-hand, as I have held it low,
The little jackals that flee so fast were feasting all in a row:
If I had bowed my head on my breast, as I have held it high,
The kite that whistles above us now were gorged till she could
    not fly."
Lightly answered the Colonel's son: "Do good to bird and
    beast,
But count who come for the broken meats before thou makest
    a feast.
If there should follow a thousand swords to carry my bones
    away,
Belike the price of a jackal's meal were more than a thief could
    pay.
They will feed their horse on the standing crop, their men on
    the garnered grain.
The thatch of the byres will serve their fires when all the
    cattle are slain.
But if thou thinkest the price be fair,—thy brethren wait to sup,
The hound is kin to the jackal-spawn,—howl, dog, and call
    them up!
And if thou thinkest the price be high, in steer and gear and
    stack,
Give me my father's mare again, and I'll fight my own way
    back!"
Kamal has gripped him by the hand and set him upon his feet.
"No talk shall be of dogs," said he, "when wolf and gray wolf
    meet.
May I eat dirt if thou hast hurt of me in deed or breath;
What dam of lances brought thee forth to jest at the dawn with
    Death?"

Lightly answered the Colonel's son: "I hold by the blood of my clan:

Take up the mare for my father's gift—by God, she has carried a man!"

The red mare ran to the Colonel's son, and nuzzled against his breast;

"We be two strong men," said Kamal then, "but she loveth the younger best.

So she shall go with a lifter's dower, my turquoise-studded rein,

My 'broidered saddle and saddle-cloth, and silver stirrups twain."

The Colonel's son a pistol drew, and held it muzzle-end,

"Ye have taken the one from a foe," said he; "will ye take the mate from a friend?"

"A gift for a gift," said Kamal straight; "a limb for the risk of a limb.

Thy father has sent his son to me, I'll send my son to him!"

With that he whistled his only son, that dropped from a mountain-crest—

He trod the ling like a buck in spring, and he looked like a lance in rest.

"Now here is thy master," Kamal said, "who leads a troop of the Guides,

And thou must ride at his left side as shield on shoulder rides.

Till Death or I cut loose the tie, at camp and board and bed,

Thy life is his—thy fate it is to guard him with thy head.

So thou must eat the White Queen's meat, and all her foes are thine,

And thou must harry thy father's hold for the peace of the Border-line,

And thou must make a trooper tough and hack thy way to power—

Belike they will raise thee to Ressaldar when I am hanged in Peshawur."

They have looked each other between the eyes, and there they found no fault,

They have taken the Oath of the Brother-in-Blood on leavened
    bread and salt:
They have taken the Oath of the Brother-in-Blood on fire and
    fresh-cut sod,
On the hilt and the haft of the Khyber knife, and the Won-
    drous Names of God.
The Colonel's son he rides the mare and Kamal's boy the dun.
And two have come back to Fort Bukloh where there went
    forth but one.
And when they drew to the Quarter-Guard, full twenty
    swords flew clear—
There was not a man but carried his feud with the blood of
    the mountaineer.
"Ha' done! ha' done!" said the Colonel's son. "Put up the steel
    at your sides!
Last night ye had struck at a Border thief—to-night 'tis a man
    of the Guides!"

Oh, East is East, and West is West, and never the twain shall
    meet,
Till Earth and Sky stand presently at God's great Judgment
    Seat;
But there is neither East nor West, Border, nor Breed, nor
    Birth,
When two strong men stand face to face, though they come
    from the ends of the earth!

RUDYARD KIPLING

The Soldier

If I should die, think only this of me:
    That there's some corner of a foreign field
That is forever England. There shall be
    In that rich earth a richer dust concealed;
A dust whom England bore, shaped, made aware,
    Gave, once, her flowers to love, her ways to roam,
A body of England's, breathing English air,

Washed by the rivers, blest by suns of home.
And think, this heart, all evil shed away,
   A pulse in the eternal mind, no less
      Gives somewhere back the thoughts by England given;
Her sights and sounds; dreams happy as her day;
   And laughter, learnt of friends; and gentleness,
      In hearts at peace, under an English heaven.

RUPERT BROOKE

I Have a Rendezvous with Death

I have a rendezvous with Death
At some disputed barricade,
When Spring comes round with rustling shade
And apple blossoms fill the air—
I have a rendezvous with Death,
When Spring brings back blue days and fair.

It may be he shall take my hand
And lead me into his dark land
And close my eyes and quench my breath—
It may be I shall pass him still.
I have a rendezvous with Death
On some scarred slope of battered hill,
When Spring comes round again this year
And the first meadow-flowers appear.

God knows 'twere better to be deep
Pillowed in silk and scented down,
Where Love throbs out in blissful sleep,
Pulse nigh to pulse, and breath to breath,
Where hushed awakenings are dear . . .
But I've a rendezvous with Death
At midnight in some flaming town,
When Spring trips north again this year,
And I to my pledged word am true,
I shall not fail that rendezvous.

ALAN SEEGER

In Flanders Fields

In Flanders fields the poppies blow
Between the crosses, row on row,
   That mark our place; and in the sky
   The larks, still bravely singing, fly
Scarce heard amid the guns below.

We are the Dead. Short days ago
We lived, felt Dawn, saw sunset glow,
   Loved and were loved, and now we lie
     In Flanders fields.

Take up our quarrel with the foe:
To you from failing hands we throw
   The torch; be yours to hold it high.
   If ye break faith with us who die
We shall not sleep, though poppies grow
     In Flanders fields.

JOHN MCCRAE

Dulce et Decorum Est

Bent double, like old beggars under sacks,
Knock-kneed, coughing like hags, we cursed through sludge,
Till on the haunting flares we turned our backs,
And towards our distant rest began to trudge.
Men marched asleep. Many had lost their boots,
But limped on, blood-shod. All went lame, all blind;
Drunk with fatigue; deaf even to the hoots
Of gas-shells dropping softly behind.

Gas! Gas! Quick, boys!—An ecstasy of fumbling,
Fitting the clumsy helmets just in time,
But someone still was yelling out and stumbling
And flound'ring like a man in fire or lime.
Dim through the misty panes and thick green light,
As under a green sea, I saw him drowning.

217

In all my dreams before my helpless sight
He plunges at me, guttering, choking, drowning.

If in some smothering dreams, you too could pace
Behind the wagon that we flung him in,
And watch the white eyes wilting in his face,
His hanging face, like a devil's sick of sin,
If you could hear, at every jolt, the blood
Come gargling from the froth-corrupted lungs
Bitter as the cud
Of vile, incurable sores on innocent tongues—
My friend, you would not tell with such high zest
To children ardent for some desperate glory,
The old lie: *Dulce et decorum est
Pro patria mori.*

WILFRED OWEN

The General

"Good-morning; good-morning!" the General said
When we met him last week on our way to the line.
Now the soldiers he smiled at are most of 'em dead,
And we're cursing his staff for incompetent swine.
"He's a cheery old card," grunted Harry to Jack
As they slugged up to Arras with rifle and pack.
          .   .   .   .
But he did for them both by his plan of attack.

SIEGFRIED SASSOON

Everyone Sang
(Armistice Day, 1918)

Everyone suddenly burst out singing;
And I was filled with such delight
As prisoned birds must find in freedom

218

Winging wildly across the white
Orchards and dark-green fields; on; on; and out of sight.

Everyone's voice was suddenly lifted,
And beauty came like the setting sun.
My heart was shaken with tears, and horror
Drifted away. . . . Oh, but everyone
Was a bird; and the song was wordless; the singing will never
   be done.

SIEGFRIED SASSOON

Grass

Pile the bodies high at Austerlitz and Waterloo.
Shovel them under and let me work—
   I am the grass; I cover all.

And pile them high at Gettysburg
And pile them high at Ypres and Verdun.
Shovel them under and let me work.
Two years, ten years, and passengers ask the conductor:
   What place is this?
   Where are we now?

   I am the grass.
   Let me work.

CARL SANDBURG

BOOK SEVEN

Our Other Eden

It is our Eden too, that green and sceptered isle, and whether we have ever heard a skylark or a nightingale, seen Kew in lilac-time or sniffed chalk cliffs and moorlands, its flowers bloom in our gardens, our birds bear its birds' names, and the poetry of love for England—and for Scotland and Ireland too —is part of our inherited emotion. Our own poets do not speak to us of our own land with more tingling emotion.

This Blessed Plot . . . This England

(FROM *Richard II*, Act II, Scene I)

This royal throne of kings, this sceptered isle,
This earth of majesty, this seat of Mars,
This other Eden, demi-Paradise,
This fortress built by Nature for herself
Against infection and the hand of war,
This happy breed of men, this little world,
This precious stone set in the silver sea,
Which serves it in the office of a wall,
Or as a moat defensive to a house,
Against the envy of less happier lands;
This blessed plot, this earth, this realm, this England,
This nurse, this teeming womb of royal kings,
Fear'd by their breed and famous by their birth,
Renownèd for their deeds as far from home,
For Christian service and true chivalry
As is the sepulcher in stubborn Jewry
Of the world's ransom, blessed Mary's Son—
This land of such dear souls, this dear dear land,
Dear for her reputation through the world . . .

WILLIAM SHAKESPEARE

And Did Those Feet in Ancient Time

And did those feet in ancient time
Walk upon England's mountains green?
And was the holy Lamb of God
On England's pleasant pastures seen?

And did the Countenance Divine
Shine forth upon our clouded hills?
And was Jerusalem builded here
Among these dark Satanic Mills?

Bring me my bow of burning gold!
Bring me my arrows of desire!

223

Bring me my spear! O clouds unfold!
Bring me my chariot of fire!

I will not cease from mental fight,
Nor shall my sword sleep in my hand,
Till we have built Jerusalem
In England's green and pleasant land.

WILLIAM BLAKE

I Traveled Among Unknown Men

I traveled among unknown men,
  In lands beyond the sea;
Nor, England! did I know till then
  What love I bore to thee.

'Tis past, that melancholy dream!
  Nor will I quit thy shore
A second time; for still I seem
  To love thee more and more.

Among thy mountains did I feel
  The joy of my desire;
And she I cherished turned her wheel
  Beside an English fire.

Thy mornings showed, thy nights concealed
  The bowers where Lucy played;
And thine too is the last green field
  That Lucy's eyes surveyed.

WILLIAM WORDSWORTH

Composed upon Westminster Bridge
(September 3, 1802)

Earth has not anything to show more fair:
Dull would he be of soul who could pass by
A sight so touching in its majesty:
This City now doth, like a garment, wear

The beauty of the morning; silent, bare,
Ships, towers, domes, theaters and temples lie
Open unto the fields, and to the sky;
All bright and glittering in the smokeless air.
Never did sun more beautifully steep
In his first splendor, valley, rock, or hill;
Ne'er saw I, never felt, a calm so deep!
The river glideth at his own sweet will:
Dear God! The very houses seem asleep;
And all that mighty heart is lying still!

WILLIAM WORDSWORTH

London, 1802

Milton! thou shouldst be living at this hour:
England hath need of thee: she is a fen
Of stagnant waters: altar, sword, and pen,
Fireside, the heroic wealth of hall and bower,
Have forfeited their ancient English dower
Of inward happiness. We are selfish men;
Oh! raise us up, return to us again,
And give us manners, virtue, freedom, power.
Thy soul was like a Star, and dwelt apart;
Thou hadst a voice whose sound was like the sea:
Pure as the naked heavens, majestic, free;
So didst thou travel on life's common way,
In cheerful godliness; and yet thy heart
The lowliest duties on herself did lay.

WILLIAM WORDSWORTH

Ode to Autumn

Season of mists and mellow fruitfulness!
Close bosom-friend of the maturing sun;
Conspiring with him how to load and bless
With fruit the vines that round the thatch-eaves run;

To bend with apples the moss'd cottage-trees,
And fill all fruit with ripeness to the core;
To swell the gourd, and plump the hazel shells
With a sweet kernel; to set budding more
And still more, later flowers for the bees,
Until they think warm days will never cease;
For summer has o'erbrimmed their clammy cells.

Who hath not seen thee oft amid thy store?
Sometimes whoever seeks abroad may find
Thee sitting careless on a granary floor,
Thy hair soft-lifted by the winnowing wind;
Or on a half-reap'd furrow sound asleep,
Drowsed with the fume of poppies, while thy hook
Spares the next swath and all its twinèd flowers;
And sometimes like a gleaner thou dost keep
Steady thy laden head across a brook
Or by a cider-press, with patient look
Thou watchest the last oozings, hours by hours.

Where are the songs of Spring? Ay, where are they?
Think not of them, thou hast thy music too,
While barrèd clouds bloom the soft-dying day
And touch the stubble-plains with rosy hue;
Then in a wailful choir the small gnats mourn
Among the river-sallows, borne aloft
Or sinking as the light wind lives or dies;
And full-grown lambs loud bleat from hilly bourn;
Hedge-crickets sing, and now with treble soft
The redbreast whistles from a garden-croft;
And gathering swallows twitter in the skies.

JOHN KEATS

The Brook

I come from haunts of coot and hern,
   I make a sudden sally,
And sparkle out among the fern,
   To bicker down a valley.

By thirty hills I hurry down,
   Or slip between the ridges,
By twenty thorps, a little town,
   And half a hundred bridges.

Till last by Philip's farm I flow
   To join the brimming river,
For men may come and men may go
   But I go on for ever.

I chatter over stony ways,
   In little sharps and trebles,
I bubble into eddying bays,
   I babble on the pebbles.

With many a curve my banks I fret,
   By many a field and fallow,
And many a fairy foreland set
   With willow-weed and mallow.

I chatter, chatter as I flow
   To join the brimming river,
For men may come and men may go
   But I go on for ever.

I wind about, and in and out,
   With here a blossom sailing,
And here and there a lusty trout,
   And here and there a grayling.

And here and there a foamy flake
   Upon me, as I travel
With many a silver water-break
   Above the golden gravel,

And draw them all along, and flow
  To join the brimming river,
For men may come and men may go
  But I go on for ever.

I steal by lawns and grassy plots,
  I slide by hazel covers;
I move the sweet forget-me-nots
  That grow for happy lovers.

I slip, I slide, I gloom, I glance,
  Among my skimming swallows;
I make the netted sunbeam dance
  Against my sandy shallows.

I murmur under moon and stars
  In brambly wildernesses;
I linger by my shingly bars;
  I loiter round my cresses;

And out again I curve and flow
  To join the brimming river,
For men may come and men may go
  But I go on for ever.

ALFRED TENNYSON

My Garden

A garden is a lovesome thing, God wot!
Rose plot,
Fringed pool,
Ferned grot—
The veriest school
Of peace; and yet the fool
Contends that God is not—
Not God! in gardens! when the eve is cool?
Nay, but I have a sign;
'Tis very sure God walks in mine.

THOMAS EDWARD BROWN

Home Thoughts from Abroad

Oh, to be in England
Now that April's there,
And whoever wakes in England
Sees, some morning, unaware,
That the lowest boughs and the brushwood sheaf
Round the elm-tree bole are in tiny leaf,
While the chaffinch sings on the orchard bough
In England—now!

And after April, when May follows,
And the white-throat builds, and all the swallows!
Hark, where my blossomed pear-tree in the hedge
Leans to the field and scatters on the clover
Blossoms and dewdrops—at the bent spray's edge—
That's the wise thrush: he sings each song twice over,
Lest you should think he never could recapture
The first fine careless rapture!
And though the fields look rough with hoary dew,
All will be gay when noontide wakes anew,
The buttercups, the little children's dower
—Far brighter than this gaudy melon-flower!

ROBERT BROWNING

Weathers

I

This is the weather the cuckoo likes,
    And so do I;
When showers betumble the chestnut spikes,
    And nestlings fly;
And the little brown nightingale bills his best,
And they sit outside at the "Traveler's Rest,"
And maids come forth sprig-muslin drest,
And citizens dream of the South and West,
    And so do I.

II

This is the weather the shepherd shuns,
　　And so do I;
When beeches drip in browns and duns,
　　And thresh, and ply;
And hill-hid tides throb, throe on throe,
And meadow rivulets overflow,
And drops on gate-bars hang in a row,
And rooks in families homeward go,
　　And so do I.

THOMAS HARDY

The Hounds of Spring
(FROM *Atalanta in Calydon*)

When the hounds of spring are on winter's traces,
　　The mother of months in meadow or plain
Fills the shadows and windy places
　　With lisp of leaves and ripple of rain;
And the brown bright nightingale amorous
Is half assuaged for Itylus,
For the Thracian ships and the foreign faces,
　　The tongueless vigil, and all the pain.

Come with bows bent and with emptying of quivers,
　　Maiden most perfect, lady of light,
With a noise of winds and many rivers,
　　With a clamour of waters, and with might;
Bind on thy sandals, O thou most fleet,
Over the splendour and speed of thy feet;
For the faint east quickens, the wan west shivers,
　　Round the feet of the day and the feet of the night.

Where shall we find her, how shall we sing to her,
　　Fold our hands round her knees, and cling?
O that man's heart were as fire and could spring to her,
　　Fire, or the strength of the streams that spring!
For the stars and the winds are unto her
As raiment, as songs of the harp-player;

For the risen stars and the fallen cling to her,
　　And the southwest-wind and the west-wind sing.

For winter's rains and ruins are over,
　　And all the season of snows and sins;
The days dividing lover and lover,
　　The light that loses, the night that wins;
And time remembered is grief forgotten,
And frosts are slain and flowers begotten,
And in green underwood and cover
　　Blossom by blossom the spring begins.

The full streams feed on flower of rushes,
　　Ripe grasses trammel a travelling foot,
The faint fresh flame of the young year flushes
　　From leaf to flower and flower to fruit;
And fruit and leaf are as gold and fire,
And the oat is heard above the lyre,
And the hoofèd heel of a satyr crushes
　　The chestnut-husk at the chestnut-root.

And Pan by noon and Bacchus by night,
　　Fleeter of foot than the fleet-foot kid,
Follows with dancing and fills with delight
　　The Mænad and the Bassarid;
And soft as lips that laugh and hide
The laughing leaves of the trees divide,
And screen from seeing and leave in sight
　　The god pursuing, the maiden hid.

The ivy falls with the Bacchanal's hair
　　Over her eyebrows hiding her eyes;
The wild vine slipping down leaves bare
　　Her bright breast shortening into sighs;
The wild vine slips with the weight of its leaves,
But the berried ivy catches and cleaves
To the limbs that glitter, the feet that scare
　　The wolf that follows, the fawn that flies.

ALGERNON CHARLES SWINBURNE

April

April, April,
Laugh thy girlish laughter;
Then, the moment after,
Weep thy girlish tears!
April, that mine ears
Like a lover greetest,
If I tell thee, sweetest,
All my hopes and fears,
April, April,
Laugh thy girlish laughter,
But, the moment after,
Weep thy golden tears!

WILLIAM WATSON

Loveliest of Trees

Loveliest of trees, the cherry now
Is hung with bloom along the bough,
And stands about the woodland ride
Wearing white for Eastertide.

Now, of my threescore years and ten,
Twenty will not come again,
And take from seventy springs a score,
It only leaves me fifty more.

And since to look at things in bloom
Fifty springs are little room,
About the woodlands I will go
To see the cherry hung with snow.

A. E. HOUSMAN

Puck's Song

(ENLARGED FROM *Puck of Pook's Hill*)

See you the ferny ride that steals
Into the oak-woods far?
O that was whence they hewed the keels
That rolled to Trafalgar.

And mark you where the ivory clings
To Bayham's mouldering walls?
O there we cast the stout railings
That stand around St. Paul's.

See you the dimpled track that runs
All hollow through the wheat?
O that was where they hauled the guns
That smote King Philip's fleet.

(Out of the Weald, the secret Weald,
Men sent in ancient years
The horse-shoes red at Flodden Field
The arrows at Poitiers!)

See you our little mill that clacks,
So busy by the brook?
She has ground her corn and paid her tax
Ever since Domesday Book.

See you our stilly woods of oak,
And the dread ditch beside?
O that was where the Saxons broke
On the day that Harold died.

See you the windy levels spread
About the gates of Rye?
O that was where the Northmen fled,
When Alfred's ships came by.

See you our pastures wide and lone,
Where the red oxen browse?
O there was a City thronged and known
Ere London boasted a house.

233

And see you, after rain, the trace
Of mound and ditch and wall?
O that was a Legion's camping-place,
When Caesar sailed from Gaul.

And see you marks that show and fade,
Like shadows on the Downs?
O they are the lines the Flint Men made,
To guard their wondrous towns.

Trackway and Camp and City lost,
Salt Marsh where now is corn—
Old Wars, old Peace, old Arts that cease,
And so was England born!

She is not any common Earth,
Water or wood or air,
But Merlin's Isle of Gramarye,
Where you and I will fare!

RUDYARD KIPLING

The Barrel-Organ

There's a barrel-organ caroling across a golden street
  In the City as the sun sinks low;
And the music's not immortal; but the world has made it sweet
  And fulfilled it with the sunset glow;
And it pulses through the pleasures of the City and the pain
  That surround the singing organ like a large eternal light;
And they've given it a glory and a part to play again
  In the Symphony that rules the day and night.

And now it's marching onward through the realms of old
    romance,
  And trolling out a fond, familiar tune,
And now it's roaring cannon down to fight the King of
    France,
  And now it's prattling softly to the moon,

And all around the organ there's a sea without a shore
  Of human joys and wonders and regrets;
To remember and to recompense the music evermore
  For what the cold machinery forgets. . . .

        Yes; as the music changes,
          Like a prismatic glass,
        It takes the light and ranges
          Through all the moods that pass;
        Dissects the common carnival
          Of passions and regrets,
        And gives the world a glimpse of all
          The colors it forgets.

        And there *La Traviata* sighs
          Another sadder song;
        And there *Il Trovatore* cries
          A tale of deeper wrong;
        And bolder knights to battle go
          With sword and shield and lance,
        Than ever here on earth below
          Have whirled into—*a dance!*—

Go down to Kew in lilac-time, in lilac-time, in lilac-time;
  Go down to Kew in lilac-time (it isn't far from London!)
And you shall wander hand in hand with love in summer's
      wonderland;
  Go down to Kew in lilac-time (it isn't far from London!)

The cherry-trees are seas of bloom and soft perfume and
      sweet perfume,
  The cherry-trees are seas of bloom (and oh, so near to
      London!)
And there they say, when dawn is high and all the world's a
      blaze of sky
  The cuckoo, though he's very shy, will sing a song of
      London. . . .

The nightingale is rather rare and yet they say you'll hear
      him there

At Kew, at Kew in lilac-time (and oh, so near to London!)
The linnet and the throstle, too, and after dark the long halloo
And golden-eyed *tu-whit, tu-whoo* of owls that ogle
London.

For Noah hardly knew a bird of any kind that isn't heard
At Kew, at Kew in lilac-time (and oh, so near to London!)
And when the rose begins to pout and all the chestnut spires
are out
You'll hear the rest without a doubt, all chorussing for
London:—

Come down to Kew in lilac-time, in lilac-time, in lilac-time;
Come down to Kew in lilac-time (it isn't far from London!)
And you shall wander hand in hand with love in summer's
wonderland;
Come down to Kew in lilac-time (it isn't far from London!)

And then the troubadour begins to thrill the golden street,
In the City as the sun sinks low;
And in all the gaudy busses there are scores of weary feet
Marking time, sweet time, with a dull mechanic beat,
And a thousand hearts are plunging to a love they'll never
meet,
Through the meadows of the sunset, through the poppies and
the wheat,
In the land where the dead dreams go.

Verdi, Verdi, when you wrote *Il Trovatore* did you dream
Of the City when the sun sinks low,
Of the organ and the monkey and the many-colored stream
On the Piccadilly pavement, of the myriad eyes that seem
To be litten for a moment with a wild Italian gleam
As *A che la morte* parodies the world's eternal theme
And pulses with the sunset-glow? . . .

And it's buy a bunch of violets for the lady
(*It's lilac-time in London; it's lilac-time in London!*)
Buy a bunch of violets for the lady
While the sky burns blue above:

On the other side the street you'll find it shady
(*It's lilac-time in London; it's lilac-time in London!*)
But buy a bunch of violets for the lady
And tell her she's your own true love.

.　　　.　　　.

There's a barrel-organ caroling across a golden street
In the City as the sun sinks glittering and slow;
And the music's not immortal; but the world has made it sweet
And enriched it with the harmonies that make a song complete
In the deeper heavens of music where the night and morning
meet
As it dies into the sunset glow;
And it pulses through the pleasures of the City and the pain
That surround the singing organ like a large eternal light,
And they've given it a glory and a part to play again
In the Symphony that rules the day and night.

And there, as the music changes
The song runs round again;
Once more it turns and ranges
Through all its joy and pain:
Dissects the common carnival
Of passions and regrets;
And the wheeling world remembers all
The wheeling song forgets.

Once more *La Traviata* sighs
Another sadder song:
Once more *Il Trovatore* cries
A tale of deeper wrong;
Once more the knights to battle go
With sword and shield and lance
Till once, once more, the shattered foe
Has whirled into—*a dance!*

Come down to Kew in lilac-time, in lilac-time, in lilac-time;
Come down to Kew in lilac-time (it isn't far from London!)

And you shall wander hand in hand with love in summer's
wonderland;
Come down to Kew in lilac-time (it isn't far from London!)

ALFRED NOYES

A Widow's Weeds

A poor old Widow in her weeds
Sowed her garden with wild-flower seeds;
Not too shallow, and not too deep,
And down came April—drip—drip—drip.
Up shone May, like gold, and soon
Green as an arbour grew leafy June.
And now all summer she sits and sews
Where willow herb, comfrey, bugloss blows,
Teasle and tansy, meadowsweet,
Campion, toadflax, and rough hawksbit;
Brown bee orchis, and Peals of Bells;
Clover, burnet, and thyme she smells;
Like Oberon's meadows her garden is
Drowsy from dawn till dusk with bees.
Weeps she never, but sometimes sighs,
And peeps at her garden with bright brown eyes;
And all she has is all she needs—
A poor old Widow in her weeds.

WALTER DE LA MARE

The Old Vicarage, Grantchester
(Café des Westens, Berlin, May, 1912)

Just now the lilac is in bloom,
All before my little room;
And in my flower-beds, I think,
Smile the carnation and the pink.
And down the borders, well I know,
The poppy and the pansy blow . . .

Oh! there the chestnuts, summer through,
Beside the river make for you
A tunnel of green gloom, and sleep
Deeply above; and green and deep
The stream mysterious glides beneath,
Green as a dream and deep as death.
—Oh, damn! I know it! and I know
How the May fields all golden show,
And when the day is young and sweet,
Glide gloriously the bare feet
That run to bathe . . .
                                    Du lieber Gott!
Here am I, sweating, sick, and hot,
And there the shadowed waters fresh
Lean up to embrace the naked flesh.

Unkempt about those hedges blows
An English unofficial rose;
And there the unregulated sun
Slopes down to rest when day is done,
And wakes a vague, unpunctual star,
A slippered Hesper; and there are
Meads toward Haslingfield and Coton
Where *das Betreten's* not *verboten.*

I only know that you may lie
Day long and watch the Cambridge sky,
And, flower-lulled in sleepy grass,
Hear the cool lapse of hours pass,
Until the centuries blend and blur
In Grantchester, in Grantchester. . . .
Still in the dawnlit waters cool
His ghostly Lordship swims his pool,
And tries the strokes, essays the tricks,
Long learnt on Hellespont, or Styx.
Dan Chaucer hears his river still
Chatter beneath a phantom mill.

Tennyson notes, with studious eye,
How Cambridge waters hurry by. . . .
And in that garden, black and white,
Creep whispers through the grass all night;
And spectral dance, before the dawn,
A hundred vicars down the lawn;
Curates, long dust, will come and go
On lissom, clerical, printless toe;
And oft between the boughs is seen
The sly shade of a Rural Dean. . . .
Till, at a shiver in the skies,
Vanishing with Satanic cries,
The prim ecclesiastical rout
Leaves but a startled sleeper-out,
Gray heavens, the first bird's drowsy calls,
The falling house that never falls. . . .

    Ah God! to see the branches stir
Across the moon at Grantchester!
To smell the thrilling-sweet and rotten
Unforgettable, unforgotten
River-smell, and hear the breeze
Sobbing in the little trees.
Say, do the elm-clumps greatly stand
Still guardians of that holy land?
The chestnuts shade, in reverend dream,
The yet unacademic stream?
Is dawn a secret shy and cold
Anadyomene, silver-gold?
And sunset still a golden sea
From Haslingfield to Madingley?
And after, ere the night is born,
Do hares come out about the corn?
Oh, is the water sweet and cool,
Gentle and brown, above the pool?
And laughs the immortal river still

Under the mill, under the mill?
Say, is there Beauty yet to find?
And Certainty? And Quiet kind?
Deep meadows yet, for to forget
The lies, and truths, and pain? . . . oh! yet
Stands the Church clock at ten to three?
And is there honey still for tea?

RUPERT BROOKE

In the Highlands

In the highlands, in the country places,
Where the old plain men have rosy faces,
      And the young fair maidens
            Quiet eyes;
Where essential silence cheers and blesses,
And for ever in the hill-recesses
      Her more lovely music
            Broods and dies.—

O to mount again where erst I haunted;
Where the old red hills are bird-enchanted,
      And the low green meadows
            Bright with sward;
And when even dies, the million-tinted,
And the night has come, and planets glinted,
      Lo, the valley hollow
            Lamp-bestarred!

O to dream, O to awake and wander
There, and with delight to take and render,
      Through the trance of silence,
            Quiet breath!
Lo! for there, among the flowers and grasses,
Only the mightier movement sounds and passes;
      Only winds and rivers,
            Life and Death.

ROBERT LOUIS STEVENSON

The Lake Isle of Innisfree

I will arise and go now, and go to Innisfree,
And a small cabin build there, of clay and wattles made;
Nine bean rows will I have there, a hive for the honey bee,
    And live alone in the bee-loud glade.

And I shall have some peace there, for peace comes dropping
        slow,
Dropping from the veils of the morning to where the cricket
        sings;
There midnight's all a glimmer, and noon a purple glow,
    And evening full of the linnet's wings.

I will arise and go now, for always night and day
I hear lake water lapping with low sounds by the shore;
While I stand on the roadway, or on the pavements gray,
    I hear it in the deep heart's core.

W. B. YEATS

Recessional

God of our fathers, known of old—
    Lord of our far-flung battle line—
Beneath whose awful hand we hold
    Dominion over palm and pine—
Lord God of Hosts, be with us yet,
    Lest we forget—lest we forget!

The tumult and the shouting dies—
    The Captains and the Kings depart—
Still stands Thine ancient sacrifice,
    An humble and a contrite heart.
Lord God of Hosts, be with us yet,
    Lest we forget—lest we forget!

Far-called, our navies melt away—
    On dune and headland sinks the fire—

Lo, all our pomp of yesterday
　　Is one with Nineveh and Tyre!
Judge of the Nations, spare us yet,
　　Lest we forget—lest we forget!

If, drunk with sight of power, we loose
　　Wild tongues that have not Thee in awe—
Such boasting as the Gentiles use,
　　Or lesser breeds without the Law—
Lord God of Hosts, be with us yet,
　　Lest we forget—lest we forget!

For heathen heart that puts her trust
　　In reeking tube and iron shard—
All valiant dust that builds on dust,
　　And guarding, calls not Thee to guard,—
For frantic boast and foolish word,
　　Thy mercy on Thy people, Lord!

RUDYARD KIPLING

BOOK EIGHT

America Singing

The Memories and the Portents

The first American poets were here before the Pilgrims or the Conquistadores arrived, and those who understand their tongues assure us that they were and are great poets. But to transmute their rhythms into English requires more than a translation of words; it demands an interpretation of a cosmos. Natalie Curtis, Mary Austin and others who have translated "Amerind" poetry took vast liberties with Indian texts, and produced results as patently Anglo-Saxon, in a different way, as Longfellow's "Hiawatha." The one American Indian poem here included is scrupulously Indian, though it was called a "free translation" by its transcriber, an anthropologist of distinction as well, obviously, as a poet.

We have ballads to remind us of the white man's past on this continent. Some of them were written by poets in their studies. Some were composed as songs for the stage. Some grew, as folk songs do, out of everyday experience. Most of them deal with life in the open spaces, in a premachine age.

An odd little group of railroad poems is embedded in this section, but, though the names of the authors of the others are more famous, the words of "Casey Jones," supposedly

written by Casey's Negro fireman, are certainly the most familiar. All of them deal with the steam-engine age, already almost as remote as the horse-and-buggy age.

Our American skylines are often described as poetry in stone and steel, but when Hart Crane attempted to put Manhattan Island and Brooklyn Bridge into poetry, he had to go back to Rip Van Winkle. The modern American cities are still waiting for their poets.

I Hear America Singing

I hear America singing, the varied carols I hear,
Those of mechanics, each one singing his as it should be blithe
      and strong,
The carpenter singing his as he measures his plank or beam,
The mason singing his as he makes ready for work, or leaves
      off work,
The boatman singing what belongs to him in his boat, the
      deck-hand singing on the steamboat deck,
The shoemaker singing as he sits on his bench, the hatter sing-
      ing as he stands,
The wood-cutter's song, the ploughboy's on his way in the
      morning, or at noon intermission or at sundown,
The delicious singing of the mother, or of the young wife at
      work, or of the girl sewing or washing,
Each singing what belongs to him or her and to none else,
The day what belongs to the day—at night the party of young
      fellows, robust, friendly,
Singing with open mouths their strong melodious songs.

WALT WHITMAN

Dawn Boy's Song

Where my kindred dwell, there I wander.
Child of the White Corn am I, there I wander.
The Red Rock House, there I wander.
Where dark prayer-sticks are at the doorway, there I wander.
With the pollen of dawn upon my trail. There I wander.
At the altar, the striped cotton hangs with pollen. There I
      wander.
Going around with it. There I wander.
Taking another, I depart with it. With it I wander.
In the house of long life, there I wander.
In the house of happiness, there I wander.
Beauty before me, with it I wander.
Beauty behind me, with it I wander.

247

Beauty below me, with it I wander.
Beauty above me, with it I wander.
In old age travelling, with it I wander.
On the beautiful trail am I, with it I wander.

A NAVAHO CHANT

TRANSLATED BY WASHINGTON MATTHEWS

(In the ancient days, a Navaho explained to Washington Matthews more than a half century ago, you climbed up from the ground to the White House on a rainbow. You cannot climb that way now. In those days Hastseyalti instructed Dawn Boy how to get there, taught him the prayers and songs he must know, and what sacrifices he must make—fragments of turquoise and white shell, corn and larkspur pollen. When Dawn Boy got his first view of the White House he began to sing, and a rainbow appeared, and as Dawn Boy walked on the rainbow a great wind began to blow, raising a dust that blinded the lightnings, bears and snakes, sentinels at the White House, so that Dawn Boy could enter sprinkling pollen on a trail of daylight, showing his gifts and singing this song.)

Hiawatha's Childhood

(FROM *The Song of Hiawatha*)

Downward through the evening twilight,
In the days that are forgotten,
In the unremembered ages,
From the full moon fell Nokomis,
She a wife, but not a mother.

She was sporting with her women,
Swinging in a swing of grape-vines,
When her rival, the rejected,
Full of jealousy and hatred,
Cut the leafy swing asunder,
Cut in twain the twisted grape-vines,
And Nokomis fell affrighted
Downward through the evening twilight,
On the Muskoday, the meadow,
On the prairie full of blossoms.
"See! a star falls!" said the people;
"From the sky a star is falling!"

There among the ferns and mosses,
There among the prairie lilies,
On the Muskoday, the meadow,
In the moonlight and the starlight,
Fair Nokomis bore a daughter.
And she called her name Wenonah,
As the first-born of her daughters.
And the daughter of Nokomis
Grew up like the prairie lilies,
Grew a tall and slender maiden,
With the beauty of the moonlight,
With the beauty of the starlight.

And Nokomis warned her often,
Saying oft, and oft repeating,
"O, beware of Mudjekeewis,
Of the West-Wind, Mudjekeewis;
Listen not to what he tells you;
Lie not down upon the meadow,
Stoop not down among the lilies,
Lest the West-Wind come and harm you!"

But she heeded not the warning,
Heeded not those words of wisdom,
And the West-Wind came at evening,
Walking lightly o'er the prairie,
Whispering to the leaves and blossoms,
Bending low the flowers and grasses,
Found the beautiful Wenonah,
Lying there among the lilies,
Wooed her with his words of sweetness,
Wooed her with his soft caresses,
Till she bore a son in sorrow,
Bore a son of love and sorrow.

Thus was born my Hiawatha,
Thus was born the child of wonder,
But the daughter of Nokomis,

Hiawatha's gentle mother,
In her anguish died deserted
By the West-Wind, false and faithless,
By the heartless Mudjekeewis.

       •   •   •

By the shores of Gitche Gumee,
By the shining Big-Sea-Water,
Stood the wigwam of Nokomis,
Daughter of the Moon, Nokomis.
Dark behind it rose the forest,
Rose the black and gloomy pine-trees,
Rose the firs with cones upon them;
Bright before it beat the water,
Beat the clear and shining water,
Beat the shining Big-Sea-Water.

There the wrinkled, old Nokomis
Nursed the little Hiawatha,
Rocked him in his linden cradle.
Bedded soft in moss and rushes,
Safely bound with reindeer sinews;
Stilled his fretful wail by saying
"Hush! the Naked Bear will hear thee!"
Lulled him into slumber, singing,
"Ewa-yea! my little owlet!
Who is this, that lights the wigwam?
With his great eyes lights the wigwam?
Ewa-yea! my little owlet!"

       •   •   •

At the door on summer evenings
Sat the little Hiawatha;
Heard the whispering of the pine-trees,
Heard the lapping of the water,
Sounds of music, words of wonder;
"Minne-wawa!" said the pine-trees,
"Mudway-aushka!" said the water.

Saw the fire-fly, Wah-wah-taysee,
Flitting through the dusk of evening,
With the twinkle of its candle
Lighting up the brakes and bushes,
And he sang the song of children,
Sang the song Nokomis taught him:
"Wah-wah-taysee, little fire-fly,
Little flitting, white-fire insect,
Little, dancing, white-fire creature,
Light me with your little candle,
Ere upon my bed I lay me,
Ere in sleep I close my eyelids!"

Saw the moon rise from the water
Rippling, rounding from the water,
Saw the flecks and shadows on it,
Whispered, "What is that, Nokomis?"
And the good Nokomis answered:
"Once a warrior, very angry,
Seized his grandmother, and threw her
Up into the sky at midnight;
Right against the moon he threw her;
'Tis her body that you see there."

Saw the rainbow in the heaven,
In the eastern sky the rainbow,
Whispered, "What is that, Nokomis?"
And the good Nokomis answered:
" 'Tis the heaven of flowers you see there;
All the wild-flowers of the forest,
All the lilies of the prairie,
When on earth they fade and perish,
Blossom in that heaven above us."

When he heard the owls at midnight,
Hooting, laughing, in the forest,
"What is that?" he cried in terror;
"What is that" he said, "Nokomis?"

And the good Nokomis answered:
"That is but the owl and owlet,
Talking in their native language,
Talking, scolding at each other."

Then the little Hiawatha
Learned of every bird its language,
Learned their names and all their secrets,
How they built their nests in Summer,
Where they hid themselves in Winter,
Talked with them whene'er he met them,
Called them "Hiawatha's Chickens."

Of all beasts he learned the language,
Learned their names and all their secrets,
How the beavers built their lodges,
Where the squirrels hid their acorns,
How the reindeer ran so swiftly,
Why the rabbit was so timid,
Talked with them whene'er he met them,
Called them "Hiawatha's Brothers." . . .

HENRY WADSWORTH LONGFELLOW

The Landing of the Pilgrim Fathers
(November 19, 1620)

The breaking waves dashed high
  On a stern and rock-bound coast,
And the woods, against a stormy sky,
  Their giant branches tossed;

And the heavy night hung dark
  The hills and waters o'er,
When a band of exiles moored their bark
  On the wild New England shore.

Not as the conqueror comes,
  They, the true-hearted, came:

Not with the roll of the stirring drums,
　　And the trumpet that sings of fame;

Not as the flying come,
　　In silence and in fear,—
They shook the depths of the desert's gloom
　　With their hymns of lofty cheer.

Amidst the storm they sang,
　　And the stars heard, and the sea;
And the sounding aisles of the dim woods rang
　　To the anthem of the free!

The ocean-eagle soared
　　From his nest by the white wave's foam,
And the rocking pines of the forest roared;
　　This was their welcome home!

There were men with hoary hair
　　Amidst that pilgrim-band;
Why had they come to wither there,
　　Away from their childhood's land?

There was woman's fearless eye,
　　Lit by her deep love's truth;
There was manhood's brow, serenely high,
　　And the fiery heart of youth.

What sought they thus afar?
　　Bright jewels of the mine?
The wealth of seas, the spoils of war?—
　　They sought a faith's pure shrine!

Aye, call it holy ground,
　　The soil where first they trod!
They have left unstained what there they found—
　　Freedom to worship God!

FELICIA D. HEMANS

253

Paul Revere's Ride

(April 18-19, 1775)

Listen, my children, and you shall hear
Of the midnight ride of Paul Revere,
On the eighteenth of April, in Seventy-five;
Hardly a man is now alive
Who remembers that famous day and year.

He said to his friend, "If the British march
By land or sea from the town tonight,
Hang a lantern aloft in the belfry arch
Of the North Church tower as a signal light,—
One, if by land, and two, if by sea;
And I on the opposite shore will be,
Ready to ride and spread the alarm
Through every Middlesex village and farm,
For the country folk to be up and to arm."

Then he said, "Good-night!" and with muffled oar
Silently rowed to the Charlestown shore,
Just as the moon rose over the bay,
Where swinging wide at her moorings lay
The Somerset, British man-of-war;
A phantom ship, with each mast and spar
Across the moon like a prison bar,
And a huge black hulk, that was magnified
By its own reflection in the tide.

PAUSE.

Meanwhile, his friend, through alley and street,
Wanders and watches with eager ears,
Till in the silence around him he hears
The muster of men at the barrack door,
The sound of arms, and the tramp of feet,
And the measured tread of the grenadiers,
Marching down to their boats on the shore.

Then he climbed the tower of the Old North Church,
By the wooden stairs, with stealthy tread,

To the belfry-chamber overhead,
And startled the pigeons from their perch
On the sombre rafters, that round him made
Masses and moving shapes of shade,—
By the trembling ladder, steep and tall,
To the highest window in the wall,
Where he paused to listen and look down
A moment on the roofs of the town,
And the moonlight flowing over all.

Beneath in the churchyard, lay the dead,
In their night-encampment on the hill,
Wrapped in silence so deep and still
That he could hear, like a sentinel's tread,
The watchful night-wind, as it went
Creeping along from tent to tent,
And seeming to whisper, "All is well!"
A moment only he feels the spell
Of the place and the hour, and the secret dread
Of the lonely belfry and the dead;
For suddenly all his thoughts are bent
On a shadowy something far away,
Where the river widens to meet the bay,—
A line of black that bends and floats
On the rising tide, like a bridge of boats.

Meanwhile, impatient to mount and ride,
Booted and spurred, with a heavy stride
On the opposite shore walked Paul Revere.
Now he patted his horse's side,
Now gazed at the landscape far and near,
Then, impetuous, stamped the earth,
And turned and tightened his saddle-girth;
But mostly he watched with eager search
The belfry-tower of the Old North Church,
As it rose above the graves on the hill,
Lonely and spectral and sombre and still.
And lo! as he looks, on the belfry's height

A glimmer, and then a gleam of light!
He springs to the saddle, the bridle he turns,
But lingers and gazes, till full on his sight
A second lamp in the belfry burns!

A hurry of hoofs in a village street,
A shape in the moonlight, a bulk in the dark,
And beneath, from the pebbles, in passing, a spark
Struck out by a steed flying fearless and fleet:
That was all! And yet, through the gloom and the light,
The fate of a nation was riding that night;
And the spark struck out by that steed, in his flight,
Kindled the land into flame with its heat.

He has left the village and mounted the steep,
And beneath him, tranquil and broad and deep,
Is the Mystic, meeting the ocean tides;
And under the alders that skirt its edge,
Now soft on the sand, now loud on the ledge,
Is heard the tramp of his steed as he rides.

It was twelve by the village clock
When he crossed the bridge into Medford town.
He heard the crowing of the cock,
And the barking of the farmer's dog,
And felt the damp of the river fog,
That rises after the sun goes down.

It was one by the village clock,
When he galloped into Lexington.
He saw the gilded weathercock
Swim in the moonlight as he passed.
And the meeting-house windows blank and bare,
Gaze at him with a spectral glare,
As if they already stood aghast
At the bloody work they would look upon.

It was two by the village clock,
When he came to the bridge in Concord town.
He heard the bleating of the flock,

And the twitter of birds among the trees,
And felt the breath of the morning breeze
Blowing over the meadows brown.
And one was safe and asleep in his bed
Who at the bridge would be first to fall,
Who that day would be lying dead
Pierced by a British musket-ball.

You know the rest. In the books you have read,
How the British Regulars fired and fled,—
How the farmers gave them ball for ball,
From behind each fence and farm-yard wall,
Chasing the red-coats down the lane,
Then crossing the fields to emerge again
Under the trees at the turn of the road,
And only pausing to fire and load.

So through the night rode Paul Revere;
And so through the night went his cry of alarm
To every Middlesex village and farm,—
A cry of defiance and not of fear,
A voice in the darkness, a knock at the door,
And a word that shall echo forevermore!
For, borne on the night-wind of the past,
Through all our history, to the last,
In the hour of darkness and peril and need,
The people will waken and listen to hear
The hurrying hoof-beats of that steed,
And the midnight message of Paul Revere.

HENRY WADSWORTH LONGFELLOW

Nancy Hanks

If Nancy Hanks
Came back as a ghost,
Seeking news
Of what she loved most,
She'd ask first

"Where's my son?
What's happened to Abe
What's he done?

"Poor little Abe,
Left all alone
Except for Tom,
Who's a rolling stone;
He was only nine
The year I died.
I remember still
How hard he cried.

"Scraping along
In a little shack,
With hardly a shirt
To cover his back,
And a prairie wind
To blow him down,
Or pinching times
If he went to town.

"You wouldn't know
About my son?
Did he grow tall?
Did he have fun?
Did he learn to read?
Did he get to town?
Do you know his name?
Did he get on?"

ROSEMARY BENÉT

Barbara Frietchie

Up from the meadows rich with corn,
Clear in the cool September morn,

The clustered spires of Frederick stand
Green-walled by the hills of Maryland.

Round about them orchards sweep,
Apple and peach tree fruited deep,

Fair as the garden of the Lord
To the eyes of the famished rebel horde,

On that pleasant morn of the early fall
When Lee marched over the mountain-wall;

Over the mountains winding down,
Horse and foot, into Frederick town.

Forty flags with their silver stars,
Forty flags with their crimson bars,

Flapped in the morning wind: the sun
Of noon looked down, and saw not one.

Up rose old Barbara Frietchie then,
Bowed with her fourscore years and ten;

Bravest of all in Frederick town,
She took up the flag the men hauled down;

In her attic window the staff she set,
To show that one heart was loyal yet.

Up the street came the rebel tread,
Stonewall Jackson riding ahead.

Under his slouched hat left and right
He glanced; the old flag met his sight.

"Halt!"—the dust-brown ranks stood fast.
"Fire!"—out blazed the rifle-blast.

It shivered the window, pane and sash;
It rent the banner with seam and gash.

Quick, as it fell, from the broken staff
Dame Barbara snatched the silken scarf.

She leaned far out on the window-sill,
And shook it forth with a royal will.

"Shoot, if you must, this old gray head,
But spare your country's flag," she said.

A shade of sadness, a blush of shame,
Over the face of the leader came;

The nobler nature within him stirred
To life at that woman's deed and word;

"Who touches a hair of yon gray head
Dies like a dog! March on!" he said.

All day long through Frederick street
Sounded the tread of marching feet:

All day long that free flag tossed
Over the heads of the rebel host.

Ever its torn folds rose and fell
On the loyal winds that loved it well;

And through the hill-gaps sunset light
Shone over it with a warm good-night.

Barbara Frietchie's work is o'er,
And the Rebel rides on his raids no more.

Honor to her! and let a tear
Fall, for her sake, on Stonewall's bier.

Over Barbara Frietchie's grave,
Flag of Freedom and Union, wave!

Peace and order and beauty draw
Round thy symbol of light and law;

And ever the stars above look down
On thy stars below in Frederick town!

JOHN GREENLEAF WHITTIER

Sheridan's Ride

(October 19, 1864)

Up from the South, at break of day,
Bringing to Winchester fresh dismay,
The affrighted air with a shudder bore,
Like a herald in haste, to the chieftain's door,
The terrible grumble, and rumble, and roar,
Telling the battle was on once more,
   And Sheridan twenty miles away.

And wider still those billows of war
Thundered along the horizon's bar;
And louder yet into Winchester rolled
The roar of that red sea uncontrolled,
Making the blood of the listener cold,
As he thought of the stake in that fiery fray,
   And Sheridan twenty miles away.

But there is a road from Winchester town,
A good, broad highway leading down:
And there, through the flush of the morning light,
A steed as black as the steeds of night
Was seen to pass, as with eagle flight;
As if he knew the terrible need,
He stretched away with his utmost speed;
Hills rose and fell, but his heart was gay,
   With Sheridan fifteen miles away.

Still sprang from those swift hoofs, thundering south,
The dust, like smoke from the cannon's mouth,
Or the trail of a comet, sweeping faster and faster,
Foreboding to traitors the doom of disaster.
The heart of the steed and the heart of the master
Were beating like prisoners assaulting their walls,
Impatient to be where the battle-field calls;
Every nerve of the charger was strained to full play,
   With Sheridan only ten miles away.

Under his spurning feet, the road
Like an arrowy Alpine river flowed,
And the landscape sped away behind
Like an ocean flying before the wind;
And the steed, like a bark fed with furnace ire,
Swept on, with his wild eye full of fire;
But lo! he is nearing his heart's desire;
He is snuffing the smoke of the roaring fray,
   With Sheridan only five miles away.

The first that the general saw were the groups
Of stragglers, and then the retreating troops;
What was done? what to do? a glance told him both,
Then, striking his spurs, with a terrible oath,
He dashed down the line, 'mid a storm of huzzas,
And the wave of retreat checked its course there, because
The sight of the master compelled it to pause.
With foam and with dust the black charger was gray;
By the flash of his eye, and the red nostril's play,
He seemed to the whole great army to say:
"I have brought you Sheridan all the way
   From Winchester town to save the day!"

Hurrah! hurrah for Sheridan!
Hurrah! hurrah for horse and man!
And when their statues are placed on high,
Under the dome of the Union sky,
The American soldier's Temple of Fame,
There, with the glorious general's name,
Be it said, in letters both bold and bright:
"Here is the steed that saved the day
By carrying Sheridan into the fight,
   From Winchester—twenty miles away!"

THOMAS BUCHANAN READ

O Captain! My Captain!

O Captain! my Captain! our fearful trip is done,
The ship has weather'd every rack, the prize we sought is won,
The port is near, the bells I hear, the people all exulting,
While follow eyes the steady keel, the vessel grim and daring;
    But O heart! heart! heart!
      O the bleeding drops of red,
        Where on the deck my Captain lies,
        Fallen cold and dead.

O Captain! my Captain! rise up and hear the bells;
Rise up—for you the flag is flung—for you the bugle trills,
For you bouquets and ribbon'd wreaths—for you the shores
                  a-crowding,
For you they call, the swaying mass, their eager faces turning;
    Here Captain! dear father!
      The arm beneath your head!
        It is some dream that on the deck,
        You've fallen cold and dead.

My Captain does not answer, his lips are pale and still,
My father does not feel my arm, he has no pulse nor will,
The ship is anchor'd safe and sound, its voyage closed and done,
From fearful trip the victor ship comes in with object won;
    Exult O shores, and ring O bells!
      But I with mournful tread,
        Walk the deck my Captain lies
        Fallen cold and dead.

WALT WHITMAN

Abraham Lincoln Walks at Midnight

(in Springfield, Illinois)

It is portentous, and a thing of state
That here at midnight, in our little town
A mourning figure walks, and will not rest,
Near the old court-house pacing up and down.

Or by his homestead, or in shadowed yards
He lingers where his children used to play,
Or through the market, on the well-worn stones
He stalks until the dawn-stars burn away.

A bronzed, lank man! His suit of ancient black,
A famous high top-hat and plain worn shawl
Make him the quaint great figure that men love,
The prairie-lawyer, master of us all.

He cannot sleep upon his hillside now.
He is among us:—as in times before!
And we who toss and lie awake for long,
Breathe deep, and start, to see him pass the door.

His head is bowed. He thinks of men and kings.
Yea, when the sick world cries, how can he sleep?
Too many peasants fight, they know not why;
Too many homesteads in black terror weep.

The sins of all the war-lords burn his heart.
He sees the dreadnaughts scouring every main.
He carries on his shawl-wrapped shoulders now
The bitterness, the folly and the pain.

He cannot rest until a spirit-dawn
Shall come;—the shining hope of Europe free:
The league of sober folk, the workers' earth
Bringing long peace to Cornland, Alp and Sea.

It breaks his heart that kings must murder still,
That all his hours of travail here for men
Seem yet in vain. And who will bring white peace
That he may sleep upon his hill again?

VACHEL LINDSAY

The New Colossus
(written in aid of the Statue of Liberty Fund, 1883)

Not like the brazen giant of Greek fame
With conquering limbs astride from land to land;
Here at our sea-washed, sunset gates shall stand
A mighty woman with a torch, whose flame
Is the imprisoned lightning, and her name
Mother of Exiles. From her beacon-hand
Glows world-wide welcome; her mild eyes command
The air-bridged harbor that twin cities frame.
"Keep, ancient lands, your storied pomp!" cries she
With silent lips. "Give me your tired, your poor,
Your huddled masses yearning to breathe free,
The wretched refuse of your teeming shore.
Send these, the homeless, tempest-tossed to me,
I lift my lamp beside the golden door!"

EMMA LAZARUS

The Railroad

What's the railroad to me?
I never go to see
Where it ends.
It fills a few hollows,
And makes banks for the swallows,
It sets the sand a-blowing,
And the blackberries a-growing.

HENRY DAVID THOREAU

The Railway Train

I like to see it lap the miles,
And lick the valleys up,
And stop to feed itself at tanks;
And then, prodigious, step

Around a pile of mountains,
And, supercilious, peer
In shanties by the side of roads;
And then a quarry pare

To fit its sides, and crawl between,
Complaining all the while
In horrid, hooting stanza;
Then chase itself down hill

And neigh like Boanerges;
Then, punctual as a star,
Stop—docile and omnipotent—
At its own stable door.

EMILY DICKINSON

To a Locomotive in Winter

Thee for my recitative,
Thee in the driving storm even as now, the snow, the winter-
    day declining,
Thee in thy panoply, thy measur'd dual throbbing and thy beat
    convulsive,
Thy black cylindric body, golden brass and silvery steel,
Thy ponderous side-bars, parallel and connecting rods, gyrat-
    ing, shuttling at thy sides,
Thy metrical, now swelling pant and roar, now tapering in the
    distance,
Thy great protruding head-light fix'd in front,
Thy long, pale, floating vapor-pennants, tinged with delicate
    purple,
The dense and murky clouds out-belching from thy smoke-
    stack,
Thy knitted frame, thy springs and valves, the tremulous
    twinkle of thy wheels,
Thy train of cars behind, obedient, merrily following,
Through gale or calm, now swift, now slack, yet steadily
    careering;

Type of the modern—emblem of motion and power—pulse of
      the continent,
For once come serve the Muse and merge in verse, even as here
      I see thee,
With storm and buffeting gusts of wind and falling snow,
By day thy warning ringing bell to sound its notes,
By night thy silent signal lamps to swing.
Fierce-throated beauty!
Roll through my chant with all thy lawless music, thy swinging
      lamps at night,
Thy madly-whistled laughter, echoing, rumbling like an earth-
      quake, rousing all,
Law of thyself complete, thine own track firmly holding,

(No sweetness debonair of tearful harp or glib piano thine,)
Thy trills of shrieks by rocks and hills return'd,
Launch'd o'er the prairies wide, across the lakes,
To the free skies unpent and glad and strong.

W A L T   W H I T M A N

Casey Jones

Come, all you rounders, if you want to hear
A story 'bout a brave engineer.
Casey Jones was the rounder's name
On a six-eight wheeler, boys, he won his fame.
The caller called Casey at a half past four,
Kissed his wife at the station door,
Mounted to the cabin with his orders in his hand
And he took his farewell trip to that promised land:

    Casey Jones, mounted to the cabin,
    Casey Jones, with his orders in his hand,
    Casey Jones, mounted to the cabin,
    And he took his farewell trip to the promised land.

"Put in your water and shovel in your coal,
Put your head out the window, watch them drivers roll,
I'll run her till she leaves the rail

'Cause I'm eight hours late with the western mail."
He looked at his watch and his watch was slow,
He looked at the water and the water was low,
He turned to his fireman and then he said,
"We're goin' to reach Frisco, but we'll all be dead:"

 Casey Jones, goin' to reach Frisco,
 Casey Jones, but we'll all be dead,
 Casey Jones, goin' to reach Frisco,
 "We're goin' to reach Frisco, but we'll all be dead."

Casey pulled up that Reno Hill,
He tooted for the crossing with an awful shrill,
The switchman knew by the engine's moan
That the man at the throttle was Casey Jones.
He pulled up within two miles of the place
Number Four stared him right in the face.
He turned to the fireman, said "Boy, you'd better jump,
'Cause there's two locomotives that's a-goin' to bump."

 Casey Jones, two locomotives,
 Casey Jones, that's a-goin' to bump,
 Casey Jones, two locomotives,
 "There's two locomotives that's a-goin' to bump."

Casey said just before he died,
"There's two more roads that I'd like to ride."
The fireman said what could they be?
"The Southern Pacific and the Santa Fe."
Mrs. Casey sat on her bed a-sighin',
Just received a message that Casey was dyin'.
Said, "Go to bed, children, and hush your cryin',
'Cause you got another papa on the Salt Lake Line:"

 Mrs. Casey Jones, got another papa,
 Mrs. Casey Jones, on that Salt Lake Line,
 Mrs. Casey Jones, got another papa,
 "And you've got another papa on the Salt Lake Line."

Attributed to T. LAWRENCE SEIBERT

Bury Me Not on the Lone Prairie

"O bury me not on the lone prairie,"
These words came low and mournfully
From the pallid lips of a youth who lay
On his dying bed at the close of day. . . .

"O bury me not on the lone prairie
Where the wild coyote will howl o'er me.
In a narrow grave just six by three,
O bury me not on the lone prairie. . . .

"O bury me not on the lone prairie
Where the buffalo paws o'er the prairie sea,
Where the buzzard sails and the wind goes free—
O bury me not on the lone prairie. . . ."

But we buried him there on the lone prairie,
Where the owl all night hoots mournfully,
And the blizzard beats and the wind blows free
O'er his lonely grave on the lone prairie.

ANONYMOUS

Van Winkle
(FROM *The Bridge*)

Macadam, gun-grey as the tunny's belt,
Leaps from Far Rockaway to Golden Gate:
Listen! the miles a hurdy-gurdy grinds—
Down gold arpeggios mile on mile unwinds.

Times earlier, when you hurried off to school
—It is the same hour though a later day—
You walked with Pizarro in a copybook,
And Cortez rode up, reining tautly in—
Firmly as coffee grips the taste,—and away!

There was Priscilla's cheek close in the wind,
And Captain Smith, all beard and certainty,

And Rip Van Winkle bowing by the way,—
"Is this Sleepy Hollow, friend—?" And he—

And Rip forgot the office hours,
                    and he forgot the pay;
        Van Winkle sweeps a tenement
                    way down on Avenue A,—

The grind-organ says . . . Remember, remember
The cinder pile at the end of the backyard
Where we stoned the family of young
Garter snakes under . . . And the monoplanes
We launched—with paper wings and twisted
Rubber bands . . . Recall—recall
                    the rapid tongues
That flittered from under the ash heap day
After day whenever your stick discovered
Some sunning inch of unsuspecting fibre—
It flashed back at your thrust, as clean as fire.

And Rip was slowly made aware
        that he, Van Winkle, was not here
    nor there. He woke and swore he'd seen Broadway
        a Catskill daisy chain in May—

So memory, that strikes a rhyme out of a box
Or splits a random smell of flowers through glass—
Is it the whip stripped from the lilac tree
One day in spring my father took to me,
Or is it the Sabbatical, unconscious smile
My mother almost brought me once from church,
And once only, as I recall—?

It flickered through the snow screen, blindly
It forsook her at the doorway, it was gone
Before I had left the window. It
Did not return with the kiss in the hall.

Macadam, gun-grey as the tunny's belt,
Leaps from Far Rockaway to Golden Gate . . .

Keep hold of that nickel for car-change, Rip,—
Have you got your *"Times"*—?
And hurry along, Van Winkle—it's getting late!

HART CRANE

Chicago

Hog Butcher for the World,
Tool Maker, Stacker of Wheat,
Player with Railroads and the Nation's Freight Handler;
Stormy, husky, brawling,
City of the Big Shoulders:
They tell me you are wicked and I believe them, for I have seen
      your painted women under the gas lamps luring the
      farm boys.
And they tell me you are crooked and I answer: Yes, it is true
      I have seen the gunman kill and go free to kill again.
And they tell me you are brutal and my reply is: On the faces
      of women and children I have seen the marks of
      wanton hunger.
And having answered so I turn once more to those who sneer
      at this my city, and I give them back the sneer and
      I say to them:
Come and show me another city with lifted head singing so
      proud to be alive and coarse and strong and cunning.
Flinging magnetic curses amid the toil of piling job on job,
      here is a tall bold slugger set vivid against the little
      soft cities;
Fierce as a dog with tongue lapping for action, cunning as a
      savage pitted against the wilderness,
      Bareheaded,
      Shoveling,
      Wrecking,
      Planning,
      Building, breaking, rebuilding.
Under the smoke, dust all over his mouth, laughing with white
      teeth,

Under the terrible burden of destiny laughing as a young man
    laughs,
Laughing even as an ignorant fighter laughs who has never lost
    a battle,
Bragging and laughing that under his wrist is the pulse, and
    under his ribs the heart of the people,
                                   Laughing!
Laughing the stormy, husky, brawling laughter of Youth, half-
    naked, sweating, proud to be Hog Butcher, Tool
    Maker, Stacker of Wheat, Player with Railroads and
    Freight Handler to the Nation.

CARL SANDBURG

My Old Kentucky Home

The sun shines bright in the old Kentucky home;
   'Tis summer, the darkeys are gay;
The corn-top's ripe, and the meadow's in the bloom,
   While the birds make music all the day.
The young folks roll on the little cabin floor,
   All merry, all happy and bright;
By-'n'-by hard times comes a-knocking at the door:—
   Then my old Kentucky home, good-night!

They hunt no more for the possum and the coon,
   On the meadow, the hill and the shore;
They sing no more by the glimmer of the moon,
   On the bench by the old cabin door.
The day goes by like a shadow o'er the heart,
   With sorrow, where all was delight;
The time has come when the darkeys have to part:—
   Then my old Kentucky home, good-night!

The head must bow, and the back will have to bend,
   Wherever the darkey may go;
A few more days and the troubles all will end,
   In the field where the sugar-canes grow.

A few more days for to tote the weary load,—
   No matter, 'twill never be light;
A few more days till we totter on the road:—
   Then my old Kentucky home, good-night!

      Weep no more, my lady,
         O, weep no more to-day!
      We will sing one song for the old Kentucky home,
         For the old Kentucky home, far away.

STEPHEN FOSTER

Old Virginny

Carry me back to old Virginny,
There's where the cotton and the corn and taters grow;
There's where the birds warble sweet in the springtime,
There's where this old darky's* heart am long'd to go,
There's where I labored all day in the cotton,
There's where I worked in the fields of yellow corn,
No place on earth do I love more sincerely,
Than old Virginny, the state where I was born.

Carry me back to old Virginny,
There let me live till I wither and decay;
Long by the old Dismal Swamp have I wandered,
There's where this old darky's life will pass away.
Massa and Missus have gone long before me,
Soon we will meet on that bright and golden shore,
There we'll be happy and free from all sorrow,
There's where we'll meet and we'll never part no more.

JAMES A. BLAND

* The author (and composer) of this, the state song of Virginia, was the
son of a slave.

What Is Africa to Me?

(FROM *Heritage*)

What is Africa to me:
Copper sun or scarlet sea,
Jungle star or jungle track,
Strong bronzed men, or regal black
Women from whose loins I sprang
When the birds of Eden sang?
One three centuries removed
From the scenes his fathers loved,
Spicy grove, cinnamon tree,
What is Africa to me?

So I lie, who all day long
Want no sound except the song
Sung by wild barbaric birds
Goading massive jungle herds,
Juggernauts of flesh that pass
Trampling tall defiant grass
Where young forest lovers lie,
Plighting troth beneath the sky.
So I lie, who always hear,
Though I cram against my ear
Both my thumbs, and keep them there,
Great drums throbbing through the air.
So I lie, whose fount of pride,
Dear distress, and joy allied,
Is my somber flesh and skin,
With the dark blood dammed within
Like great pulsing tides of wine
That, I fear, must burst the fine
Channels of the chafing net
Where they surge and foam and fret.

Africa? A book one thumbs
Listlessly, till slumber comes.
Unremembered are her bats

Circling through the night, her cats
Crouching in the river reeds,
Stalking gentle flesh that feeds
By the river brink; no more
Does the bugle-throated roar
Cry that monarch claws have leapt
From the scabbards where they slept.
Silver snakes that once a year
Doff the lovely coats you wear,
Seek no covert in your fear
Lest a mortal eye should see;
What's your nakedness to me?
Here no leprous flowers rear
Fierce corollas in the air;
Here no bodies sleek and wet
Dripping mingled rain and sweat,
Tread the savage measures of
Jungle boys and girls in love.

What is last year's snow to me,
Last year's anything? The tree
Budding yearly must forget
How its past arose or set—
Bough and blossom, flower, fruit,
Even what shy bird with mute

Wonder at her travail there,
Meekly labored in its hair.
One three centuries removed
From the scenes his fathers loved,
Spicy grove, cinnamon tree,
What is Africa to me?

COUNTEE CULLEN

Droning a drowsy syncopated tune,
Rocking back and forth to a mellow croon,
   I heard a Negro play.
Down on Lenox Avenue the other night
By the pale dull pallor of an old gas light
   He did a lazy sway. . . .
   He did a lazy sway. . . .
To the tune o' those Weary Blues.
With his ebony hands on each ivory key
He made that poor piano moan with melody.
   O Blues!
Swaying to and fro on his rickety stool
He played that sweet raggy tune like a musical fool.
   Sweet Blues!
Coming from a black man's soul.
   O Blues!
In a deep song voice with a melancholy tone
I heard that Negro sing, that old piano moan—
   "Ain't got nobody in all this world,
   Ain't got nobody but ma self.
   I's gwine to quit ma frownin'
   And put ma troubles on the shelf."
Thump, thump, thump went his foot on the floor.
He played a few chords then he sang some more—
   "I got the Weary Blues
   And I can't be satisfied.
   Got the Weary Blues
   And can't be satisfied—
   I ain't happy no mo'
   And I wish that I had died."
And far into the night he crooned that tune.
The stars went out and so did the moon.
The singer stopped playing and went to bed
While the Weary Blues echoed through his head.
He slept like a rock or a man that's dead.

LANGSTON HUGHES

If We Must Die

If we must die—let it not be like hogs
Hunted and penned in an inglorious spot,
While round us bark the mad and hungry dogs,
Making their mark at our accursèd lot.
If we must die—oh, let us nobly die,
So that our precious blood may not be shed
In vain; then even the monsters we defy
Shall be constrained to honor us though dead:
Oh, kinsmen! We must meet the common foe;
Though far outnumbered, let us still be brave,
And for their thousand blows deal one death-blow!
What though before us lies the open grave?
Like men we'll face the murderous, cowardly pack,
Pressed to the wall, dying, but—fighting back!

CLAUDE MCKAY

Lift Every Voice and Sing

Lift every voice and sing
Till earth and heaven ring,
Ring with the harmonies of Liberty;
Let our rejoicing rise
High as the listening skies,
Let it resound loud as the rolling sea.
Sing a song full of the faith that the dark past has taught us,
Sing a song full of the hope that the present has brought us.
Facing the rising sun of our new day begun,
Let us march on till victory is won.

Stony the road we trod,
Bitter the chastening rod,
Felt in the days when hope unborn had died;
Yet with a steady beat,
Have not our weary feet
Come to the place for which our fathers sighed?

277

We have come over a way that with tears has been watered,
We have come, treading our path through the blood of the
      slaughtered,
Out from the gloomy past
Till now we stand at last
Where the white gleam of our bright star is cast.

God of our weary years,
God of our silent tears,
Thou who hast brought us thus far on the way;
Thou who hast by Thy might
Led us into the light,
Keep us forever in the path, we pray.
Lest our feet stray from the places, our God, where we met
      Thee,
Lest our hearts drunk with the wine of the world, we forget
      Thee;
Shadowed beneath Thy hand,
May we forever stand.
True to our God, True to our native land.

JAMES WELDON JOHNSON

(This poem was written for a Lincoln's birthday celebration in Jacksonville, Florida, in 1900, set to music by the author's brother, J. Rosamond Johnson, and sung by a chorus of five hundred Negro children. The song was mimeographed for the occasion, but remembered and spread far beyond Jacksonville. Someone dubbed it the "Negro National Hymn," and today it is sung by millions.)

America the Beautiful

O beautiful for spacious skies,
    For amber waves of grain,
For purple mountain majesties
    Above the fruited plain!
      America! America!
    God shed His grace on thee,
And crown thy good with brotherhood
    From sea to shining sea!

O beautiful for pilgrim feet,
  Whose stern, impassioned stress
A thoroughfare for freedom beat
  Across the wilderness!
    America! America!
  God mend thine every flaw,
Confirm thy soul in self-control,
  Thy liberty in law!

O beautiful for heroes proved
  In liberating strife,
Who more than self their country loved,
  And mercy more than life!
    America! America!
  May God thy gold refine,
Till all success be nobleness,
  And every gain divine!

O beautiful for patriot dream
  That sees beyond the years
Thine alabaster cities gleam
  Undimmed by human tears!
    America! America!
  God shed His grace on thee
And crown thy good with brotherhood
  From sea to shining sea!

KATHERINE LEE BATES

BOOK NINE

America Singing

The Seasons

Of thee they sang. Our American poets have sung of the American countryside, its lichened rocks and wild untempled hills, its contrary seasons, its flowers and trees and birds and fogs. And these outdoor poems, almost all of them written by native or transplanted New Englanders, are the most evocative yet written in America.

Why New England's stony pastures should have inspired better poetry than the cotton fields and quail country of the Old South, the sleepy bayous of Louisiana, the limitless skies of Kansas and the Dakotas (and also of Texas) or the rugged Western mountains and the painted deserts is something of a mystery, even to those of us who love them and have elected to live among them. But fact is fact and poetry is poetry. Even Sidney Lanier's "Chattahoochee" and Robinson Jeffers' "Edge of the Pacific" do not quite prove the contrary.

In Just-spring

in Just-
spring   when the world is mud-
luscious the little
lame balloonman

whistles   far   and wee

and eddieandbill come
running from marbles and
piracies and it's
spring

when the world is puddle-wonderful

the queer
old balloonman whistles
far   and   wee
and bettyandisbel come dancing

from hop-scotch and jump-rope and

it's
spring
and
    the
       goat-footed

balloonMan   whistles
far
and
wee

E. E. CUMMINGS

The Mountain Sat upon the Plain

The mountain sat upon the plain
In his eternal chair,

283

His observation omnifold,
His inquest everywhere.

The seasons prayed around his knees,
Like children round a sire:
Grandfather of the days is he,
Of dawn the ancestor.

EMILY DICKINSON

The Robin Is the One

The robin is the one
That interrupts the morn
With hurried, few, express reports
When March is scarcely on.

The robin is the one
That overflows the noon
With her cherubic quantity,
An April but begun.

The robin is the one
That speechless from her nest
Submits that home and certainty
And sanctity are best.

EMILY DICKINSON

Pink, Small and Punctual (Arbutus)

Pink, small and punctual,
Aromatic, low,
Covert in April,
Candid in May,

Dear to the moss,
Known by the knoll,
Next to the robin
In every human soul.

Bold little beauty,
Bedecked with thee,
Nature forswears
Antiquity.

EMILY DICKINSON

Mending Wall

Something there is that doesn't love a wall,
That sends the frozen-ground-swell under it,
And spills the upper boulders in the sun;
And makes gaps even two can pass abreast.
The work of hunters is another thing:
I have come after them and made repair
Where they have left not one stone on a stone,
But they would have the rabbit out of hiding,
To please the yelping dogs. The gaps I mean,
No one has seen them made or heard them made,
But at spring mending-time we find them there.
I let my neighbor know beyond the hill;
And on a day we meet to walk the line
And set the wall between us once again.
We keep the wall between us as we go.
To each the boulders that have fallen to each.
And some are loaves and some so nearly balls
We have to use a spell to make them balance:
"Stay where you are until our backs are turned!"
We wear our fingers rough with handling them.
Oh, just another kind of outdoor game,
One on a side. It comes to little more:
There where it is we do not need the wall:
He is all pine and I am apple-orchard.
My apple trees will never get across
And eat the cones under his pines, I tell him.
He only says, "Good fences make good neighbors."
Spring is the mischief in me, and I wonder

If I could put a notion in his head:
"*Why* do they make good neighbors? Isn't it
Where there are cows? But here there are no cows.
Before I built a wall I'd ask to know
What I was walling in or walling out,
And to whom I was like to give offense.
Something there is that doesn't love a wall,
That wants it down!" I could say "elves" to him,
But it's not elves exactly, and I'd rather
He said it for himself. I see him there
Bringing a stone grasped firmly by the top
In each hand, like an old-stone savage armed.
He moves in darkness, as it seems to me,
Not of woods only and the shade of trees.
He will not go behind his father's saying,
And he likes having thought of it so well
He says again, "Good fences make good neighbors."

ROBERT FROST

Trespass

No, I had set no prohibiting sign,
And yes, my land was hardly fenced.
Nevertheless the land was mine:
I was being trespassed on and against.

Whoever the surly freedom took
Of such an unaccountable stay
Busying by my woods and brook
Gave me a strangely, restless day.

He might be opening leaves of stone,
The picture-book of the trilobite,
For which the region round was known,
And in which there was little property right.

'Twas not the value I stood to lose
In specimen crab in specimen rock,

But his ignoring what was whose
That made me look again at the clock.

Then came his little acknowledgment:
He asked for a drink at the kitchen door,
An errand he may have had to invent,
But it made my property mine once more.

ROBERT FROST

Spring

(FROM *The Biglow Papers; Sunthin' in the Pastoral Line*)

. . . I, country-born an' bred, know where to find
Some blooms thet make the season suit the mind,
An' seem to metch the doubtin' bluebird's notes,—
Half-vent'-rin' liverworts in furry coats,
Bloodroots, whose rolled-up leaves ef you oncurl,
Each on 'em 's cradle to a baby-pearl,—
But these are jes' Spring's pickets; sure ez sin,
The rebble frosts 'll try to drive 'em in;
For half our May's so awfully like May n't,
't would rile a Shaker or an evrige saint;
Though I own up I like our back'ard springs
Thet kind o' haggle with their greens an' things,
An' when you 'most give up, 'uthout more words
Toss the fields full of blossoms, leaves, an' birds;
Thet's Northun natur', slow an' apt to doubt,
But when it *doos* get stirred, there's no gin-out!

Fust come the blackbirds, clatt'rin' in tall trees,
An' settlin' things in windy Congresses,—
Queer politicians, though, for I'll be skinned
Ef all on 'em don't head aginst the wind.
'fore long the trees begin to show belief,—
The maple crimsons to a coral-reef,
Then saffern swarms swing off from all the willers
So plump they look like yaller caterpillars,

Then grey hossches' nuts leetle hands unfold
Softer 'n a baby's be at three days old:
Thet's robin-redbreast's almanick; he knows
Thet arter this ther' 's only blossom-snows;
So, choosin' out a handy crotch and spouse,
He goes to plast'rin' his adobe house.

Then seems to come a hitch,—things seem to lag behind,
Till some fine mornin' Spring makes up her mind,
An 'ez, when snow-swelled rivers cresh their dams
Heaped-up with ice thet dovetails in an' jams,
A leak comes spirtin' thru some pin-hole cleft,
Grows stronger, fercer, tears out right an' left,
Then all the waters bow themselves an' come
Suddin, in one gret slope o' shedderin' foam,
Jes' so our Spring gits everythin' in tune
An' gives one leap from Aperl into June:
Then all comes crowdin' in; afore you think
Young oak-leaves mist the side-hill woods with pink;
The catbird in the laylock-bush is loud;
The orchards turn to heaps o' rosy cloud;
Red-cedars blossom tu, though few folks know it,
An' look all dipt in sunshine like a poet;
The lime-trees pile their solid stacks o' shade
An' drows'ly simmer with the bees' sweet trade;
In ellum-shrouds the flashin' hang-bird clings
An' for the summer vy'ge his hammock slings;
All down the loose-walled lanes in archin' bowers
The barb'ry droops its strings o' golden flowers,
Whose shrinkin' hearts the school-gals love to try
With pins,—they'll worry yourn so, boys, bimeby!
But I don't love your cat'logue style,—do you?—
Ez ef to sell off Natur' by vendoo;
One word with blood in 't 's twice ez good ez two:
'nuff sed, June's bridesman, poet o' the year,
Gladness on wings, the bobolink, is here;
Half-hid in tip-top apple-blooms he swings,

Or climbs against the breeze with quiverin' wings,
Or, givin' way to 't in a mock despair,
Runs down, a brook o' laughter, thru the air.

JAMES RUSSELL LOWELL

The Rhodora

In May, when sea-winds pierced our solitudes,
I found the fresh Rhodora in the woods,
Spreading its leafless blooms in a damp nook,
To please the desert and the sluggish brook.
The purple petals, fallen in the pool,
Made the black water with their beauty gay;
Here might the red-bird come his plumes to cool,
And court the flower that cheapens his array.

Rhodora! if the sages ask thee why
This charm is wasted on the earth and sky,
Tell them, dear, that if eyes were made for seeing,
Then Beauty is its own excuse for being:
Why thou wert there, O rival of the rose!
I never thought to ask, I never knew:
But, in my simple ignorance, suppose
The self-same Power that brought me there brought you.

RALPH WALDO EMERSON

June
(FROM The Vision of Sir Launfal)

. . . What is so rare as a day in June?

Then, if ever, come perfect days;
Then Heaven tries earth if it be in tune,
    And over it softly her warm ear lays:
Whether we look, or whether we listen,
We hear life murmur, or see it glisten;
    Every clod feels a stir of might,

An instinct within it that reaches and towers,
And, groping blindly above it for light,
    Climbs to a soul in grass and flowers;
The flush of life may well be seen
    Thrilling back over hills and valleys;
The cowslip startles in meadows green,
    The buttercup catches the sun in its chalice,
And there's never a leaf nor a blade too mean
    To be some happy creature's palace;
The little bird sits at his door in the sun,
    Atilt like a blossom among the leaves,
And lets his illumined being o'errun
    With the deluge of summer it receives;
His mate feels the eggs beneath her wings,
And the heart in her dumb breast flutters and sings;
He sings to the wide world and she to her nest,—
In the nice ear of Nature which song is the best?

Now is the high-tide of the year,
    And whatever of life hath ebbed away
Comes flooding back with a ripply cheer
    Into every bare inlet and creek and bay;
Now the heart is so full that a drop overfills it,
We are happy now because God wills it;
No matter how barren the past may have been,
'Tis enough for us now that the leaves are green;
We sit in the warm shade and feel right well
How the sap creeps up and the blossoms swell;
We may shut our eyes, but we cannot help knowing
That skies are clear and the grass is growing;
The breeze comes whispering in our ear
That dandelions are blossoming near,
    That maize has sprouted, that streams are flowing,
That the river is bluer than the sky,
That the robin is plastering his house hard by;
And if the breeze kept the good news back,
For other couriers we should not lack;
    We could guess it all by yon heifer's lowing,—

And hark! how clear bold chanticleer,
Warmed with the new wine of the year,
   Tells all in his lusty crowing!

Joy comes, grief goes, we do not know how;
Everything is happy now. . . .

JAMES RUSSELL LOWELL

The Pedigree of Honey

The pedigree of honey
Does not concern the bee;
A clover, any time, to him,
Is aristocracy.

EMILY DICKINSON

I'll Tell You How the Sun Rose

I'll tell you how the sun rose,—
A ribbon at a time.
The steeples swam in amethyst,
The news like squirrels ran.

The hills untied their bonnets,
The bobolinks begun.
Then I said softly to myself,
"That must have been the sun!"

But how he set I know not.
There seemed a purple stile
Which little yellow boys and girls
Were climbing all the while

Till when they reached the other side,
A dominie in gray
Put gently up the evening bars,
And led the flock away.

EMILY DICKINSON

Come In

As I came to the edge of the woods,
Thrush music—hark!
Now if it was dusk outside,
Inside it was dark.

Too dark in the woods for a bird
By sleight of wing
To better its perch for the night,
Though it still could sing.

The last of the light of the sun
That had died in the west
Still lived for one song more
In a thrush's breast.

Far in the pillared dark
Thrush music went—
Almost like a call to come in
To the dark and lament.

But no, I was out for stars:
I would not come in.
I meant not even if asked,
And I hadn't been.

ROBERT FROST

The Mountain

The mountain held the town as in a shadow.
I saw so much before I slept there once:
I noticed that I missed stars in the west,
Where its black body cut into the sky.
Near me it seemed: I felt it like a wall
Behind which I was sheltered from a wind.
And yet between the town and it I found,
When I walked forth at dawn to see new things,
Were fields, a river, and beyond, more fields.

The river at the time was fallen away,
And made a widespread brawl on cobblestones;
But the signs showed what it had done in spring:
Good grassland gullied out, and in the grass
Ridges of sand, and driftwood stripped of bark.
I crossed the river and swung round the mountain.
And there I met a man who moved so slow
With white-faced oxen in a heavy cart,
It seemed no harm to stop him altogether.

'What town is this?' I asked.
                              'This? Lunenburg.'
Then I was wrong: the town of my sojourn,
Beyond the bridge, was not that of the mountain,
But only felt at night its shadowy presence.
'Where is your village? Very far from here?'

'There is no village—only scattered farms.
We were but sixty voters last election.
We can't in nature grow to many more:
That thing takes all the room!' He moved his goad.
The mountain stood there to be pointed at.
Pasture ran up the side a little way.
And then there was a wall of trees with trunks;
After that only tops of trees, and cliffs
Imperfectly concealed among the leaves.
A dry ravine emerged from under boughs
Into the pasture.
                  'That looks like a path.
Is that the way to reach the top from here?—
Not for this morning, but some other time:
I must be getting back to breakfast now.'

'I don't advise your trying from this side.
There is no proper path, but those that *have*
Been up, I understand, have climbed from Ladd's.
That's five miles back. You can't mistake the place:
They logged it there last winter some way up.
I'd take you, but I'm bound the other way.'

'You've never climbed it?'

                                        'I've been on the sides,
Deer-hunting and trout-fishing. There's a brook
That starts up on it somewhere—I've heard say
Right on the top, tip-top—a curious thing,
But what would interest you about the brook,
It's always cold in summer, warm in winter.
One of the great sights going is to see
It steam in winter like an ox's breath,
Until the bushes all along its banks
Are inch-deep with the frosty spines and bristles—
You know the kind. Then let the sun shine on it!'

'There ought to be a view around the world
From such a mountain—if it isn't wooded
Clear to the top.' I saw through leafy screens
Great granite terraces in sun and shadow,
Shelves one could rest a knee on getting up—
With depths behind him sheer a hundred feet.
Or turn and sit on and look out and down,
With little ferns in crevices at his elbow.

'As to that I can't say. But there's the spring,
Right on the summit, almost like a fountain.
That ought to be worth seeing.'
                                        'If it's there.
You never saw it?'

                            'I guess there's no doubt
About its being there. I never saw it.
It may not be right on the very top:
It wouldn't have to be a long way down
To have some head of water from above,
And a *good distance* down might not be noticed
By anyone who'd come a long way up.
One time I asked a fellow climbing it
To look and tell me later how it was.'

'What did he say?'
                        'He said there was a lake
Somewhere in Ireland on a mountain top.'

'But a lake's different. What about the spring?'

'He never got up high enough to see.
That's why I don't advise your trying this side.
He tried this side. I've always meant to go
And look myself, but you know how it is:
It doesn't seem so much to climb a mountain
You've worked around the foot of all your life.
What would I do? Go in my overalls,
With a big stick, the same as when the cows
Haven't come down to the bars at milking time?
Or with a shotgun for a stray black bear?
'Twouldn't seem real to climb for climbing it.'

'I shouldn't climb it if I didn't want to—
Not for the sake of climbing. What's its name?'

'We call it Hor: I don't know if that's right.'

'Can one walk around it? Would it be too far?'

'You can drive round and keep in Lunenburg.
But it's as much as ever you can do,
The boundary lines keep in so close to it.
Hor is the township, and the township's Hor—
And a few houses sprinkled round the foot,
Like boulders broken off the upper cliff,
Rolled out a little further than the rest.'

'Warm in December, cold in June, you say?'

'I don't suppose the water's changed at all.
You and I know enough to know it's warm
Compared with cold, and cold compared with warm,
But all the fun's in how you say a thing.'

'You've lived here all your life?'

'Ever since Hor

Was no bigger than a—' What, I did not hear.
He drew the oxen toward him with light touches
Of his slim goad on nose and offside flank,
Gave them their marching orders and was moving.

ROBERT FROST

Wind in the Grass

Are you so weary? Come to the window;
Lean, and look at this.
Something swift runs under the grass
With a little hiss.

Now you see it rippling off,
Reckless, under the fence,
Are you so tired? Unfasten your mind
And follow it hence.

MARK VAN DOREN

Former Barn Lot

Once there was a fence here,
    And the grass came and tried—
Leaning from the pasture—
    To get inside.

But colt feet trampled it,
    Turning it brown;
Until the farmer moved
    And the fence fell down.

Then any bird saw,
    Under the wire,
Grass nibbling inward
    Like green fire.

MARK VAN DOREN

God Made a Little Gentian

God made a little gentian;
It tried to be a rose
And failed, and all the summer laughed.
But just before the snows
There came a purple creature
That ravished all the hill;
And summer hid her forehead,
And mockery was still.
The frosts were her condition;
The Tyrian would not come
Until the North evoked it,
"Creator! shall I bloom?"

EMILY DICKINSON

The Sheaves

Where long the shadows of the wind had rolled,
Green wheat was yielding to the change assigned;
And as by some vast magic undivined
The world was turning slowly into gold.
Like nothing that was ever bought or sold
It waited there, the body and the mind;
And with a mighty meaning of a kind
That tells the more the more it is not told.

So in a land where all days are not fair,
Fair days went on till on another day
A thousand golden sheaves were lying there,
Shining and still, but not for long to stay—
As if a thousand girls with golden hair
Might rise from where they slept and go away.

EDWIN ARLINGTON ROBINSON

When the Frost Is on the Punkin

When the frost is on the punkin and the fodder's in the shock,
And you hear the kyouck and gobble of the struttin' turkey-
cock,
And the clackin' of the guineys, and the cluckin' of the hens,
And the rooster's hallylooyer as he tiptoes on the fence;
O, it's then's the times a feller is a-feelin' at his best,
With the risin' sun to greet him from a night of peaceful rest,
As he leaves the house, bareheaded, and goes out to feed the
stock,
When the frost is on the punkin and the fodder's in the shock.

They's something kind o' harty-like about the atmusfere
When the heat of summer's over and the coolin' fall is here—
Of course we miss the flowers, and the blossoms on the trees,
And the mumble of the hummin'-birds and buzzin' of the bees;
But the air's so appetizin'; and the landscape through the haze
Of a crisp and sunny morning of the airly autumn days
Is a pictur' that no painter has the colorin' to mock—
When the frost is on the punkin and the fodder's in the shock.

The husky, rusty russel of the tossels of the corn,
And the raspin' of the tangled leaves as golden as the morn;
The stubble in the furries—kind o' lonesome-like but still
A-preachin' sermuns to us of the barns they growed to fill;
The strawstack in the medder, and the reaper in the shed;
The hosses in their stalls below—the clover overhead!—
O, it sets my hart a-clickin' like the tickin' of a clock
When the frost is on the punkin and the fodder's in the shock.

Then your apples is all getherd, and the ones a feller keeps
Is poured round the cellar-floor in red and yeller heaps;
And your cider-makin's over, and your wimmern-folks is
through
With their mince and apple-butter, and their souse and
saussage too! . . .
I don't know how to tell it—but ef such a thing could be

As the Angels wantin' boardin', and they'd call around on me—
I'd want to 'commodate 'em—all the whole-indurin' flock—
When the frost is on the punkin and the fodder's in the shock.

JAMES   WHITCOMB   RILEY

Stopping by Woods on a Snowy Evening

Whose woods these are I think I know.
His house is in the village though;
He will not see me stopping here
To watch his woods fill up with snow.

My little horse must think it queer
To stop without a farmhouse near
Between the woods and frozen lake
The darkest evening of the year.

He gives his harness bells a shake
To ask if there is some mistake.
The only other sound's the sweep
Of easy wind and downy flake.

The woods are lovely, dark and deep,
But I have promises to keep,
And miles to go before I sleep,
And miles to go before I sleep.

ROBERT   FROST

Birches

When I see birches bend to left and right
Across the lines of straighter darker trees,
I like to think some boy's been swinging them.
But swinging doesn't bend them down to stay.
Ice-storms do that. Often you must have seen them
Loaded with ice a sunny winter morning
After a rain. They click upon themselves

As the breeze rises, and turn many-colored
As the stir cracks and crazes their enamel.
Soon the sun's warmth makes them shed crystal shells
Shattering and avalanching on the snow-crust—
Such heaps of broken glass to sweep away
You'd think the inner dome of heaven had fallen.
They are dragged to the withered bracken by the load,
And they seem not to break; though once they are bowed
So low for long, they never right themselves:
You may see their trunks arching in the woods
Years afterward, trailing their leaves on the ground
Like girls on hands and knees that throw their hair
Before them over their heads to dry in the sun.
But I was going to say when Truth broke in
With all her matter-of-fact about the ice-storm
I should prefer to have some boy bend them
As he went out and in to fetch the cows—
Some boy too far from town to learn baseball,
Whose only play was what he found himself,
Summer or winter, and could play alone.
One by one he subdued his father's trees
By riding them down and over again
Until he took the stiffness out of them,
And not one but hung limp, not one was left
For him to conquer. He learned all there was
To learn about not launching out too soon
And so not carrying the tree away
Clear to the ground. He always kept his poise
To the top branches, climbing carefully
With the same pains you use to fill a cup
Up to the brim, and even above the brim.
Then he flung outward, feet first, with a swish,
Kicking his way down through the air to the ground.

So was I once myself a swinger of birches.
And so I dream of going back to be.
It's when I'm weary of considerations,

And life is too much like a pathless wood
Where your face burns and tickles with the cobwebs
Broken across it, and one eye is weeping
From a twig's having lashed across it open.
I'd like to get away from earth awhile
And then come back to it and begin over.
May no fate willfully misunderstand me
And half grant what I wish and snatch me away
Not to return. Earth's the right place for love:
I don't know where it's likely to go better.
I'd like to go by climbing a birch tree
And climb black branches up a snow-white trunk
Toward heaven, till the tree could bear no more,
But dipped its top and set me down again.
That would be good both going and coming back
One could do worse than be a swinger of birches.

ROBERT FROST

Fog

The fog comes
on little cat feet.
It sits looking
over harbor and city
on silent haunches
and then moves on.

CARL SANDBURG

The Sky Is Low

The sky is low, the clouds are mean,
A travelling flake of snow
Across a barn or through a rut
Debates if it will go.

A narrow wind complains all day
How some one treated him;
Nature, like us, is sometimes caught
Without her diadem.

EMILY DICKINSON

The Storm
(FROM *Snowbound*)

The sun that brief December day
Rose cheerless over hills of gray,
And, darkly circled, gave at noon
A sadder light than waning moon.
Slow tracing down the thickening sky
Its mute and ominous prophecy,
A portent seeming less than threat,
It sank from sight before it set.
A chill no coat, however stout,
Of homespun stuff could quite shut out,
A hard, dull bitterness of cold,
That checked, mid-vein, the circling race
Of life-blood in the sharpened face,
The coming of the snow-storm told.
The wind blew east; we heard the roar
Of Ocean on his wintry shore,
And felt the strong pulse throbbing there
Beat with low rhythm our inland air.

Meanwhile we did our nightly chores,
Brought in the wood from out of doors,
Littered the stalls, and from the mows
Raked down the herd's-grass for the cows:
Heard the horse whinnying for his corn;
And, sharply clashing horn on horn,
Impatient down the stanchion rows
The cattle shake their walnut bows;
While, peering from his early perch

Upon the scaffold's pile of birch,
The cock his crested helmet bent
And down his querulous challenge sent.

Unwarmed by any sunset light
The gray day darkened into night,
A night made hoary with the swarm
And whirl-dance of the blinding storm,
As zigzag, wavering to and fro,
Crossed and recrossed the wingèd snow:
And ere the early bedtime came
The white drift piled the window-frame,
And through the glass the clothes-line posts
Looked in like tall and sheeted ghosts.

So all night long the storm roared on:
The morning broke without a sun;
In tiny spherule traced with lines
Of Nature's geometric signs,
In starry flake, and pellicle
All day the hoary meteor fell;
And, when the second morning shone,
We looked upon a world unknown,
On nothing we could call our own.
Around the glistening wonder bent
The blue walls of the firmament,
No cloud above, no earth below,—
A universe of sky and snow!
The old familiar sights of ours
Took marvellous shapes; strange domes and towers
Rose up where sty or corn-crib stood,
Or garden-wall, or belt of wood;
A smooth white mound the brush-pile showed,
A fenceless drift what once was road;
The bridle-post an old man sat
With loose-flung coat and high cocked hat;
The well-curb had a Chinese roof;
And even the long sweep, high aloof,

In its slant splendor, seemed to tell
Of Pisa's leaning miracle. . . .

All day the gusty north-wind bore
The loosening drift its breath before;
Low circling round its southern zone,
The sun through dazzling snow-mist shone.
No church-bell lent its Christian tone
To the savage air, no social smoke
Curled over woods of snow-hung oak.
A solitude made more intense
By dreary-voiced elements,
The shrieking of the mindless wind,
The moaning tree-boughs swaying blind,
And on the glass the unmeaning beat
Of ghostly finger-tips of sleet.
Beyond the circle of our hearth
No welcome sound of toil or mirth
Unbound the spell, and testified
Of human life and thought outside.
We minded that the sharpest ear
The buried brooklet could not hear,
The music of whose liquid lip
Had been to us companionship,
And, in our lonely life, had grown
To have an almost human tone.

As night drew on, and, from the crest
Of wooded knolls that ridged the west,
The sun, a snow-blown traveller, sank
From sight beneath the smothering bank,
We piled, with care, our nightly stack
Of wood against the chimney-back,—
The oaken log, green, huge, and thick,
And on its top the stout back-stick;
The knotty forestick laid apart,
And filled between with curious art
The ragged brush; then, hovering near,

We watched the first red blaze appear,
Heard the sharp crackle, caught the gleam
On whitewashed wall and sagging beam,
Until the old, rude-furnished room
Burst, flower-like, into rosy bloom;
While radiant with a mimic flame
Outside the sparkling drift became,
And through the bare-boughed lilac-tree
Our own warm hearth seemed blazing free.
The crane and pendent trammels showed,
The Turks' heads on the andirons glowed;
While childish fancy, prompt to tell
The meaning of the miracle,
Whispered the old rhyme: *"Under the tree,*
When fire outside burns merrily,
There the witches are making tea."

The moon above the eastern wood
Shone at its full; the hill-range stood
Transfigured in the silver flood,
Its blown snows flashing cold and keen,
Dead white, save where some sharp ravine
Took shadow, or the sombre green
Of hemlocks turned to pitchy black
Against the whiteness at their back.
For such a world and such a night
Most fitting that unwarming light,
Which only seemed where'er it fell
To make the coldness visible.

Shut in from all the world without,
We sat the clean-winged hearth about,
Content to let the north-wind roar
In baffled rage at pane and door,
While the red logs before us beat
The frost-line back with tropic heat;
And ever, when a louder blast
Shook beam and rafter as it passed,

The merrier up its roaring draught
The great throat of the chimney laughed;
The house-dog on his paws outspread
Laid to the fire his drowsy head,
The cat's dark silhouette on the wall
A couchant tiger's seemed to fall;
And, for the winter fireside meet,
Between the andirons' straddling feet,
The mug of cider simmered slow,
The apples sputtered in a row,
And, close at hand, the basket stood
With nuts from brown October's wood.

What matter how the night behaved?
What matter how the north-wind raved?
Blow high, blow low, not all its snow
Could quench our hearth-fire's ruddy glow. . . .

We sped the time with stories old,
Wrought puzzles out, and riddles told. . . .
Our father rode again his ride
On Memphremagog's wooded side;
Sat down again to moose and samp
In trapper's hut and Indian camp;
Lived o'er the old idyllic ease
Beneath St. François' hemlock-trees. . . .
Or, nearer home, our steps he led
Where Salisbury's level marshes spread
    Mile-wide as flies the laden bee;
Where merry mowers, hale and strong,
Swept, scythe on scythe, their swaths along
    The low green prairies of the sea.
We shared the fishing off Boar's Head,
    And round the rocky Isles of Shoals
    The hake-broil on the drift-wood coals;
The chowder on the sand-beach made,
Dipped by the hungry, steaming hot,
With spoons of clam-shell from the pot.

306

Our mother, while she turned her wheel
Or run the new-knit stocking-heel,
Told how the Indian hordes came down
At midnight on Cocheco town,
And how her own great-uncle bore
His cruel scalp-mark to fourscore.
Recalling, in her fitting phrase,
   So rich and picturesque and free,
   (The common unrhymed poetry
Of simple life and country ways),
The story of her early days,—
She made us welcome to her home;
Old hearths grew wide to give us room. . . .
We heard the hawks at twilight play,
The boat-horn on Piscataqua,
The loon's weird laughter far away;
We fished her little trout-brook, knew
What flowers in wood and meadow grew,
What sunny hillsides autumn-brown
She climbed to shake the ripe nuts down,
Saw where in sheltered cove and bay
The ducks' black squadron anchored lay,
And heard the wild geese calling loud
Beneath the gray November cloud. . . .

Our uncle, innocent of books,
Was rich in lore of fields and brooks,
The ancient teachers never dumb
Of Nature's unhoused lyceum.
In moons and tides and weather wise,
He read the clouds as prophecies,
And foul or fair could well divine,
By many an occult hint and sign,
Holding the cunning-warded keys
To all the woodcraft mysteries;
Himself to Nature's heart so near
That all her voices in his ear

Of beast or bird had meanings clear. . . .
A simple, guileless, childlike man,
Content to live where life began;
Strong only on his native grounds,
The little world of sights and sounds
Whose girdle was the parish bounds,
Whereof his fondly partial pride
The common features magnified,
As Surrey hills to mountains grew
In White of Selborne's loving view,—
He told how teal and loon he shot,
And how the eagle's eggs he got,
The feats on pond and river done,
The prodigies of rod and gun;
Till, warming with the tales he told,
Forgotten was the outside cold,
The bitter wind unheeded blew,
From ripening corn the pigeons flew,
The partridge drummed i' the wood, the mink
Went fishing down the river-brink.
In fields with bean or clover gay,
The woodchuck, like a hermit gray,
   Peered from the doorway of his cell;
The muskrat plied the mason's trade,
And tier by tier his mud-walls laid;
And from the shagbark overhead
   The grizzled squirrel dropped his shell. . . .

Brisk wielder of the birch and rule,
The master of the district school
Held at the fire his favored place,
Its warm glow lit a laughing face
Fresh-hued and fair, where scarce appeared
The uncertain prophecy of beard.
He teased the mitten-blinded cat,
Played cross pins on my uncle's hat,
Sang songs, and told us what befalls

In classic Dartmouth's college halls.
Born the wild Northern hills among,
From whence his yeoman father wrung
By patient toil subsistence scant,
Not competence and not yet want,
He early gained the power to pay
His cheerful, self-reliant way;
Could doff at ease his scholar's gown
To peddle wares from town to town;
Or through the long vacation's reach
In lonely lowland districts teach,
Where all the droll experience found
At stranger hearths in boarding round,
The moonlit skater's keen delight,
The sleigh-drive through the frosty night,
The rustic party, with its rough
Accompaniment of blind-man's-buff,
And whirling plate, and forfeits paid,
His winter task a pastime made.
Happy the snow-locked homes wherein
He tuned his merry violin,
Or played the athlete in the barn,
Or held the good dame's winding-yarn,
Or mirth-provoking versions told
Of classic legends rare and old,
Wherein the scenes of Greece and Rome
Had all the commonplace of home,
And little seemed at best the odds
'Twixt Yankee pedlers and old gods;
Where Pindus-born Arachthus took
The guise of any grist-mill brook,
And dread Olympus at his will
Became a huckleberry hill. . . .

At last the great logs, crumbling low,
Sent out a dull and duller glow,
The bull's-eye watch that hung in view,

Ticking its weary circuit through,
Pointed with mutely warning sign
Its black hand to the hour of nine.
That sign the pleasant circle broke:
My uncle ceased his pipe to smoke,
Knocked from its bowl the refuse gray,
And laid it tenderly away;
Then roused himself to safely cover
The dull red brands with ashes over.
And while, with care, our mother laid
The work aside, her steps she stayed
One moment, seeking to express
Her grateful sense of happiness
For food and shelter, warmth and health,
And love's contentment more than wealth. . . .

Within our beds awhile we heard
The wind that round the gables roared,
With now and then a ruder shock,
Which made our very bedsteads rock.
We heard the loosened clapboards tost,
The board-nails snapping in the frost;
And on us, through the unplastered wall,
Felt the light sifted snow-flakes fall.
But sleep stole on, as sleep will do
When hearts are light and life is new;
Faint and more faint the murmurs grew,
Till in the summer-land of dreams
They softened to the sound of streams,
Low stir of leaves, and dip of oars,
And lapsing waves on quiet shores. . . .

JOHN GREENLEAF WHITTIER

Song of the Chattahoochee

Out of the hills of Habersham
Down the valleys of Hall,
I hurry amain to reach the plain,
Run the rapid and leap the fall,
Split at the rock and together again,
Accept my bed, or narrow or wide,
And flee from folly on every side
With a lover's pain to attain the plain
    Far from the hills of Habersham,
    Far from the valleys of Hall.

All down the hills of Habersham,
    All through the valleys of Hall,
The rushes cried, *Abide, abide,*
The willful waterweeds held me thrall,
The laving laurel turned my tide,
The ferns and the fondling grass said *Stay,*
The dewberry dipped for to work delay,
And the little reeds sighed, *Abide, abide,*
    Here in the hills of Habersham,
    Here in the valleys of Hall.

High o'er the hills of Habersham,
    Veiling the valleys of Hall,
The hickory told me manifold
Fair tales of shade, the poplar tall
Wrought me her shadowy self to hold,
The chestnut, the oak, the walnut, the pine,
Overleaning, with flickering meaning and sign,
Said, *Pass not, so cold, these manifold*
    Deep shades of the hills of Habersham,
    These glades in the valley of Hall.

And oft in the hills of Habersham,
    And oft in the valleys of Hall,
The white quartz shone, and the smooth brook-stone
Did bar me of passage with friendly brawl,

And many a luminous jewel lone
—Crystals clear or acloud with mist,
Ruby, garnet and amethyst—
Made lures with the lights of streaming stone
                In the clefts of the hills of Habersham,
                In the beds of the valley of Hall.

                But oh, not the hills of Habersham,
                And oh, not the valleys of Hall
Avail: I am fain for to water the plain.
Downward the voices of Duty call—
Downward, to toil and be mixed with the main,
The dry fields burn, and the mills are to turn,
And a myriad flowers mortally yearn,
And the lordly main from beyond the plain
                Calls o'er the hills of Habersham,
                Calls through the valleys of Hall.

                                    SIDNEY LANIER

Continent's End

At the equinox when the earth was veiled in a late rain,
        wreathed with wet poppies, waiting spring,
The ocean swelled for a far storm and beat its boundary, the
        ground-swell shook the beds of granite.

I gazing at the boundaries of granite and spray, the established
        sea-marks, felt behind me
Mountain and plain, the immense breadth of the continent,
        before me the mass and doubled stretch of water.

I said: You yoke the Aleutian seal-rocks with the lava and
        coral sowings that flower the south,
Over your flood the life that sought the sunrise faces ours that
        has followed the evening star.

The long migrations meet across you and it is nothing to you,
        you who have forgotten us, mother.

You were much younger when we crawled out of the womb
    and lay in the sun's eye on the tideline.

It was long and long ago; we have grown proud since then and
    you have grown bitter; life retains
Your mobile soft unquiet strength; and envies hardness, the
    insolent quietness of stone.

The tides are in our veins, we still mirror the stars, life is your
    child, but there is in me
Older and harder than life and more impartial, the eye that
    watched before there was an ocean.

That watched you fill our beds out of the condensation of
    thin vapor and watched you change them,
That saw you soft and violent wear your boundaries down,
    eat rock, shift places with the continents.

Mother, though my song's measure is like your surf-beat's
    ancient rhythm I never learned it of you.
Before there was any water there were tides of fire, both our
    tones flow from the older fountain.

ROBINSON JEFFERS

"Light"

Poets have always had a higher capacity for laughter than have those who write about poetry. There is a distressingly orthodox tendency to isolate verses with a lilt of laughter in them to a supposedly inferior category known as "light verse."

"Light verse" is impossible to define; it refuses to be sequestered. Shakespeare wrote "light verse." In fact, most of the Elizabethan lyrics included in Book One of this collection are "light verse"; so are many here grouped under "Memories of Childhood," and the Kipling verses included among "Echoes of War." Kipling, to be sure, has been a problem for anthologists and college professors. He is so distressingly vernacular, and recent, too; and the professors always find it easier to bid their students study "light verse" when it has been hallowed by the passage of a few centuries, while ignoring it if modern. Yet Kipling's poems have already contributed more phrases to the common patois of the English language than any other poet's since Shakespeare. In this book he appears among his compeers, as a poet of love and war and the sea.

The poems here called "Light" have in common only an occasional shy or open smile, and their refusal to fit easily under the more solemn titles of other sections of this book.

"Light"

Poets have always had a higher capacity for laughter than have those who write about poetry. There is a disagreeable orthodoxy tendency to isolate verse, with a lift of laughter, in their to a supposedly inferior category, known as "light verse." "Light verse," it is impossible to define, is impossible to be registered. Shakespeare wrote "light verse." In fact, most of the Elizabethan lyrics included in Book One of this collection are "light verse," to are many here grouped under "Humorous of Childhood," and the Kipling verses included among "Poems of War." Nursing, to be sure, has been a problem, for analof the and foolage ponderers. He is to dismiss lightly certainties, the verse, too, and the prof....more answer and accustuer to bid ....th ....more thickly "light verse," whose it has been ballaided by the poets... of free emotion, whichit lightify if it would. At Kimyly poems have already contributed more powers to the compendiums of the English Language than any other poets..... the Shakespeare, in this book he appears among his most grave, as poet of love uncensored of man.

The poem here called "Light," is in no collection on occasional that was a bit while, and thus refuses to be taken under the poet, belongs thore of a rather seathing to the liou

Fable

The mountain and the squirrel
Had a quarrel,
And the former called the latter "Little Prig";
Bun replied,
"You are doubtless very big;
But all sorts of things and weather
Must be taken in together,
To make up a year
And a sphere.
And I think it no disgrace
To occupy my place.
If I'm not so large as you,
You are not so small as I,
And not half so spry.
I'll not deny you make
A very pretty squirrel track;
Talents differ; all is well and wisely put;
If I cannot carry forests on my back,
Neither can you crack a nut."

RALPH WALDO EMERSON

Jabberwocky

'Twas brillig, and the slithy toves
  Did gyre and gimble in the wabe;
All mimsy were the borogoves,
  And the mome raths outgrabe.

"Beware the Jabberwock, my son!
  The jaws that bite, the claws that catch!
Beware the Jubjub bird, and shun
  The frumious Bandersnatch!"

He took his vorpal sword in hand:
  Long time the manxome foe he sought.—
So rested he by the Tumtum tree,
  And stood awhile in thought.

And as in uffish thought he stood,
  The Jabberwock, with eyes of flame,
Came whiffling through the tulgey wood,
  And burbled as it came!

One, two! One, two! And through and through
  The vorpal blade went snicker-snack!
He left it dead, and with its head
  He went galumphing back.

"And hast thou slain the Jabberwock?
  Come to my arms, my beamish boy!
O frabjous day! Callooh! Callay!"
  He chortled in his joy.

'Twas brillig, and the slithy toves
  Did gyre and gimble in the wabe;
All mimsy were the borogoves,
  And the mome raths outgrabe.

LEWIS CARROLL
(CHARLES LUTWIDGE DODGSON)

The Walrus and the Carpenter

The sun was shining on the sea,
  Shining with all his might:
He did his very best to make
  The billows smooth and bright—
And this was odd, because it was
  The middle of the night.

The moon was shining sulkily,
  Because she thought the sun
Had got no business to be there
  After the day was done—
"It's very rude of him," she said,
  "To come and spoil the fun!"

318

The sea was wet as wet could be,
The sands were dry as dry.
You could not see a cloud because
No cloud was in the sky:
No birds were flying overhead—
There were no birds to fly.

The Walrus and the Carpenter
Were walking close at hand;
They wept like anything to see
Such quantities of sand:
"If this were only cleared away,"
They said, "it *would* be grand!"

"If seven maids with seven mops
Swept it for half a year,
Do you suppose," the Walrus said,
"That they could get it clear?"
"I doubt it," said the Carpenter,
And shed a bitter tear.

"O Oysters, come and walk with us!"
The Walrus did beseech.
"A pleasant walk, a pleasant talk,
Along the briny beach:
We cannot do with more than four,
To give a hand to each."

The eldest Oyster looked at him,
But never a word he said:
The eldest Oyster winked his eye,
And shook his heavy head—
Meaning to say he did not choose
To leave the oyster-bed.

But four young Oysters hurried up,
All eager for the treat:
Their coats were brushed, their faces washed,
Their shoes were clean and neat—

And this was odd, because, you know,
   They hadn't any feet.

Four other Oysters followed them,
   And yet another four;
And thick and fast they came at last,
   And more, and more, and more—
All hopping through the frothy waves,
   And scrambling to the shore.

The Walrus and the Carpenter
   Walked on a mile or so,
And then they rested on a rock
   Conveniently low:
And all the little Oysters stood
   And waited in a row.

"The time has come," the Walrus said,
   "To talk of many things;
Of shoes—and ships—and sealing-wax—
   Of cabbages—and kings—
And why the sea is boiling hot—
   And whether pigs have wings."

"But wait a bit," the Oysters cried,
   "Before we have our chat;
For some of us are out of breath,
   And all of us are fat!"
"No hurry!" said the Carpenter.
   They thanked him much for that.

"A loaf of bread," the Walrus said,
   "Is what we chiefly need:
Pepper and vinegar besides
   Are very good indeed—
Now if you're ready, Oysters dear,
   We can begin to feed."

"But not on us!" the Oysters cried,
   Turning a little blue.

"After such kindness, that would be
    A dismal thing to do!"
"The night is fine," the Walrus said.
    "Do you admire the view?

"It was so kind of you to come!
    And you are very nice!"
The Carpenter said nothing but
    "Cut us another slice:
I wish you were not quite so deaf—
    I've had to ask you twice!"

"It seems a shame," the Walrus said,
    "To play them such a trick,
After we've brought them out so far,
    And made them trot so quick!"
The Carpenter said nothing but
    "The butter's spread too thick!"

"I weep for you," the Walrus said:
    "I deeply sympathize."
With sobs and tears he sorted out
    Those of the largest size,
Holding his pocket-handkerchief
    Before his streaming eyes.

"O Oysters," said the Carpenter,
    "You've had a pleasant run!
Shall we be trotting home again?"
    But answer came there none—
And this was scarcely odd, because
    They'd eaten every one.

LEWIS CARROLL
(CHARLES LUTWIDGE DODGSON)

'Twas on the shores that round our coast
  From Deal to Ramsgate span,
That I found alone on a piece of stone
  An elderly naval man.

His hair was weedy, his beard was long,
  And weedy and long was he,
And I heard this wight on the shore recite,
  In a singular minor key:

"Oh, I am a cook and a captain bold,
  And the mate of the *Nancy* brig,
And a bo'sun tight, and a midshipmite,
  And the crew of the captain's gig."

And he shook his fists and he tore his hair,
  Till I really felt afraid,
For I couldn't help thinking the man had been drinking,
  And so I simply said:

"Oh, elderly man, it's little I know
  Of the duties of men of the sea,
But I'll eat my hand if I understand
  How you can possibly be

"At once a cook, and a captain bold,
  And the mate of the *Nancy* brig,
And a bo'sun tight, and a midshipmite,
  And the crew of the captain's gig."

Then he gave a hitch to his trousers, which
  Is a trick all seamen larn,
And having got rid of a thumping quid,
  He spun this painful yarn:

" 'Twas in the good ship *Nancy Bell*
  That we sailed to the Indian sea,
And there on a reef we come to grief,
  Which has often occurred to me.

"And pretty nigh all of the crew was drowned
    (There was seventy-seven o' soul),
And only ten of the *Nancy's* men
    Said 'here' to the muster-roll.

"There was me and the cook and the captain bold
    And the mate of the *Nancy* brig,
And the bo'sun tight, and a midshipmite,
    And the crew of the captain's gig.

"For a month we'd neither wittles nor drink,
    Till a-hungry we did feel,
So we drawed a lot, and accordin', shot
    The captain for our meal.

"The next lot fell to the *Nancy's* mate,
    And a delicate dish he made;
Then our appetite with the midshipmite
    We seven survivors stayed.

"And then we murdered the bo'sun tight,
    And he much resembled pig;
Then we wittled free, did the cook and me,
    On the crew of the captain's gig.

"Then only the cook and me was left,
    And the delicate question, 'Which
Of us two goes to the kettle?' arose
    And we argued it out as sich.

"For I loved that cook as a brother, I did,
    And the cook he worshipped me;
But we'd both be blowed if we'd either be stowed
    In the other chap's hold, you see.

" 'I'll be eat if you dines off me,' says Tom,
    'Yes, that,' I says, 'you'll be,—
'I'm boiled if I die, my friend,' " quoth I,
    And 'Exactly so,' quoth he.

"Says he, 'Dear James, to murder me,
    Were a foolish thing to do,

For don't you see that you can't cook *me*,
　　While I can—and will—cook *you!*'

"So he boils the water, and takes the salt,
　　And the pepper in portions true
(Which he never forgot), and some chopped shalot,
　　And some sage and parsley too.

" 'Come here,' says he, with a proper pride,
　　Which his smiling features tell,
' 'Twill soothing be if I let you see
　　How extremely nice you'll smell.'

"And he stirred it round and round and round,
　　And he sniffed at the foaming froth;
When I ups with his heels, and smothers his squeals
　　In the scum of the boiling broth.

"And I eat that cook in a week or less,
　　And—as I eating be
The last of his chops, why, I almost drops,
　　For a wessel in sight I see!

.　　　.　　　.

"And I never larf, and I never smile,
　　And I never lark nor play,
But I sit and croak, and a single joke
　　I have—which is to say:

"Oh, I am a cook and a captain bold
　　And the mate of the *Nancy* brig,
And a bo'sun tight, *and* a midshipmite,
　　And the crew of the captain's gig!"

W. S. GILBERT

When awful darkness and silence reign
Over the great Gromboolian plain,
   Through the long, long wintry nights;—
When the angry breakers roar
As they beat on the rocky shore;—
   When Storm-clouds brood on the towering heights
Of the Hills of the Chankly Bore:—

Then, through the vast and gloomy dark,
There moves what seems like a fiery spark,
   A lonely spark with silvery rays
   Piercing the coal-black night,—
   A Meteor strange and bright:—
Hither and thither the vision strays,
   A single lurid light.

Slowly it wanders,—pauses,—creeps,—
Anon it sparkles,—flashes and leaps;
And ever as onward it gleaming goes
A light on the Bong-tree stems it throws.
And those who watch at that midnight hour
From Hall or Terrace, or lofty Tower,
Cry, as the wild light passes along,—
      'The Dong!—the Dong!
   'The wandering Dong through the forest goes!
      'The Dong! the Dong!
   'The Dong with a luminous Nose!'

      Long years ago
   The Dong was happy and gay,
Till he fell in love with a Jumbly Girl
   Who came to those shores one day,
For the Jumblies came in a sieve, they did,—
Landing at eve near the Zemmery Fidd
      Where the Oblong Oysters grow,
   And the rocks are smooth and gray.
And all the woods and the valleys rang

With the Chorus they daily and nightly sang,—
    'Far and few, far and few,
    Are the lands were the Jumblies live;
    Their heads are green, and their hands are blue,
    And they went to sea in a sieve.'

Happily, happily passed those days!
    While the cheerful Jumblies staid;
    They danced in circlets all night long,
    To the plaintive pipe of the lively Dong,
    In moonlight, shine, or shade.
For day and night he was always there
By the side of the Jumbly Girl so fair,
With her sky-blue hands, and her sea-green hair.
Till the morning came of that hateful day
When the Jumblies sailed in their sieve away,
And the Dong was left on the cruel shore
Gazing—gazing for evermore,—
Ever keeping his weary eyes on
That pea-green sail on the far horizon,—
Singing the Jumbly Chorus still
As he sate all day on the grassy hill,—
    'Far and few, far and few,
    Are the lands where the Jumblies live;
    Their heads are green, and their hands are blue,
    And they went to sea in a sieve.'

But when the sun was low in the West,
    The Dong arose and said;—
—'What little sense I once possessed
    Has gone quite out of my head!'—
And since that day he wanders still
By lake and forest, marsh and hill,
Singing—'O somewhere, in valley or plain
'Might I find my Jumbly Girl again!
'For ever I'll seek by lake and shore
'Till I find my Jumbly Girl once more!'

Playing a pipe with silvery squeaks,
Since then his Jumbly Girl he seeks,
And because by night he could not see,
He gathered the bark of the Twangum Tree
    On the flowery plain that grows.
    And he wove him a wondrous Nose,—
A Nose as strange as a Nose could be!
Of vast proportions and painted red,
And tied with cords to the back of his head.
    —In a hollow rounded space it ended
    With a luminous Lamp within suspended,
        All fenced about
        With a bandage stout
        To prevent the wind from blowing it out;—
    And with holes all round to send the light,
    In gleaming rays on the dismal night.

And now each night, and all night long,
Over those plains still roams the Dong;
And above the wail of the Chimp and Snipe
You may hear the squeak of his plaintive pipe
While ever he seeks, but seeks in vain
To meet with his Jumbly Girl again;
Lonely and wild—all night he goes,—
The Dong with a luminous Nose!
And all who watch at the midnight hour,
From Hall or Terrace, or lofty Tower,
Cry, as they trace the Meteor bright,
Moving along through the dreary night,—
    'This is the hour when forth he goes,
    'The Dong with a luminous Nose!
    'Yonder—over the plain he goes;
        'He goes!
        'He goes;
    'The Dong with a luminous Nose!'

                                    EDWARD LEAR

Miniver Cheevy, child of scorn,
　Grew lean while he assailed the seasons;
He wept that he was ever born,
　And he had reasons.

Miniver loved the days of old
　When swords were bright and steeds were prancing;
The vision of a warrior bold
　Would set him dancing.

Miniver sighed for what was not,
　And dreamed, and rested from his labors;
He dreamed of Thebes and Camelot,
　And Priam's neighbors.

Miniver mourned the ripe renown
　That made so many a name so fragrant;
He mourned Romance, now on the town,
　And Art, a vagrant.

Miniver loved the Medici,
　Albeit he had never seen one;
He would have sighed incessantly
　Could he have been one.

Miniver cursed the commonplace
　And eyed a khaki suit with loathing;
He missed the medieval grace
　Of iron clothing.

Miniver scorned the gold he sought,
　But sore annoyed was he without it;
Miniver thought, and thought, and thought,
　And thought about it.

Miniver Cheevy, born too late,
　Scratched his head and kept on thinking;
Miniver coughed, and called it fate,
　And kept on drinking.

EDWIN ARLINGTON ROBINSON

Morals

(FROM *Further Fables for Our Time*)

Get it right or let it alone.
The conclusion you jump to may be your own.

Where most of us end up there is no knowing;
But the hellbent get where they are going.

The saddest words of pen or tongue
Are wisdom's wasted on the young.

Who would avoid life's wriest laughter
Should not attain the thing he's after.

Though statisticians in our time have never kept the score,
Man wants a great deal here below and Woman even more.

Men of all degrees should form this prudent habit:
Never serve a rabbit stew before you catch the rabbit.

JAMES THURBER

The Elephant

A tail behind, a trunk in front,
Complete the usual elephant.
The tail in front, the trunk behind,
Is what you very seldom find.

If you for specimens should hunt
With trunks behind and tails in front,
The hunt would occupy you long,
The force of habit is so strong.

A. E. HOUSMAN

329

The Rum Tum Tugger

The Rum Tum Tugger is a Curious Cat:
If you offer him pheasant he would rather have grouse.
If you put him in a house he would much prefer a flat,
If you put him in a flat then he'd rather have a house.
If you set him on a mouse then he only wants a rat,
If you set him on a rat then he'd rather chase a mouse.
Yes the Rum Tum Tugger is a Curious Cat—
  And there isn't any call for me to shout it:
    For he will do
    As he do do
      And there's no doing anything about it!

The Rum Tum Tugger is a terrible bore:
When you let him in, then he wants to be out;
He's always on the wrong side of every door,
And as soon as he's at home, then he'd like to get about.
He likes to lie in the bureau drawer,
But he makes such a fuss if he can't get out.
Yes the Rum Tum Tugger is a Curious Cat—
  And there isn't any use for you to doubt it:
    For he will do
    As he do do
      And there's no doing anything about it!

The Rum Tum Tugger is a curious beast:
His disobliging ways are a matter of habit.
If you offer him fish then he always wants a feast;
When there isn't any fish then he won't eat rabbit.
If you offer him cream then he sniffs and sneers,
For he only likes what he finds for himself;
So you'll catch him in it right up to the ears,
If you put it away on the larder shelf.
The Rum Tum Tugger is artful and knowing,
The Rum Tum Tugger doesn't care for a cuddle;
But he'll leap on your lap in the middle of your sewing,
For there's nothing he enjoys like a horrible muddle.

Yes the Rum Tum Tugger is a Curious Cat—
   And there isn't any need for me to spout it:
      For he will do
      As he do do
         And there's no doing anything about it!

                              T. S. ELIOT

The Cat

Observe the Cat upon this page.
Philosophers in every age,
The very *wisest* of the wise
Have tried her mind to analyze
In vain, for nothing can they learn.
She baffles them at every turn
Like Mister Hamlet in the play.
She leads their reasoning astray;
She feigns an interest in string
Or yarn or any rolling thing.
Unlike the Dog, she does not care
With common Man her thoughts to share.
She teaches us that in life's walk
'T is better to let others talk,
And listen while *they* say instead
The foolish things *we* might have said.

                     OLIVER HERFORD

The Dog

Here is the Dog. Since time began,
The Dog has been the friend of Man.
The Dog loves Man because he shears
His coat and clips his tail and ears.
Man loves the Dog because he'll stay
And listen to his talk all day,
And wag his tail and show delight

At all his jokes, however trite.
His bark is far worse than his bite,
So people say. They may be right;
Yet if to make a choice I had,
I'd choose his bark, however bad.

OLIVER HERFORD

The Chimpanzee

Children, behold the Chimpanzee:
He sits on the ancestral tree
From which we sprang in ages gone.
I'm glad we sprang: had we held on,
We might, for aught that I can say,
Be horrid Chimpanzees today.

OLIVER HERFORD

The Yak

As a friend to the children commend me the Yak.
    You will find it exactly the thing:
It will carry and fetch, you can ride on its back,
    Or lead it about with a string.

The Tartar who dwells on the plains of Tibet
    (A desolate region of snow)
Has for centuries made it a nursery pet,
    And surely the Tartar should know!

Then tell your papa where the Yak can be got,
    And if he is awfully rich,
He will buy you the creature—or else he will *not*
    (I cannot be positive which).

HILAIRE BELLOC

The Frog

Be kind and tender to the Frog,
  And do not call him names,
As "Slimy-Skin," or "Polly-wog,"
  Or likewise, "Ugly James."

Or "Gape-a-grin," or "Toad-gone-wrong,"
  Or "Billy-Bandy-knees";
The Frog is justly sensitive
  To epithets like these.

No animal will more repay
  A treatment kind and fair,
At least, so lonely people say
Who keep a frog (and, by the way,
  They are extremely rare).

HILAIRE BELLOC

Habits of the Hippopotamus

The hippopotamus is strong
  And huge of head and broad of bustle;
The limbs on which he rolls along
  Are big with hippopotomuscle.

He does not greatly care for sweets
  Like ice cream, apple pie or custard,
But takes to flavor what he eats
  A little hippopotomustard.

The hippopotamus is true
  To all his principles and just;
He always tries his best to do
  The things one hippopotomust.

He never rides in trucks or trams
  In taxicabs or omnibuses,
And so keeps out of traffic jams
  And other hippopotomusses.

ARTHUR GUITERMAN

The Hippopotamus

Behold the hippopotamus!
We laugh at how he looks to us,
And yet in moments dank and grim
I wonder how we look to him.
Peace, peace, thou hippopotamus!
We really look all right to us,
As you no doubt delight the eye
Of other hippopotami.

OGDEN NASH

The Ant

The ant has made himself illustrious
Through constant industry industrious.
So what?
Would you be calm and placid
If you were full of formic acid?

OGDEN NASH

The Eel

I don't mind eels
Except as meals.

OGDEN NASH

Envoy

Go, Songs

Go, songs, for ended is our brief, sweet play;
  Go, children of swift joy and tardy sorrow:
And some are sung, and that was yesterday,
  And some unsung, and that may be to-morrow.

Go forth; and if it be o'er stony way,
  Old joy can lend what newer grief must borrow:
And it was sweet, and that was yesterday,
  And sweet is sweet, though purchased with sorrow.

Go, songs, and come not back from your far way;
  And if men ask you why you smile and sorrow,
Tell them ye grieve, for your hearts know To-day,
  Tell them ye smile, for your eyes know To-morrow.

FRANCIS THOMPSON

INDEX BY AUTHORS

337

INDEX BY TITLES

INDEX BY FIRST LINES

About the Author

Lewis Gannett wrote millions of words—the equivalent of dozens of books—in his column "Books and Things" in the quarter-century in which he was the daily book reviewer of the New York *Herald Tribune*. One book, *Sweet Land*, grew out of a Western trip reported in that column; another, *Cream Hill*, out of his country weekends. He is editor of the *Mainstream in America* series.

The minister's home in Rochester, New York, in which Mr. Gannett grew up was "full of awareness of poetry." But his last published poem he believes appeared in F.P.A.'s column in the *Tribune* in 1916, under the pseudonym "Luigi," when Mr. Gannett was a cub reporter on the old New York *World*.

"I never dreamed of becoming a critic," says Mr. Gannett. He went to Harvard (class of 1913) to become a biologist, but took his bachelor's degree in philosophy, his master's in economics, then seeking "something closer to life," got a job on the *World*. In the First World War he served with the Quakers in France; in the Second he left his book-review desk to become a correspondent on the Western front. "You can't write about books if you know only books," he says.

Mr. Gannett now lives the year round near West Cornwall, Conn. His wife is an artist; his son is in the Foreign Service; his daughter, author of the "Dragon" books for children, is married to an artist-professor; he has eleven grandchildren.